CHURCHILL'S GREAT ESCAPES

★★★★★★★
Seven Incredible Escapes Made by WWII HEROES
★★★★★★★

DAMIEN LEWIS

CITADEL PRESS
Kensington Publishing Corp.
www.kensingtonbooks.com

CITADEL PRESS BOOKS are published by

Kensington Publishing Corp.
900 Third Avenue
New York, NY 10022

All Kensington titles, imprints, and distributed lines are available at special quantity discounts for bulk purchases for sales promotions, premiums, fund-raising, educational, or institutional use. Special book excerpts or customized printings can also be created to fit specific needs. For details, write or phone the office of the Kensington sales manager: Kensington Publishing Corp., 900 Third Avenue, New York, NY 10022, attn: Sales Department; phone 1-800-221-2647.

CITADEL PRESS and the Citadel logo are Reg. U.S. Pat. & TM Off.

First hardcover edition: May 2022

First trade paperback edition: April 2024
ISBN: 978-0-8065-4210-2

ISBN: 978-0-8065-4211-9 (ebook)

10 9 8 7 6 5 4 3 2 1

Printed in the United States of America

Kensington Books by Damien Lewis

Churchill's Shadow Raiders

Churchill's Hellraisers

Churchill's Band of Brothers

Churchill's Great Escapes

Churchill's Brothers in Arms

For the great escapees as depicted in these pages.
And for all who slipped the clutches of the enemy,
so as to continue the fight against Nazi tyranny.

The hero is commonly the simplest and obscurest of men.

Henry David Thoreau

Contents

Author's Note

There are sadly few survivors from the Second World War operations depicted in these pages. Throughout the period of researching and writing this book I have sought to be in contact with as many as possible, plus surviving family members of those who have passed away. If there are further witnesses to the stories told here who are inclined to come forward, please do get in touch, as I will endeavour to include further recollections of the operations portrayed in this book in future editions.

The time spent by Allied servicemen and women as Special Service volunteers was often traumatic and wreathed in layers of secrecy, and many chose to take their stories to their graves. Memories tend to differ and apparently none more so than those concerning operations behind enemy lines. The written accounts that do exist tend to differ in their detail and timescale, and locations and chronologies are sometimes contradictory. Nevertheless, I have endeavoured to provide an accurate sense of place, timescale and narrative to the story as depicted in these pages.

Where various accounts of a mission appear to be particularly confused, the methodology I have used to reconstruct where, when and how events took place is the 'most likely' scenario. If two or more testimonies or sources point to a particular time or place or sequence of events, I have opted to use that account as most likely.

The above notwithstanding, any mistakes herein are entirely of my own making, and I would be happy to correct any in future editions. Likewise, while I have attempted to locate the copyright holders of the photos, sketches and other images and material used in this book, this has not always been straightforward or easy. Again, I would be happy to correct any mistakes in future editions.

CHURCHILL'S
GREAT ESCAPES

Preface

In 2016 I had the good fortune to be approached by an influential member of the Special Air Service regiment, who asked if I would be interested in telling the story of how the SAS had hunted down Hitler's war criminals in the immediate aftermath of the Second World War. I had heard about this incredible tale, but knew that without access to solid source material – Second World War-era reports, war diaries, personal recollections – it would be impossible to relate. That individual offered me all of this and more, for which I am hugely grateful. The resulting book – *The Nazi Hunters* – is one that I am immensely proud to have written.

At one stage in the story related in that book, in the autumn of 1944, a Canadian airman was shot down over the border between occupied France and Germany. That man, Flight Officer Ronald Lewis 'Lew' Fiddick, managed to evade the enemy and, with the help of the French resistance, linked up with SAS forces operating deep behind the lines in the Vosges Mountains of north-eastern France. Those men would go on to form the core of the SAS Nazi-hunting unit that would track down some of the most elusive war criminals, until their operations were brought to a precipitate end in 1948.

The SAS's hit-and-run exploits in the Vosges were legendary. Aiming to 'cut the head off the Nazi snake', this elite, behind-the-lines unit targeted senior enemy officers, shooting apart and blowing up their staff cars, before melting away, wraith-like, into the Vosges' dark forests and hills. But Fiddick's story particularly stood out. Made an honorary member of the SAS following the dramatic way he slipped the enemy's clutches after his aircraft was shot down, his subsequent escape and evasion took him from the war-torn Vosges all the way back to friendly lines.

From there I developed a fascination for similar tales of astounding bravery, resourcefulness and endurance, as members of the SAS risked all to evade enemy capture from the earliest years of the unit's formation until the end of the Second World War, and across all nations in which they served. There are scores of such stories, and my selection of the seven related here reflects the many theatres and wide means by which such escapes were executed, and features some of the key individuals involved. Suffice to say, a dozen more volumes of such tales could be written, featuring similarly compelling and dramatic tales.

The seven stories I've chosen embody the wider esprit de corps and attitude of the Special Forces' great escapees of the Second World War. Of course, the incredible endeavours portrayed here were not the exclusive domain of the SAS: other elite forces and indeed regular units have their own share of similarly heroic tales. But as the SAS pioneered and perfected such escape and evasion techniques, it is only right that the stories of their exploits should lead the way.

So, in that spirit let me take you to the first in a dramatic series of escapes and evasions, which last from the earliest years of the Second World War until its very final stages.

Great Escape One

ESCAPE FROM COLOSSUS

The fleet of eight Armstrong Whitworth Whitley medium bombers flitted across the moonlit Sicilian countryside, destination mainland Italy. Inside the aircraft were thirty-six raiders hell-bent on pulling off a mission of unprecedented daring, but one on which the odds were stacked against anyone returning alive. Forming part of No. 11 Special Air Service Battalion – the forerunner to the Special Air Service proper – they included some of the British Army's finest.

Four days earlier they had been shivering in the bitter winter rain and fog of an English winter, as the seemingly invincible Nazi war machine attempted to bomb the island nation into submission. Now, they were poised to execute an utterly audacious operation, one that had the personal blessing of Winston Churchill – dropping into the heart of Mussolini's Fascist Italy, to blow up that nation's life-giving watercourse, the Aqueduct Pugliese, which supplied fresh drinking water to three million Italian souls.

If they succeeded, they would destroy not only the water supply for the major cities in the south of the country, but also that supplying the country's key ports, including Taranto and Brindisi, which were vital to Italy's campaign in North Africa. Depriving those ports of water could shut them down completely, massively boosting Britain's fortunes in the war.

According to the raiders' commanding officer, Major Trevor Allan Gordon – 'Tag' – Pritchard, their mission, codenamed Operation Colossus, would be 'an experiment to see just what we can do. We're pioneers, or guinea pigs, whichever way you prefer to look at it.' They were indeed guinea pigs, for this was to be the first ever airborne operation by Allied forces, no Allied troops ever having parachuted into combat before.

One of Pritchard's men, Lieutenant George Paterson, of Canadian origin and a sapper – a demolitions expert – by trade, was to play a pivotal role. At six-foot-three, Paterson – known as 'the Big Canadian' – was an easy-going but tough giant of a man, hailing from the city of Kelowna, in British Columbia. But as they flew towards the target Paterson's mind was consumed by one thing only – the sense of his nerves knotted tight in his stomach.

Over his headphones, Paterson heard the Whitley's pilot announce that they were twenty minutes away from jump-hour. Shaking his corporal, Jack Watson, awake, he began to rouse the others. His men had seemed to suffer few of the nerves that he had, for most had slept soundly through the long flight.

With the red jump-light switching to green, Paterson took a grip on his fears and leapt into the darkness, drifting down towards the shadowed countryside. Below and above him the fellow men in his stick were likewise suspended beneath swathes of parachute silk. As his eyes adjusted to the light, he caught sight of the aqueduct, its silhouette bold and clear on the mountain-side.

Once safely on the ground, he and his men broke out their weapons and explosives from the containers, which had also been dropped by the Whitley. Armed up, they began to climb the ravine leading to the aqueduct itself. In the distance, a faint rumble of explosions broke the silence. That had to be two Whitley bombers carrying out their diversionary attacks on Foggia rail yard, a vital link in Italy's wartime logistics. Hopefully, any watchers who had seen the fleet of British aircraft fly overhead would presume that all had been engaged upon that bombing mission. That at least was the plan.

As Paterson and his men reached the aqueduct, the mission commander, Pritchard, brought them up to speed. On two counts there was bad news. One: the Whitley carrying the main team of sappers was missing, along with the bulk of their explosives. Paterson being the only sapper remaining, it now fell to him to come up with a plan to demolish the aqueduct. Two: as the raiders gathered together all their explosives, the sum total amounted to less than seven hundred pounds in weight, or just a third of the amount they'd expected. Some was lost on the missing aircraft, while the rest must have frozen solid in the Whitley's bomb-racks, and failed to drop.

Undaunted, Paterson went about assessing the target. The mission briefings had stated that the aqueduct's three piers were constructed of masonry, but Paterson soon discovered the grim truth: they were made of reinforced concrete, and that took much more explosive power to destroy. The plan had been to blow all three piers, shattering the aqueduct from end to end. That was now impossible, with such limited explosives to hand and knowing the true nature of the aqueduct's construction. All Paterson could suggest was that they concentrate all their charges on the one pier, and hope for the best. He began packing the crates of explosives against the target, before adding the detonators and a length of fuse, at which point he informed Pritchard that all was ready.

At 0029 hours on 11 February 1941, with everyone backed away a safe distance, Paterson lit the fuse and rushed to join Pritchard in the cover of some boulders. But as the seconds ticked by there was no detonation. Eventually, Paterson decided to go and see what was wrong, taking Pritchard for company. After creeping forward a few yards, they were stopped in their tracks by a sound like a massive clap of thunder erupting before them.

A whirlwind of debris erupted skywards, showering the men with clouds of blasted rocks and mud. As the thick pall of dust and smoke dissipated, the two men held their breath in hope: had the charges done the trick? The air cleared to reveal a beautiful sight: half of the aqueduct was down. The target pier had been demolished completely, and another was leaning badly, leaving the precious water of the Apulian Aqueduct cascading down the ravine and away into the valley beyond.

Against all odds, Operation Colossus had succeeded. It was now that Tag Pritchard revealed to his raiders their escape plan: they were to trek westwards through the Apennine Mountains, which form the spine of Italy, making for a coastal rendez-vous with a British submarine, HMS *Triumph*. Six days hence, *Triumph* was scheduled to pluck them off Italy's western shores and to safety – but only if they could make it.

With no time to lose, the men split into smaller parties, in an effort to escape and evade a vengeful enemy. Major Pritchard led one group of would-be escapees, along with Lieutenant Anthony Deane-Drummond, his second in command. Lieutenant Paterson took charge of another. They formed up and headed into the snowbound mountains, in a desperate effort to avoid capture and whatever grim fate would then follow.

Paterson led the way with his group, heading up the mountain slope over treacherous ground. In no time they were ankle-deep in freezing mud, which sucked at their every step. Husbanding their precious reserves of water, they stopped to quench their thirst at every stream they came to. Just before dawn, they took refuge in a shallow ravine. Over portable stoves they brewed tea, before trying to eat their pemmican, the fatty porridge that constituted their main rations. But its heavy, greasy consistency made the men gag, and those who did manage to get it down them soon found it paying an unwelcome return visit.

Sticking to the cover of that ravine, they hid during the hours of daylight, only setting out again come nightfall. Moving through the high peaks of the Apennines, the going proved horrendous, as Pritchard and his men struggled to keep going in the bitter cold. Despite a second night's hard march, they'd barely managed to cover seventeen miles come daybreak, their every footfall dogged by treacherous ice and snow.

Having lain up in hiding for a second day, Paterson decided they had no choice but to risk taking to a road, to speed them in the direction they needed to travel. They were exhausted, frozen stiff, famished and their progress through the mountains was proving too slow to make the rendezvous with the British submarine. By contrast, taking to that night-dark road enabled them to cover six miles in the first two hours. Spirits lifted. Paterson pushed them on at pace, moving past a crossroads, before coming to a stone bridge. But they were barely over that, when a group of heavily armed Carabinieri – the Italian military police force – burst out of hiding, weapons at the ready.

At first, Paterson and his men tried to argue that they were German troops on a night exercise, but it fooled no one. By now local villagers had gathered: men, women and children, over a hundred of them, and some armed with shotguns. Sensing resistance was futile, Paterson and his men were rounded up and taken to a small village. Handcuffed, they were packed onto mule carts for the journey to the local town gaol. At gunpoint, they were ordered into the cells, whereupon they discovered that some of their fellow Operation Colossus raiders, including their CO, Tag Pritchard, were already present, having been taken captive just a few hours earlier.

After an uncomfortable night in the cells, the Operation Colossus captives were transported to the city of Naples, by train. On arrival, they were driven to the military prison – an archaic building that resembled a medieval dungeon. There, Paterson was thrust into a cell, his guard stating in broken English that he was to be shot. The grim reality finally hit home. In the cell that night, believing he faced imminent execution, Paterson thought about his family back in Canada and his life before the war – studying hard, drinking beer with his mates – and of the pretty blonde typist he had had his eye on. Come daybreak, he was led into another room, to undergo interrogation by the Questura, Fascist Italy's secret police. But despite their many attempts to extract information, and the death threats, Paterson maintained a rigid silence.

Days passed, and Paterson still hadn't been executed. Instead, he was informed that as they were parachutists, the Operation Colossus captives were to be treated as Air Force POWs – prisoners of war. When they were sent to an Italian airbase, as a temporary holding camp, conditions dramatically improved. The commanding officer there, a Colonel Montalba, appeared to be a compassionate, principled individual. He ensured they had decent food, a bath every second day and that they were allowed exercise. Essentials such as toothbrushes, soap and towels were even provided.

But when Colonel Montalba wasn't around, the Questura continued their pursuit of the Colossus raiders. One morning, a Questura photographer and finger-printing expert arrived. Pritchard refused to cooperate, stating that they were prisoners of war, not common criminals. On returning to his base, a furious Colonel Montalba tore apart the Questura's equipment, smashing the photographer's plates and his camera, plus the finger-printing kits.

After three weeks of this relatively benign existence, the prisoners were summoned into Colonel Montalba's office. With great cheer he announced they were to be moved to a camp in the mountains, at Sulmona. It promised magnificent scenery, excellent food and plenty of wine and cigarettes, as well as the company of their fellow British POWs, Colonel Montalba declared. It was regrettable, he added, that the only thing they would not be allowed was the company of women!

In due course Paterson and his fellow POWs travelled by train through snowy peaks and dense pine forests, with only the occasional village breaking up the scenery. Finally, the small town of Sulmona came into view. Guarded by thirty-five Carabinieri, the Colossus captives were taken on a five-mile march to the prison gates. Upon arrival, they were confined to cramped cells with little to do, and with no fellow POWs for company. The men became irritable and downhearted. Colonel Montalba's promises of the good life – of fine food, wine, company and song – seemed to have been wildly exaggerated.

Several weeks into their incarceration at PG 78 Sulmona, a Colonel Fisk from the American Embassy, in Rome, arrived to check they were being treated fairly. Paterson and the others pleaded with him to get them moved to somewhere they could exercise and where they could mix with fellow POWs. Shortly afterwards, they were transferred to the officers' compound. The huts there were bigger, there was space to exercise, but best of all, they were finally among their fellow captives. Paterson was assigned a bed in a hut called 'Dominion House', which housed Australians, New Zealanders, South Africans and British among its number.

In his new surroundings, Paterson learned that their Italian captors even provided each POW with half a litre of wine per day. Most saved up the wine over several days, in order to throw a special party. But at Dominion House the inmates had got into the habit of drinking all the wine they could right away. With Paterson on hand, there was hope that they might rely on the Big Canadian's self-discipline and iron will to curb their excessive boozing, and he was duly appointed Dominion House Wine Secretary.

With Paterson's strictures over the wine ration rigorously imposed, escape became uppermost on the captives' minds. But with Sulmona lying four hundred miles from the Swiss frontier – neutral Switzerland offering the nearest promise of safety – those few who had previously attempted to escape had all been recaptured and returned to the camp.

Even so, the men of No. 11 SAS – Britain's first ever airborne forces, who were all volunteers for hazardous duties – remained undaunted. They had been subjected to months of harsh 'commando style' training in Britain, plus the rigours of learning parachute jumping, including from static towers, tethered balloons and aircraft; they were in no mood to sit out the remainder of the war as POWs.

At Sulmona Paterson befriended an RAF fighter pilot called Garry Garrad-Cole, among other POWs. Garrad-Cole asked him if he'd like to join an escape attempt they were planning. Paterson, fired up by the thought of some action at last, replied: 'You're damn right I would!'

Garrad-Cole had managed to escape once before, in the company of a naval lieutenant. They had reached Italy's eastern – Adriatic – coast but had been caught in the process of stealing a boat to make good their getaway. The plan of escape now was to dig a tunnel leading from inside the broom cupboard of their hut, out under the camp's perimeter. Garrad-Cole showed Paterson where several floor tiles had been removed, revealing a dark and narrow shaft. Each day the excavated soil was passed around the hut inmates, before being discreetly dribbled out via their trouser legs and scattered around the camp.

Over the coming day, the tunnel excavation progressed well, and Paterson felt his spirits lift in anticipation of the break-out. But one morning a mule, loaded with supplies, suddenly disappeared down a large hole, as it made its way along the path running just outside the camp perimeter. Within minutes, the escape shaft had been discovered.

Even so, Paterson and Garrad-Cole weren't inclined to give up. Some weeks later they managed to execute a daring dash past the wire, but Paterson only got as far as a ditch, before some angry farmers descended upon him with their hunting rifles at the ready. Garrad-Cole was also quickly recaptured. Sentenced to thirty days' solitary confinement, by the time they were released

rationing within the camp had become severe. The Italians, realising that the war was unlikely to be over anytime soon, had
switched the prisoners' diet to a few slices of stale black bread
and a watery vegetable stew.

The weeks passed, and Paterson and his fellow prisoners grew
increasingly despondent. They seemed to be permanently plagued
by hunger and could foresee no opportunities for breaking out.
Finally, all of the Special Forces officers were brought before the
Colonel of Sulmona POW camp. He informed them that as they
were the main instigators of all the escape attempts, they were
to be shipped off to another place of incarceration, one that was
far more secure.

Following a long train journey under close guard, Paterson
and his fellows arrived at an ancient, glowering monastery in
the town of San Romano, central Italy. The monastery had been
split into two, with one section still occupied by the monks, but
the other walled off and tightly patrolled. Inside, there were some
fifty Greek POWs, who greeted the new arrivals warmly. Despite
their lack of a common language, the Greeks immediately offered
to share their Red Cross food parcels with the newcomers, who
they could see were half-starved.

His spirits somewhat reinvigorated, Paterson once again began
considering thoughts of escape. During the first few weeks at
their new place of internment, he carefully studied the POWs'
section of the building, but every conceivable exit was covered by
rifle-posts and machine-gun emplacements. However, the monks'
quarters, on the far side of a bricked-off corridor, remained unex-
plored.

One of Paterson's fellow Operation Colossus raiders decided to
attempt a reconnaissance of the monks' quarters, by pronouncing

himself a Roman Catholic and demanding that he be allowed to attend services in the chapel. Under heavy guard he began his daily visits, each time gathering vital intelligence of the monastery's layout. From this information Paterson, an engineer by trade, drew up an accurate plan of the building. It revealed that behind the bricked-off corridor separating the POWs from the monks lay a rarely used cloister – a covered walkway. If they could remove a few bricks, they might be able to slip into the cloister and make good their getaway.

It was a sound plan, but they would need a distraction to cover the racket made by chiselling away the bricks. A few weeks back the Greeks had gathered together enough wine and goodies from the Red Cross parcels to throw a party in honour of St George, the patron saint of England. Now, Paterson and his fellow escapees figured it was time to return the gesture with a party all of their own. With luck, the drunken singing would provide the perfect cover as they excavated a hole in the wall.

Over the next fortnight they got busy. Identity cards that might pass a fleeting inspection were cleverly forged. Clothing was shared around and careful alterations made to enable the men to blend in as civilians in the outside world. Routes were planned and money put aside.

The evening for the party arrived. Paterson played his role as the genial host, passing around the wine to intoxicate the Greeks – who were known to be enthusiastic singers – while remaining stone-cold sober himself. Behind the scenes, others got busy attacking the wall. After a short while they succeeded in getting one brick free. They reported to Paterson that it was tricky to break the mortar without making too much noise, but that they should be ready in an hour or so.

With the party in full swing, word reached Paterson that the hole was nearly big enough. It was time for Paterson and the group of British officers to slip away unnoticed. They raced for their rooms to make their final preparations, disguising themselves as best they could as civilians. No sooner had they done so than Lieutenant Deane-Drummond, one of Paterson's fellow Operation Colossus raiders, came tearing down the corridor.

'It's all off!' Deane-Drummond cried. 'One of the bloody monks heard a brick drop and decided to investigate. He's just yelled for the guard. They'll be here in minutes. Hide everything incriminating and let's get to bed.'

Paterson, Deane-Drummond and the others had barely slipped under the sheets, when the Carabinieri came storming into their rooms, announcing that there had been an escape attempt. Paterson protested their innocence, claiming that none of them had been involved. The accusations were deeply unjust, for they were all fast asleep, he insisted. Paterson's play-acting would have succeeded had it not been for one of the Carabinieri discovering his carefully drawn plans of the monastery, hidden under his bedside table.

As punishment, Paterson was marched off for a month's solitary confinement. He told himself, ruefully, that perhaps the peace and quiet would do him good. But he wasn't to be alone for long. Most of the British officers joined him, as the Italian guards decided to punish them all. Even so, Paterson remained determined to break out.

The first of the Operation Colossus raiders to do so would be Lt Deane-Drummond. Faking mastoiditis – an infection of the bone behind the ear – Deane-Drummond got himself moved to Florence Military Hospital. Early one morning he managed to sneak past his guard on the ward and catch a train to Milan, some three hundred kilometres north and that much closer to Switzerland. From there he travelled on to Como, which lies on the Italian side of the Swiss border, and managed to slip across the frontier.

Having made it into neutral Switzerland, Deane-Drummond proceeded to cross the border into France, in the company of some fellow escapees, making his way to an isolated beach lying some twenty miles east of the French port city of Marseilles. It was there that a small British naval vessel, disguised as a Spanish fishing trawler, managed to land during the dead of night and rescue them all.

But Deane-Drummond's successful breakout, coupled with the escape attempts of Paterson and fellow POWs, turned the attitude of the Italian camp guards distinctly hostile. Come late summer, Paterson and fellows were informed they were to be transferred to Gavi, a camp twenty miles north of the city of Genoa. Supposedly escape-proof, it was at the Gavi camp that the most mutinous and restive Allied prisoners were held.

On their arrival, Paterson could see why. Perched high on one side of the mountain was an ancient fortress, surrounded by sheer drops on all sides and accessed by a narrow winding road. Each wall of the fortress was lined by machine-gun posts and squads of patrolling guards. By now, Paterson had been in captivity for eighteen months, and the very sight of the Gavi camp sent his spirits plunging. But, he reminded himself, nowhere was one hundred per cent escape-proof. There had to be a way.

During the long months of incarceration, Paterson had learned to adapt to his circumstances. Keeping mind and body active was key. Learning languages, mathematics, art – anything, so long as it didn't give the mind too long to brood. At Gavi, he busied himself with Italian, and they even managed to organise a drama club and a casino to pass the days.

As the months ground by, fresh POWs arrived, bringing encouraging news of the war. The battle for North Africa had been won, and Sicily had been taken by Allied troops. Then came news that was like a bolt from the blue. Benito Mussolini, Italy's Fascist dictator, was removed from power. Seeing which way the wind was blowing in the war, Italy's leaders had signed an armistice with the Allies on 3 September 1943. When this was made public on the 8th, most of the Italian guards at Gavi seemed euphoric. They announced that the war would soon be over and they would all be going home.

Gavi's fearsome machine-gun posts were left unmanned and the sentry boxes unattended, as guards and prisoners mingled in celebration. With the gates left unguarded, all the prisoners could have walked out, but they'd received word via secret channels that they should stay where they were, the better to assist with their repatriation in due course. Sadly, this 'stay put' order, instigated by Allied high command, would backfire catastrophically.

As morning came, the jovial atmosphere evaporated. When Paterson gazed out from the fortress, he realised that the guards were back at their posts. More chillingly, he could see the distinctive grey uniforms of a unit of German troops moving through the valley below.

'We will be shot if any of us let you go,' confided one of the Italian guards, dejectedly.

The routine at Gavi returned to what it had been before, while the German forces remained in position, to pressure the Italians into keeping a close watch. Then, in mid-September 1943, the

Germans dismissed the Italian guards and moved into the fortress themselves. The prisoners were told to prepare to be moved early the next morning. Paterson and his fellow detainees realised this could mean only one thing: they were about to be shipped to Germany, the very last place they wanted to go.

Desperate to escape, several tried to hide in out-of-the-way-sheds, cupboards, attics and disused storerooms, only to be discovered. Their last-ditch attempts delayed the journey for twenty-four hours, but no more. Finally the prisoners were lined up and strip-searched, before being loaded aboard a convoy of trucks. As the POWs sat there, silent and downcast, Paterson knew that once they were in Germany there would be little chance of ever breaking away.

After travelling all day, the convoy pulled into a freight yard in the northern Italian region of Lombardy. There, they were ushered into a goods warehouse, where several hundred POWs were crammed together. Word reached Paterson that they were to be taken by train over the Brenner Pass, the dramatic mountain chasm that straddles the border between Italy and Austria, and onwards into Germany. Paterson realised that their worst nightmare was about to begin.

Under the hot September sun it seemed like an eternity before they were marched towards a long line of goods wagons. Interspersed between them were groups of heavily armed SS troopers, who would be riding in open vans. Once Paterson and the others had been herded inside the wooden-sided carriages, the doors slid shut and were locked tightly closed.

With a sharp blast on the whistle, the train lurched forward. Inside Paterson's wagon, it was hot, airless and very nearly dark. As the locomotive steamed northwards, the men's hunger began to stir. From Red Cross supplies they'd brought with them they pulled out whatever biscuits, raisins and chocolate remained. It wasn't long before the conversation turned to escape.

One of those riding on that train was Major David Stirling, the founder of the SAS, who had been taken prisoner while on operations in the North African desert in January 1943. Stirling had escaped almost immediately from his German captors but was quickly retaken by a force of Italian troops, who delighted in having got one over on their German brothers-in-arms by recapturing 'The Phantom Major', as Field Marshal Erwin Rommel had dubbed Stirling.

Stirling would go on to make repeated escape attempts, and he and Paterson had become friends in the Italian POW camps, bonding over their shared desire to be free. In short, the determination to break out from that train, as it steamed north towards Germany, was palpable, and the conversation ebbed back and forth about how best they might do so. Finally, a group of South African POWs figured it was worth seeing if they could cut a hole through the wooden planking that formed the carriage's sides.

'Anyone manage to bring a knife?' someone ventured.

One man handed over a small pocket-knife, while another produced an item he'd managed to get his hands on shortly before their departure, very much with escape in mind – a pair of heavy-duty dental pliers with the tips shaped like a parrot's beak. With the use of those improvised excavation tools, a small hole was torn through to the outside, at the point where their car linked with the next.

A buzz of excitement rippled through the carriage, as the prisoners realised their chances of escape were now very real. But as luck would have it the train began to slow, before eventually coming to a stop. Thinking quickly, Paterson urged one of the men to stuff the hole with his sweater. Thus blocked up, when the guards passed, checking all the carriages were in order, the damage should remain undetected.

After fifteen minutes, the train began to move once more and no one had raised the alarm. The cutters set to work again, tearing at the wood, desperate to be free. Every now and again the train would slow and stop, to let other locomotives pass; each time the men stuffed the hole with their clothing. Finally, at just after midnight, the gap was declared big enough for a man to squeeze through.

Filling their pockets with as much food and cigarettes as possible, each of the would-be escapees lined up, and waited for the train to slow enough to chance a leap. Two South Africans went first, followed by another pair of desperate fugitives. As Paterson poked his head out, readying himself to follow, he saw one of the figures ahead of him inch his way onto the coupling linking the two carriages. Suddenly, the train gave an almighty jolt, knocking the figure off his feet and throwing him beneath the wheels.

Paterson looked on in horror, but the men behind – unaware of the tragedy – were growing restless. Plucking up his courage, Paterson squeezed himself out onto the coupling. By now the train was powering down into a valley and picking up speed. He would be killed outright if he jumped. Eventually the train slowed and the Big Canadian summoned up his courage . . . and leapt. Seconds later he crashed onto the sharp stones of the gravel embankment, where, despite the pain he was in, he forced himself to lie utterly still.

Spreadeagled on the ground, Patterson's mind raced. Would

a guard see him and open fire? As the carriages flashed past, he braced himself for a burst of bullets in the back. But eventually, the red tail-light zipped by and he breathed a sigh of relief. It was to be short-lived. Some eighty yards further on, the train ground to a halt. The rattle of semi-automatic gunfire broke the silence, with bullets spraying along the tracks. Had he been spotted? If he stayed put, the guards could leap down and race back towards him, and he would be finished.

Glancing around, to his right lay only a steep mountainside; there was no escape that way. But on the opposite side of the tracks lay a scrub-covered hillside running down to a broad river. Paterson decided he would have to chance it. Jumping to his feet, he dashed over the rail-tracks, before rolling down the bank into the undergrowth on the far side. In a low crouch, he proceeded to race down the hill, brambles and branches tearing at him, his only focus being to get away. Finally, his way was barred by the river.

Knowing he had to press on, he removed his clothes and boots, bundling everything together, before strapping it onto a piece of wood lying near by. Entering the icy mountain water, he gasped. Pushing the bundle before him, he started swimming, but the current was stronger than he had imagined and it began to sweep him away. Gradually, he made progress, but then an eddy – a fierce current forming a small whirlpool – snatched his precious bundle, wrenching it from his grasp. Though he tried desperately to recover it, within seconds his possessions had been sucked out of reach.

More crawling than swimming, Paterson made the far bank, where he collapsed, struggling to catch his breath. As he looked down at himself, he realised his dire predicament: he was on the run in hostile country and stark naked. With night-time setting in he had only one choice: he would have to get moving to stay warm, hoping to find some clothing and shelter along the way. Shuffling forward and limping noticeably, he made slow progress through the darkening terrain, conscious all the time of his nakedness.

He felt terribly weary and desperately in need of sleep. To his left he spied the lights of what looked like a small village, plus a nearer farmhouse. Moving warily, he noticed an open basement window. Taking his chances, he lowered himself down to what appeared to be a vegetable storehouse. Over in one corner, he found a pile of old sacks. Craving rest, he lay down and covering himself with the makeshift bedding fell quickly asleep.

Unbeknown to Paterson, David Stirling was among those who'd failed to break free from the train carriages. 'I escaped, he didn't,' was how Paterson would write of this parting of the ways, after the war. Stirling would go on to be incarcerated in Colditz Castle, in the German state of Saxony, a high-security facility for Allied officers who were seriously 'troublesome', until the end of the war.

Hours after drifting into an exhausted sleep, Paterson awoke to footsteps moving about in the house above him. It was still barely light outside and he knew he must find clothing and seek help. When he climbed back out through the window, the morning air was cold on his skin. To the rear of the house, he saw some bedsheets hanging on a washing line. Grabbing one, he wrapped himself in it, before pounding on the farmstead's door.

Silence. Paterson knocked again and finally there was the sound of a bolt being drawn back, whereupon the door was swung open by a dark-haired girl.

'Signorina,' Paterson began, but before he could utter another word, the girl had shrieked and run off, clearly shocked by the sight of Paterson's almost naked body draped in one of their best bedsheets.

Within minutes an older woman appeared. In his make-do Italian, learned during his months in captivity, Paterson explained that he was an Allied prisoner of war on the run and desperately in need of clothing and food. Could she help? The woman, although clearly frightened, seemed sympathetic.

'You need to see the village priest,' she told him, 'for he may be able to help. My daughter will accompany you there.'

The girl reappeared. Now, she seemed more curious than shocked as she led Paterson along the village street. She stopped outside a house and knocked. An elderly woman answered. Once more, Paterson explained his predicament. The woman beckoned him inside, before leading him into a small, stark room with only a crucifix for decoration. At the table, a priest in a threadbare robe sat having his breakfast.

Paterson retold his story while the priest listened attentively. Once he was done, the holy man explained that Paterson could not stay there, for the Germans were in the next village and would surely find him. However, he would find Paterson some clothes and his housekeeper would give him a meal. Paterson felt his spirits lift at the kindly priest's offer of help.

Half an hour later, the priest returned with an assortment of garments and a pair of boots. At six-foot-three, it was a struggle for Paterson to prise himself into the clothing, which proved too tight and short, and the boots impossibly small. The priest hurried off again, and minutes later he was back with an ancient pair, with soles that were cracked and worn. But at least he could get his feet into them.

Thus attired, Paterson was led to the door and pointed towards a series of hills. 'Past those is Lake Garda,' the priest explained. 'Travel on the north side, then work south-west. You will find passes from there that lead into Switzerland. It is a long journey, may God be with you.'

Thanking the priest, Paterson set out under a warm September sun. That day he marched across meadows and up wild and rugged hills, until in the late afternoon he caught sight of Lake Garda shimmering beyond. As he headed down from the heights, hunger and tiredness overtook him. Ahead he could see a small village with a church. Perhaps the priest there might also help. As he approached, he saw the congregation leaving, after the early evening service.

When the priest appeared, Paterson moved towards him. 'Padre, I'm a Canadian officer on the run from the Germans,' he explained. 'Can you help?'

The priest, evidently well fed by the look of his plump cheeks, responded with outright hostility. 'No, not at all! You must leave immediately.'

Paterson didn't see the point in arguing. This 'holy man' clearly had sympathies with the wrong side. He hurried away. Tired, hungry and cold, and with his feet throbbing in his old, worn boots, he had no option but to make for a small clump of bushes high on a barren hillside. There, he tucked himself away for the night as best he could.

The following day matters hardly improved. With few streams near by, his thirst worsened. By afternoon he had made it to a shepherd's hut, where an elderly woman offered him some bread and milk, but with nowhere to sleep he again spent the night in the open. By morning he knew he had to find food, water and shelter, and he resigned himself to taking his chances on the road. The going would be easier and maybe he would find a church or a monastery that would take him in.

By midday, the sun was beating down and Paterson was utterly spent. He knew that if he lay out in the open, people would become curious. Fortunately, he spotted a dry culvert – a water drain – which he could crawl into and rest. By mid-afternoon the sun's heat had lessened and he dragged himself out. A sign ahead on the road declared: 'Brescia 5 Kilometres'. He knew that if he couldn't find help in that town, he was finished.

As Paterson entered the outskirts, his shabby, ill-fitting attire began to draw attention. Out in the fields he'd gone largely unnoticed; here in the town's streets he looked distinctly out of place. His mouth and lips parched with thirst, he could do nothing but stumble forward, desperately searching for somewhere he might find sanctuary.

A cyclist stopped and turned his head, staring back at Paterson. The rider, who looked to be in his thirties, was small, with dark hair and dressed like a workman. He seemed to be waiting for Paterson to catch up.

'*Inglese?*' he whispered, just as soon as Paterson was within earshot.

Paterson nodded. English was as good as Canadian around these parts, he figured.

The cyclist explained that he had helped another Englishman and he could help Paterson. Too tired to resist or argue, Paterson allowed himself to be led along narrow streets and back alleys, until they reached a courtyard where a group of children were playing.

'This is my home,' the man declared simply, introducing himself as Luigi.

Once he'd been ushered into the front room, Paterson collapsed in the nearest chair. Under Luigi's instructions, the ladies of the house got to work removing Paterson's ill-fitting boots and bathing and bandaging his blistered and bleeding feet. Spaghetti and coarse bread were produced, plus wine. Luigi explained that he and his friends loathed the 'German pigs', and would do anything they could to resist their occupation of Italy.

Paterson, feeling utterly relieved to be among friends, and with his hunger and thirst quenched, began to close his eyes. Luigi, noticing his fatigue, helped him to his feet and suggested that he stay at his sister-in-law's house, just near by. Her husband was away in the army, so there was space. Luigi led Paterson to the house, where they made for the bedroom. Opening the door, there was a panicked shriek, as a young naked woman leapt from the bed and fled, leaving an equally naked man looking more than a little embarrassed.

Luigi laughed. 'This is the other *Inglese*.'

'I'm Corporal Jack Harris,' explained the red-faced figure. 'I arrived five days back and have been looked after by these wonderful people.'

'So I see,' replied Paterson, drily, before slumping down, exhaustedly, and falling into a deep slumber.

After a few days' rest Paterson's feet started to heal, but he was anxious at just how safe he – and Harris – were. Luigi's open hatred of the Germans surely would draw unwanted attention. Harris, who was fluent in Italian – he, too, had learned it first in the POW camps – had heard Luigi and his friends talking about 'the partisans' – the Italian resistance. Maybe they would be safer out in the countryside with the partisans. As Paterson was an expert in explosives, and Harris a dab-hand at wireless communications, they would be an asset to any guerrilla force seeking to take the fight to the enemy.

They shared their idea with Luigi, who seemed equally enthused. A day or so later they set off for the country on bicycles. After several hours they arrived at the partisans' headquarters – a stone barn set amid a small pasture and surrounded by trees. Inside, amid the firelight, twenty figures were ranged around the floor. After Luigi had made the introductions, they greeted Paterson and Harris warmly. Over wine and food, they shared their stories, plus their hatred of the Germans, before sleep took over.

The following morning, Paterson and Harris set about getting to grips with the partisans' set-up, but far from being a proper fighting unit, they seemed more like a poorly run boy scout troop. There was little discipline or purpose, few weapons to speak of and hopeless security. Everyone seemed to have big dreams about what they would do to the enemy but no means to achieve it. Meanwhile, those living in the nearby villages knew the whereabouts of their camp and it was only a matter of time before someone would talk.

Paterson knew they weren't safe here. He requested Luigi's help to get them to Milan, some thirty kilometres short of the border with Switzerland. From there, they would have to find their own way across. Within a couple of days Luigi had made appropriate arrangements, furnishing Paterson and Harris with bicycles, whereupon a young woman arrived riding her own bike.

'This is your guide,' declared Luigi. 'She will take you to your next hiding place.'

After bicycling through open countryside for a day, the trio arrived at a large farmhouse. The girl knocked on the door and after a brief conversation, she beckoned Harris and Paterson to come forward. 'The Riccinis will look after you,' she announced. 'You will be safe here.' With that, she bade them farewell and cycled off.

Signora Riccini stood there with Gabi, her attractive, dark-haired daughter, welcoming Harris and Paterson like true heroes and offering assurances that they would do all they could to help. At dinner they met the man of the house – Signor Riccini – who announced that they were welcome to stay as long as they needed. Signora Riccini told them that her husband's tailor would arrange for new sets of clothing, after which she would link them up with a man who could guide them to the border.

She warned that it might take a week or so before everything was arranged. As life with the Riccinis was proving a happy and enjoyable interlude, Paterson wasn't overly worried. In Gabi, their pretty nineteen-year-old daughter, he had found a willing teacher of Italian, and despite the rationing, food was plentiful on the Riccinis' farm.

One evening there was a visitor, a Roberto Oreste, who was the man who would help get them to Switzerland. While it wouldn't be easy, Oreste knew a Spaniard living in Milan who would help. After saying their heartfelt farewells, Paterson and Harris left the Riccinis' place, setting off with Oreste for the nearest train station. Now dressed smartly, like affluent businessmen, they could pass as native Italians going about their daily routine. With no identity papers, they feared they might have to dodge the police at the railway station, but as luck would have it their smart attire saw them through.

Upon arrival in Milan they followed Oreste out of the busy station, and it wasn't long before they reached an apartment block. Oreste knocked on one of the apartment doors which was opened by a thin man with burning eyes. 'This is Pedro, my Spanish friend who hates Franco,' Oreste declared. 'He will help us.' By 'Franco', he meant General Franco, the Fascist dictator of Spain.

As a plump blonde – Pedro's girlfriend – helped them to coffee, Pedro explained that many POWs had made it across into Switzerland, but it was becoming more and more difficult, for the Germans had strengthened their border patrols. They would need a guide. Pedro knew of a woman who was strongly anti-fascist and who had friends living around the border. Her name was Maria Resta and she would be able to help.

Shortly, Paterson and Harris were taken to a luxury apartment in a fashionable neighbourhood of Milan. There they met a young woman, plainly dressed, who was Maria Resta.

She explained that she had two acquaintances who were involved in cross-border smuggling, who might be prepared to act as guides. She would have to track them down but knew the wine bars they tended to frequent. If Paterson and Harris were willing to accompany her, they would travel there that very afternoon.

The four made their way to Lecco, a resort lying at the foothills of the Bergamo Alps, in the far north of Italy and on the shores of Lake Como. Over several hours, they trailed Maria Resta around a succession of wine bars, but no one had seen or heard of her smuggler-acquaintances for some time. As dusk began to set in, Maria Resta suggested that the only sensible thing to do was to return with her to Milan.

Paterson resisted, arguing that they should try to steal a boat to get across the lake, for the Swiss border lay tantalisingly close on the far side. But Maria was adamant that hundreds of guards patrolled the area between there and the border. 'Only a guide who knows the way can get you safely across,' she warned. Paterson and Harris reluctantly took the train back to Milan. Over a late meal of spaghetti and wine, Maria suggested there was another man they should talk to. He had assisted many POWs. The following day, she led Paterson and Harris to a meeting with Signor Rossi, a well-dressed, middle-aged man who spoke near-perfect English. An engineer by trade, Signor Rossi welcomed the two fugitives into his office, asking them to explain how they had arrived in Italy. After listening attentively, he announced himself satisfied that they were who they said they were, and not Gestapo agents out to trap him.

Signor Rossi explained that his wife was English, hence his ability to speak the language so well, and that he had helped several prisoners to cross the border. He would be willing to do the same for them, but . . . He paused. If they were prepared to stay, he could put them to good use. After Italy had surrendered, hundreds of POWs had taken advantage of the resulting confusion to disappear, heading deep into the countryside. He needed help to track them down and to assist them in their escape, before the Gestapo caught up with them. Since Paterson and Harris both spoke Italian and could stay at the Riccinis', he would be grateful for their help.

He left the two to consider his surprise offer. Paterson's immediate sense was to refuse. He was tired of being on the run and he wanted to get out, especially as they were this close to the border. But upon reflection, he realised that Signor Rossi's plan had merit. The Italian had impressed him with his focus and purpose. Also, if he and Harris agreed, they would no longer be 'the hunted'. Instead, they would be able to strike back at the enemy.

'I think we should agree,' Paterson told Harris. 'He's working for our men and I'm willing to stay.'

Paterson's one concern was how it might affect the Riccinis. It was dangerous for them to have hosted POWs for just a few days, and he didn't want to further encumber them with their presence. He needn't have worried. When they returned to the Riccinis' house, Signora Riccini declared herself overjoyed that she could help foil the enemy. Gabi, too, seemed very happy at the return of Paterson, but for quite different reasons.

For a brief period life took on an easy pace for Paterson. While they weren't exactly dating, there was a wonderful flirtation going on between him and Gabi, which lifted his spirits enormously. In return, the teenager was clearly enjoying her time with a young, good-looking and dashing foreigner. Perhaps fortuitously, Signor Rossi's escape organisation began to move into action. Word reached Paterson and Harris of groups of escaped POWs hiding out in the hills, sheltering with friendly families.

Harris and Paterson travelled to their hideouts. Once there, they attempted to persuade the POWs to escape across the border. Many had built up relationships with their hosts, and were reluctant to leave, believing the Allies would soon liberate all of Italy. Paterson had to disabuse them of that fact. The Allied frontline was still many hundreds of miles away. Fighting had proven fierce, and they were unlikely to reach the north of Italy for at least a year. The chances of the fugitives being caught were high, and the families sheltering them would very likely be shot. Fortunately, in light of the dire consequences for their hosts, most agreed to make a break for Switzerland.

Several weeks into their escape work, Paterson and Harris had assisted dozens of prisoners to cross the border, but there were still more. Reports reached them of a group of partisans headquartered in the mountains, which had been embroiled in a major battle with the Germans. Word was that many of the partisans were actually escaped POWs. Leaving Harris to liaise with other escapees, Paterson and a local guide hurried into the hills, but the only evidence of the partisans they found was a helmet with a bullet hole, hundreds of empty bullet cases, plus a machine-gun pit with a smashed-up weapon.

Unable to find any of the partisans, they returned to the Riccinis. By the time they reached the farmhouse it was dark and raining. As they approached, something made Paterson stop. There were no lights showing in the front room. The Italian guide offered to investigate, suggesting that Paterson wait in the bushes to see what transpired.

As Paterson looked on, worried for his friends, the guide knocked. Suddenly, the door was flung open and the guide was ordered inside at gunpoint. Paterson froze. Within minutes, the door opened and the guide was shoved out again. Paterson watched him head back down the drive. After a few moments, he crept out of the bushes, before hurrying to catch up. It turned out that the Questura had seized the Riccinis, but Gabi had managed to get away. There was no sign of Harris anywhere.

In due course Paterson learned that both Gabi and Harris had had forewarning and had managed to slip away. They most likely had headed for Milan. With no viable base for his escape network any more, Paterson decided to follow. He made his way to Signor Rossi's house, where he recounted the entire story. Signor Rossi didn't think the Riccinis were in any great danger, since the Questura had failed to seize the real evidence – Paterson and Harris.

'But what now?' Paterson asked.

Many British soldiers still remained in the villages, Signor Rossi explained. He'd like to get them out before the winter set in. 'By the way,' he added, 'I heard from your friend Gabi. She is very worried about you and I'm sure she'll be glad to hear that you're safe.'

Agreeing to stay and help, Paterson moved in with an elderly couple who were caretakers at a local factory. They seemed quiet but friendly, and sympathetic to the cause. The next evening, there was a knock at the door. Paterson tensed, as the woman of the house went to answer. He heard a girl's voice at the door. Moments later Paterson found a sobbing Gabi hugging him, her head buried in his chest. The elderly woman quietly took her leave, shutting the door gently behind her.

'Thank goodness you're safe,' Gabi whispered. 'Hold me.'

Paterson pulled her close and moments later they kissed. Aware of the dangers their attachment posed, Paterson insisted they would have to say their goodbyes, at least for now.

If the Questura connected Gabi to him, they would arrest her, and he couldn't bear that. Eventually, Gabi accepted that he was right. They kissed each other goodbye, and Paterson watched as Gabi walked away. It was the last that he would ever see of her.

The following day, Paterson was given a tour of Milan to acquaint himself with the layout of the city. He would need to familiarise himself with it, especially as he would very likely be working alone now. They covered all the sights: the grand La Scala opera house; the Piazza del Duomo, Milan's beautiful and historic city square; plus the Gestapo headquarters and the central police station. Finally, they arrived at a forbidding mass of interconnected buildings, protected by a high stone wall and towers – San Vittore prison.

'If you get taken there, you've had it,' Paterson was warned.

Over the coming weeks, he managed to get a number of Allied prisoners smuggled over the border, but one day he was travelling back from Lake Como on the train when it pulled to an unexpected halt. Leaning out of the window, Paterson could see a group of black-shirted Fascist Youth – the notorious Milizia Volontaria per la Sicurezza Nazionale, more commonly known as the 'Blackshirts' – lining up to board the train.

'Identity check!' shouted one.

Paterson froze. He had no such ID card. His only chance was to get off and somehow get away. Hurrying back down the train, he searched for an unguarded door, but the Fascist Youth were everywhere. Pushing his way along the crowded aisle, a Blackshirt demanded he show his ID. Paterson refused, saying he'd already presented it and was in a hurry. But just as he figured he'd managed to bluff his way through, another more authoritative voice rang out.

'Just a moment, Signore.' A middle-aged, balding man in a suit blocked Paterson's way. 'I am an officer of the Questura. You must produce your identity card.'

Within moments the Blackshirts had surrounded him. 'All right, all right,' Paterson declared. 'I haven't got an ID card because I'm an escaped British officer.'

There was a moment's stunned silence, before the Blackshirts hurled themselves upon him, wrestling him to the ground. Paterson was dragged off the train and frogmarched to the local barracks. After questioning by the Questura, to which Paterson's only answer was 'I can't remember,' he was led to San Vittore prison, its dark, menacing walls and towers rising before him.

There, Paterson was received by two SS men, who manhandled him through a series of iron doors, before shoving him into a cell, the heavy door being firmly bolted behind. After a night of broken sleep, Paterson awoke to a sparse meal of watery soup and a small dry roll. Shortly, two men arrived claiming to be Gestapo. They marched Paterson out of the prison and down the street to the Gestapo headquarters. Inside, the questioning began and it proved relentless.

'How did you escape?'

'Who has helped you?'

'Where have you been living?'

'Who gave you clothes and money?'

'Have you been spying and passing information to your colleagues in Switzerland?'

Paterson knew that if he cracked and revealed any details of what he had been up to, his brave Italian helpers would pay with their lives. For hours on end, he endured the interrogation, sticking rigidly to his cover – that ever since his escape he had wandered the Italian countryside, getting help from locals, none of whose names he could remember – despite the repeated threats that he would be shot as a spy.

San Vittore prison was renowned for being escape-proof and Paterson could see why. Built in the form of a star, it had six cell blocks, each four storeys high. Exercise courtyards lay between the blocks, at the end of which rose a twelve-foot-high wall. A gravel road ran around the entire cell-block complex, with another, higher wall enclosing that. Soldiers with machine-guns lined its outer perimeter. While the guards were mostly Italian, those in charge – Gestapo and SS officers – were German. According to Paterson's fellow prisoners, they were 'sadistic monsters'. Two men in particular, Sergeant Major Schwartz and his assistant, Corporal Franz, were the masters of brutality. It wasn't long before Paterson saw this with his own eyes.

Prisoners who stepped out of line were made to crawl up and down the exercise yard on their elbows and knees, until their clothing was ripped and their skin bleeding and raw. If anyone spilt anything, Sergeant Major Schwartz would force them to lick it up with their tongue, relishing their pain and discomfiture. When Sergeant Major Schwartz tired of his brutal punishments, his side-kick, Corporal Franz, would turn on a prisoner, treating him like a human football, kicking him until he lost consciousness.

Paterson was set to work changing lice-ridden blankets and cleaning out cells. He tried to keep his head down and to remain unnoticed by the guards, but some things he witnessed were almost beyond his capacity to endure. There were men, women and children – whole families – held at San Vittore, but only temporarily. Paterson learned that they were Jews, and that they were bound for the Mauthausen concentration camp complex, in Austria.

Moved almost to tears by the plight of these families, Paterson risked passing words of encouragement to them, while trying to share what little food he could and even though he was always hungry. Witnessing their bitter plight fuelled his own thoughts of escape. If he could only get away, he could take the fight to the Nazi enemy once again – those who were responsible for perpetrating such unspeakable atrocities. But after much watchfulness and deliberation, he realised all his schemes were hopeless. San

Vittore did indeed appear to be escape-proof. He resolved that his only purpose had to be to stay alive and to remain sane for long enough to see an end to the war.

The seasons passed – winter bleeding into spring. It brought little relief for those locked up in San Vittore. As the Allied forces advanced north through Italy, the savagery of the German guards increased, with some prisoners being driven to a local quarry and shot out of hand.

Then, one early afternoon in June 1944, Paterson caught sight of someone he had hoped never to see inside the prison walls: it was Signor Rossi, the mastermind of the Milan escape network. Sandwiched between two thickset guards, the slightly built figure was hustled into an isolation cell. Paterson's heart sank. Desperately hoping to speak with Signor Rossi, he knew he would have to wait for the right moment.

The next morning, he learned that Signor Rossi had been taken for interrogation. Paterson hoped that if the Gestapo could pin nothing on him, he might be transferred into a cell along with the rest of them, but his interrogation and isolation continued for many days. Paterson had almost given up hope of seeing his friend again, when Signor Rossi appeared. It seemed that he had been given some of the same menial duties as Paterson, which placed them in the same part of the prison.

Finding themselves in an empty cell, they seized the chance to exchange a few words. It turned out that Signor Rossi had been sold out to the Gestapo by a supposed friend. They had nothing on him, barring a report that he had recently compiled, listing the number of POWs that he had helped escape.

'Nearly three thousand,' he whispered, proudly. 'They got nothing from me despite all their questioning.'

Paterson was consumed by worry for his friend. He asked what would happen to him now. 'I'll appear before a court-martial, and then most likely be shot or, if I'm lucky, locked up.'

Horrified, Paterson was determined to do something to help, despite the fact that the prison seemed escape-proof.

'There is always a way out if you have money, George,' Signor Rossi reassured him. 'One of the warders is being bribed and he'll help us escape. Plus, I want to take another three men, who were also working with me. If things go to plan, we could all be out in a week.'

Paterson could barely believe his ears. It was five days before he and Rossi spoke again. It was in the exercise yard, and Signor Rossi was casually leaning against a wall, when he beckoned Paterson over.

'Have you still got your civilian clothes?' he whispered.

'I have. They're in my cell.'

'Excellent. Here's what we're going to do.'

Signor Rossi explained that they would make their escape attempt during the guards' siesta that very day. They would dress in their civilian clothing, but with their prison overalls thrown over the top. They would carry blankets to give the impression that they were going about their menial duties, and would leave the cell block, passing through a courtyard and a gate, which would have been left open. Right then they would be positioned between the two security walls.

'Are you with me so far?' Rossi quizzed.

Paterson nodded and Rossi continued. To their right, about fifty yards away, would be a shed. Inside they would remove their prison overalls. When they came out they would find a door in the wall that was always kept locked, which meant it was never

37

guarded. A duplicate key had been made by the warder, the man that Signor Rossi had bribed. With that they would unlock the door and slip through, but the last escapee had to close the door and lock it after him. That way, they would hide the means of their escape. The door led onto the open street, where they must get away quickly and hide.

There was one last detail, Signore Rossi explained: they would have to make their escapes one by one, for a crowd of prisoners would be sure to attract the attention of the guards. Paterson returned to his cell buzzing with excitement, but at the same time he was acutely aware of what would happen if they failed. Sergeant Major Schwartz and Corporal Franz would escort them to the quarry and deliver a bullet to each of their heads. The minutes seemed to drag by, as he rehearsed the plan over and over again in his head. Finally, it was time.

Changing into his civilian clothes, he pulled his prison over-alls on top, grabbed a stack of dirty blankets and set off for the designated cell block. Guards lined the corridors, but they were either dozing or reading – siesta time – and Paterson's presence went unnoticed. As he crossed the first courtyard, he began to feel hot and sweaty, sensing the eyes that were tracking him from the guard towers above. Reaching the far side, he opened the door and slipped into the neighbouring cell block. A guard sat smoking and their eyes met, but the bundle of blankets must have convinced him that Paterson was going about his menial duties, for the bored guard looked the other way.

Paterson reached the end of the corridor, and dropped the blankets into one of the latrines, before exiting through a side door into the final courtyard. There, across the open space, lay an open gate. Trying not to run, he forced himself to keep at a steady and relaxed-looking pace. He slipped through the gate and was now on the gravel road lying between the perimeter walls. Over on the right, fifty yards away was the shed.

He snatched a glance at the sentries above: they seemed not to have noticed his presence. Counting the paces to the shed, and expecting a challenge to ring out at any moment, he reached it and slipped inside. Sweating and with his heart pounding, Paterson ripped off his prison overalls. Reshaping the fedora hat that he had hidden under one arm, he hesitated for just a moment. Would he make it those last few steps to freedom? What if a guard spotted him and opened fire?

Driving the doubts from his mind, he slipped out of the shed and took a few steps around the corner. There was the door that Signor Rossi had assured him would be left unguarded and unlocked. Turning the handle, he breathed a sigh of relief when the catch clicked and the door swung open. Stepping through and closing it behind him, Paterson found himself on the far side of the prison walls. Freedom beckoned. He heard a tram rattling towards him. If he could reach that, his getaway would be all but guaranteed.

Suddenly, Paterson's stomach gave a horrible lurch. Coming around the corner was the stocky figure of one of Corporal Franz's henchmen, with whom Paterson had already had several bruising encounters. He could not turn away, for fear he'd raise the man's suspicions. There was nothing for it but to brazen it out.

Pulling his hat brim low, Paterson stepped straight ahead. Out of the corner of his eye he could see the guard glance at him, but Paterson strode purposefully around the corner and was gone. With the nearest watchtower well behind him now, Paterson headed for the tram stop. The tram seemed to move at a snail's pace, creeping closer by the second. Moments later, Paterson stepped aboard, the bell jangled and they were off.

Incredibly, Paterson had just broken out of the supposedly escape-proof San Vittore prison in Milan.

He made his way to Maria Resta's apartment, where he knocked tentatively. The door opened and she rushed to embrace him. 'It's so good to see you, Giorgio.'

Paterson related his story to Maria and her husband, while he feasted on a meal of spaghetti, cheese, fruit and wine. Later that night he awoke, his stomach in spasms. After the near star-vation of the prison rations, he was unaccustomed to such rich food. Maria Resta's news had been hugely encouraging. Like Paterson, Signor Rossi had also escaped. He planned to head for Switzerland and was adamant that Paterson should do the same. Mentally and physically exhausted, Paterson accepted that this was the only sensible option, for he longed to be back in Britain. He had been variously held captive or on the run for three and a half years now, and he hungered for a little security and safety.

That afternoon, he ventured out onto the streets of Milan, allowing Maria Resta to take him to a local photographer, to obtain a passport-sized photo for his identity card. Fearful that he would be recaptured, Paterson did his best to steady his nerves. The plan was for a Milanese fireman, known only as 'Orlando', to accompany Paterson as far as Lake Como, just short of the border, from where a local guide would lead him across the frontier.

At noon the following day, Maria Resta took Paterson to the fire station where Orlando was waiting. After bidding a heartfelt farewell, Paterson followed Orlando to a small room at the back, where he was given a fireman's uniform to change into. With his newly forged ID card to hand, Paterson mounted a fire engine alongside Orlando, and they set off for a small farmhouse in the vicinity of Lake Como.

There, Paterson was introduced to 'Francesco', a professional smuggler. This man, according to Orlando, was 'the greatest rascal unhung'.

With Francesco in the lead, Paterson made his way up the steep hill behind the farmstead, and they were soon in open moorland. A path snaked across the high ground, while below Lake Como glistened and glinted beguilingly, small boats sailing hither and thither. It looked so picture-postcard perfect, but here the enemy's eyes were everywhere.

After an hour on that winding path, they came to a slight ridge and a small patch of bushes. Francesco dropped into a crouch, Paterson following suit. Down below was a well-worn path, which Francesco explained was the route taken by the border guards. The next patrol was due in about ten minutes. Once that had passed, Paterson would have around half an hour to make it down the slope, across the path and under the high wire fence on the far side.

They waited for the patrol. Once it had snaked by, Paterson thanked his roguish guide, before hurrying down the bank in a half-crouch. He dashed across the path before dropping to his belly and half-sliding and half-crawling under the wire fence. Once he had wormed his way through, he jumped to his feet and ran towards a clump of beckoning trees. There, he stopped for a brief moment to catch his breath, and to reflect with disbelief that after three and a half years as a prisoner of war, a fugitive, and an escape-network organiser, it seemed he was finally free.

His spirits soaring, he took to a path leading down from the high border fence. But shortly, he rounded an outcrop of rock, only to blunder into a squad of soldiers dressed in the green-grey uniform so redolent of enemy troops. For a long moment Paterson was rooted to the spot. Had he somehow erred, and re-entered Italy? Had he been betrayed by Francesco? But shortly, he realised the truth: these were not German soldiers, but Swiss.

After a polite welcome from the Swiss patrol, they advised Paterson to continue on his way, heading for Bellinzona, a town set a dozen kilometres or so from the border. There, Paterson would be formally processed by the Swiss authorities. Shortly, he reached a mountainside cottage. The woman of the house brought him milk, fresh bread, cheese and cold meat. It was delicious and he ate and drank gratefully, feeling refreshed for his onwards journey.

Upon reaching Bellinzona, there followed the formalities of an interview with a Swiss captain, after which Paterson was obliged to spend a few weeks in a nearby quarantine centre. There, to his immense joy, he was reunited with Corporal Jack Watson, his second-in-command on Operation Colossus. Watson had made his own epic escape, after discipline had collapsed in the POW camp where he was held, following Mussolini's fall.

Paterson and Watson were transferred to Montreux, on Lake Geneva, where a large number of British and Allied escaped POWs were being held. The Allies had set up offices to handle the influx of escapees, and to provide them with money to buy clothes and other essentials. On his first night, Paterson, desperate to celebrate his freedom, hit the town. Come morning, he'd spent all his money and had a stonking great headache as proof of the partying!

Deciding the Lake Geneva beaches offered a cheaper and healthier form of relaxation, he headed there for a swim. This became a daily routine. One morning, he noticed a couple talking near by. One was an utterly striking figure: she was tall, slim and blonde, with piercing blue eyes. Oddly, Paterson figured he recognised the young lady's companion, but he couldn't decide from where. And then it hit him: it was one of the many escapees that Paterson had helped usher across the border.

Remembering the man's name, he called out: 'Charles! Charles Gray.'

Gray in turn recognised Paterson and the two shook hands vigorously. It was an emotional reunion. Gray introduced his companion to Paterson. Her name was Karen, and as their eyes met Paterson felt an instant attraction. Having bid his reluctant goodbye to Gabi, Signora Riccini's raven-haired daughter, in Milan, now, on the shores of Lake Geneva, he felt the first stirrings of an equally powerful attraction. Over the days that followed, Paterson and Karen's friendship blossomed and Gray, tactfully, retired from the scene. Speaking English but with a strong trace of a French accent, the enchanting Karen, who had a Swiss father and an English mother, had been brought up in and around Geneva. But otherwise her life remained something of a mystery, and Paterson didn't pry too deeply.

He was captivated, finding they had much in common, enjoying the same kind of hobbies – swimming, dancing and hiking. Their time together almost erased the dark memories of the war, but of course in the autumn of 1944 it was still far from being won. Not long after meeting Karen, Paterson received a mystery summons. He was asked to meet with a certain Mr McTavish, in the British military's Press Office, which had been established in Montreux. Puzzled, Paterson took a taxi there one morning.

McTavish, a tall, grey-haired Scot, invited Paterson into his office, before enquiring how he was enjoying Montreux. After a little more such small talk he got straight to the point. The Press Office was actually a front. In truth, McTavish worked for the Special Operations Executive (SOE), Churchill's so-called Ministry for Ungentlemanly Warfare. SOE had been established to break all the rules of war, taking the fight to the enemy no-holds-barred. In that spirit, McTavish's job was to despatch SOE agents into Italy, seeking information that London desperately needed, or charged with acts of assassination or sabotage, or raising resistance armies.

McTavish was forever receiving requests for arms and explosives from the Italian partisans, and while some were genuine, others were not. One of his agents had been about to go in but had gone down with meningitis. Accordingly, McTavish urgently needed a replacement. Paterson had a good record. He spoke Italian and had been living with the partisans. McTavish figured that he would make an ideal SOE agent.

McTavish produced a map and explained more about the assignment he had in mind. In the mountains of northern Italy, the partisan bands were beginning to work together, and they had already cleared the enemy from a few miles of the border. Their plan was to build up their numbers and strength, before becoming strong enough to take Domodossola, a city that sits at the foot of the Italian Alps. Working from that base, if the whole of northern Italy could come together in armed rebellion, it would cut the German Army's supply lines and force them into defeat or surrender.

'I'm in contact with one of their leaders, a Colonel Monetta,' McTavish explained. 'He's a good man, and a former Italian Army officer. They have enough weapons for now, but if they get more recruits, we'll need to air-drop arms, ammunition and supplies. It's one of the reasons why I need someone like you in place.'

McTavish eyed Paterson searchingly, for the big Canadian was giving little away. Having spent so many long months on the run and being hunted through Italy, he wondered whether he really wished to return. And now there was the Karen factor to consider . . .

'There's another reason, too,' McTavish persisted. 'A whole generation of Italians have grown up under Mussolini. If they start fighting between themselves and break up into factions, it could result in civil war. London and Washington want reliable reports on any political developments, which is why we think you're the man for the job. Part soldier; part political observer.'

With that, McTavish told Paterson to let him know his decision in three or four days' time.

Paterson sought out Karen. They spent a delightful few hours wandering in the flower meadows on the hills that fringe Lake Geneva. Taking a rest, she remarked on her companion's strange mood. He seemed quiet and introspective. In truth, Paterson was inwardly in turmoil. He was torn between his affection for her and his sense of duty. He felt incapable of choosing between the company of this delightful woman and what he knew, deep down, was the right thing to do.

'Karen, I may have to go away,' he said at last. Because SOE was such a secret organ of the British war effort, he could reveal few details. But he had thought up a good cover story. 'I'm possibly going to be working for the British Consul in Locarno. They need someone who speaks reasonable Italian. Perhaps you could come down there, if I can't get away?'

Paterson had chosen Locarno, for it was the nearest Swiss town to the area of Italy he would be operating in. He figured he could maybe flit across the border now and again, if a liaison with Karen was on the cards. Her obvious keenness to visit made it even harder for Paterson to accept McTavish's offer, especially knowing that he could well be dead within a month, or taken prisoner – again.

Nevertheless, duty called.

Paterson returned to McTavish's office to accept his offer. He had one condition, he explained – that he be allowed to take along his trusty corporal, and wireless operator, Jack Watson. McTavish readily agreed.

That sorted, the Scot got straight to work, briefing Paterson about the names and backgrounds of the various partisan commanders and the cover identity they'd thought up for him. The Gestapo's suspicions that Paterson had been a spy worried McTavish. Accordingly, Paterson would take on a new identity. He would become Major George Robertson, of the Royal Engineers, who had been captured in North Africa and held at a prisoner-of-war camp in north-eastern Italy. Paterson's cover story was that he had escaped amid the chaos of the Italian surrender and had joined the partisans.

McTavish explained that he'd get Paterson properly kitted out with mountain clothing and equipment. He also advised him to make contact with John Birback, the British Vice-Consul, in Locarno, to whom he would be reporting, once he went over the border. At least having such an influential contact might boost his chances of seeing Karen, Paterson reasoned.

After the meeting with McTavish was done, Paterson tracked down Watson and explained the coming mission. 'It won't be any picnic. In fact, it may well be pure chaos. But if you're up for it, I'd like you to join me.'

Watson's reply was instant. 'I'm with you, sir.'

Over the next few days, Paterson and Watson were properly kitted out in Alpine gear. They studied maps, memorised codes and rehearsed their cover stories. Just the one weekend remained before their departure, and Paterson was determined to enjoy it in Karen's company. After dinner they went to a lakeside cabaret, before spending the rest of the evening in each other's arms. Before the weekend was out, Paterson told Karen that he loved her and that he wanted to marry her, but . . .

Anticipating his next sentence, she remarked: 'You're going back into Italy, aren't you?'

Paterson nodded. The rest didn't need saying. Once he had crossed back into that war-torn country, he didn't know whether he would ever see her again. The following morning they said their farewells, arranging to meet in Locarno. They promised each other they would get married, but neither really knew if that promise could ever be kept.

The moment of departure arrived, and Paterson and Watson were joined by Birback, the Locarno Vice-Consul. Together, they began the drive to the border. The Swiss mountains were quiet and peaceful, contrasting so markedly with what they were heading into – a war zone stalked by hatred, hunger, fear, savagery and death. Birback dropped Paterson and Watson on the approach to a bridge. He could venture no further. Wishing them good luck, he left the two men to carry on without him.

On the far side of the bridge, Paterson and Watson were

received by Colonel Monetta, McTavish's main contact among the partisans. The colonel took them to a large house, to meet the commanders of the various factions. There was Superbi, a plump and jolly fellow who was leader of the socialists. There were Arca and Didio, both young, former Italian Army officers, who commanded the Green Flames – the Catholic and democratic partisans – and the Royalists, respectively. Courageous and spirited, both were fine leaders of men.

The only commander missing was Moscatelli, the leader of the Communists, who apparently was too busy to be there. 'Probably trying to convert the peasants into Reds,' one of the others remarked, dismissively. After a toast to victory, Paterson reassured them of the Allies' support and congratulated them on their recent successes.

'Tomorrow, we will attack the German pigs and you'll see that we mean business,' piped up Arca, the Green Flames commander.

Just before dawn, everyone was in position above a German military outpost. Arca explained that the 'Tedeschi' – the Italian term they used for Germans – were quartered in the large house below. Superbi's men were in position on the far side, so the Tedeschi would be caught in a pincer movement.

One of Arca's fighters commenced the attack, opening fire, after which there was a fusillade of shots from Superbi's men as well. Shortly, the Tedeschi woke up to the assault and began to return fire. For a quarter of an hour the battle raged, with one partisan taking a bullet to the shoulder and another being fatally wounded in the head. Finally, a white shirt tied to a broomstick appeared at the window of the outpost. Moments later the German soldiers filed out, their hands raised in the air.

Over the next few days, the partisans continued their drive to rid the mountains of these isolated German outposts. Few put up more than sporadic resistance. Despite their successes, it became clear to Paterson that the partisans were prone to disorganisation and indiscipline. Ironically, the only leader with any kind of grip on his fighters proved to be the Communist, Moscatelli – the man who had snubbed Paterson at the very first meeting.

A well-built man of about thirty-five, Moscatelli had trained with the Russian Red Army in guerrilla tactics and political activism. He had been relatively successful in persuading the local peasants to join his Communist brigade. With two thousand under his command, his unit dwarfed the others, who could barely muster five hundred each. But Moscatelli lacked properly trained officers, and his fighters could prove as volatile as the rest.

Regardless, on 10 September 1944 – so just a few weeks after Paterson and Watson had joined their number – the combined forces struck against the city of Domodossola. The battle raged, but not for anything like as long as Paterson had feared. When the German garrison surrendered, Paterson was puzzled. Why, he wondered, had they accepted defeat so easily? But when he laid eyes upon the troops stationed in the city, he understood: they were made up of elderly reservists and demoralised conscripts.

Overjoyed at taking the city, the partisans seemed inclined to sit back and enjoy the fruits of their success. But Paterson was worried. Surely, the German high command could not allow such blatant insurrection within territory which they in theory still controlled. He felt sure there would be a counter-attack and the partisans would need to be ready. With ammunition in short supply, as well as ready cash to buy provisions, Paterson decided to head for Locarno. There, he would petition SOE for weaponry and cash. At least that way they might hold Domodossola.

Paterson's foray back to Locarno was all too brief: there was no time at all to rendezvous with Karen. But at least he returned to Domodossola as the hero of the hour. He brought with him 20,000 lire in a rucksack, and the promises of air-drops of weaponry to follow.

Three days later, the first air-drop was due. Together with Arca, the Green Flames commander, and a dozen of his men, Paterson headed to the drop zone, which was set on a hill to the north of the city. An hour after the allocated drop-time, there was still no sign of the plane. As each further hour passed, Paterson grew more and more concerned. They were badly in need of the weaponry and ammo, especially as there had been reports of German military activity to the south of the city.

Just prior to dawn, they decided to return to Domodossola. They would try again in a few days' time. Paterson slept for several hours but was awoken late that afternoon with troubling news. All along the defensive perimeter to their south there were reports of probing attacks by the enemy. Paterson sensed it was a sign of worse to come.

In the early hours of the morning, Colonel Monetta – the overall partisan commander – woke Paterson, with the news that he'd been dreading. An entire German battalion, supported by Fascist Italian infantry, was advancing towards the city. The partisans had managed to blow the bridge through the main pass but were being forced to fall back into the mountains.

'Didio [Royalist brigade commander] is there, gathering his brigade . . .' Colonel Monetta explained. 'He'll try and move forward and stop them, but if he fails and they get in behind us along the frontier . . .' Monetta drew his finger across his throat, in an obvious gesture: if that happened, they would be finished.

All hopes were now pinned on Didio and his fighters. Paterson woke Watson, and together with Colonel Monetta they drove towards the frontline, arriving just after dawn. The defences appeared to be in a perilous state, and Paterson was acutely aware of how the failure of that air-drop might turn the tide of the battle. With things as desperate as they were, he suggested that Watson remain with the partisans, while he would head for the Royalist brigade commander Locarno to urge the air-drops to resume.

That agreed, Paterson began the drive back north, together with Colonel Monetta. En route, they paused to speak with Didio, who was rushing his fighters to shore up the frontline. The dramatic terrain all around appeared to be eerily quiet and deserted. But in truth, German troops had infiltrated the area, unseen by Didio's partisans, and it was now that their ambush was sprung.

All of a sudden, a barrage of fire rang out from the high ground, followed by the rattle of heavy machine guns. Stunned for a moment by the suddenness of the assault, Paterson, Colonel Monetta and Didio froze, as the air was cut with bullets all around them. Moments later, they began to crawl back towards the car, as the entire valley echoed with the noise of intense battle.

It took them thirty minutes dodging from one patch of cover to another, to get close to their vehicle. But their progress had been tracked by the enemy, their very movements betraying the presence of the car. Moments later, a barrage of tracer fire ripped into the vehicle and it burst into flames. Now, they were pinned down and bereft of any means of speedy escape, or of Paterson making it back to Locarno.

Worse still, the only route of retreat lay across an open stretch of bullet-pocked road. Colonel Monetta went first, sprinting ahead and diving into cover, as a fusillade of bullets tore at his heels. As Paterson contemplated the dash before him, bursts of fire continued to rake the open road. Finally, he decided he had to go. His Tommy gun grasped closely in his hands, he leapt to his feet and sprang forward, charging across the killing ground, before diving in behind the colonel.

Didio followed, but as he took his first steps a machine gun roared into life. Didio's face contorted, his hand clutching his left knee. Moments later, Didio, just twenty-four years of age, was cut down. An easy prey now, bullets tore into his body, as it jerked violently on the ground.

'Jesus,' croaked Paterson. He felt numbed by the savagery of the sudden attack.

But this was no time to tarry. With Colonel Monetta at his side, they dashed to join a group of partisans who were sheltering in the cover of a culvert. For two hours the battle raged, as the partisans held one side of the road, and the enemy the other. But all the while the intensity of the partisans' fire seemed to be slowing, while that of the enemy grew progressively heavier. Soon, there were rounds from anti-tank guns shattering the rocks to either side.

Finally, a strange and eerie silence descended, the firing coming to an abrupt halt. Was it over? Paterson thought not. A rock was dislodged near by and a cascade of smaller stones followed. The enemy were closing in. Without a word, Paterson and Colonel Monetta burst out of the culvert, guns blazing, as they prepared to make a last stand. Paterson raised his gun to nail the nearest German, but Colonel Monetta was quicker, cutting the enemy soldier down.

Suddenly, Paterson caught a glimpse of a grey-uniformed figure creeping between the boulders. A short burst from his Tommy gun and the enemy soldier fell dead. Another burst of fire cut the air, and this time Colonel Monetta was the target. Paterson turned to see him crumple, his body ripped full of bullet holes, as he collapsed in a small pool of water. Quickly, Paterson searched out the killer. Aiming his Tommy gun, he released a savage burst, ripping into the German soldier's head and torso.

Trading bursts of fire, Paterson tried to dash up the road, retreating towards the main body of partisans. Another German crept into view. A squeeze on the trigger and . . . *click* . . . Paterson was all out of ammunition. Throwing the gun aside, he prepared to take to his heels. But seconds later he felt boots kicking away his legs, followed by a flurry of punches and blows from rifle butts. As his body hit the ground his head slammed into a boulder and everything went dark.

Paterson came to sometime later, to spy a figure striding down the hillside, wearing the distinctive uniform of a sergeant major of the German Alpine troops. The rest of the enemy came to attention in his presence.

'No shooting of the prisoners,' the figure barked out an order. 'Take them back to camp for questioning.'

Paterson was hauled to his feet, but one of the German troopers seemed to pay him particular interest. As he stared at Paterson, he suddenly cried out: 'Oberleutnant Paterson!'

In the same instant, Paterson recognised the German trooper. It was a man he had known only as 'Willi' – one of the guards at San Vittore prison. Having been recognised, there was no hope now of maintaining his cover story – that of being escaped POW Major George Robertson, of the Royal Engineers. Paterson thanked his lucky stars for one thing: no one had yet thought to search him properly and for now his – false – identity card remained hidden.

Paterson was led to a heavily guarded out-house, where he joined a clutch of other prisoners. As soon as he was able, he tore his identity card into tiny pieces, and together with his – false – dog tags, he poked it all through the cracks in the wooden floorboards. Come morning, they were hustled onto some trucks and driven south for several hours, until they reached a bleak, grey building, which someone muttered was Novara prison. There, they were herded into a large communal cell.

Early the next morning Paterson was taken off for questioning. The SS sergeant major demanded to know everything that had happened to Paterson after he had escaped from San Vittore. Overnight, Paterson had prepared his cover story: he had headed into the hills and joined the partisans. When the SS man moved on to who had sheltered him, he countered with the tried and tested ruse – he simply couldn't remember.

A month passed at Novara prison, before Paterson was told that he was to be moved. Under escort from two bulky SS men, he was taken to the local station and hustled onto a train heading east. Arriving in Milan, a car drove Paterson along streets that looked all too familiar. His heart sank as the penny dropped – he was being returned to none other than the escape-proof hellhole of San Vittore.

Upon arrival, the familiar tone of Corporal Franz's voice boomed out, only now he had been promoted to sergeant major. Worse still, when he laid eyes on Paterson, unshaven and looking very much the worse for wear, he roared with laughter.

'You look as though you've had a rough time,' he guffawed. 'Have you returned for some of our kind treatment?'

'Yes, of course. I've missed you all,' Paterson retorted.

Expecting to receive one of Franz's signature flurry of kicks, Paterson was surprised at the comparative geniality of his response. He was led to his isolation cell, and given increased rations, supposedly on orders of Sergeant Major Franz himself. It made not the slightest bit of sense, and of course the relatively benign treatment could not last.

Shortly, he was taken for interrogation. This time, his Gestapo inquisitors demanded Paterson reveal the names of all those who had helped him, or he should expect the worst. Paterson stuck to his story, answering each question as slowly and as carefully as he could, explaining that he simply did not remember. He was shown photos of men and women, and asked if he knew them. With each he shook his head.

For days the grilling continued, but now with the added threat of torture. Finally, the Gestapo officers ordered Paterson to be taken away, warning him that his lack of cooperation would very likely mean that he would be shot as a spy. Paterson slumped dejectedly in his cell. He had no doubt their threats were real, and he could see no way out.

To make matters worse, Paterson had developed a horrific rash from the scabies – microscopic mites that burrow into the skin to lay eggs – which infested the cells. He asked to see the prison doctor and was taken to the dispensary. The Italian medic proved kindly and friendly and Paterson sensed that the man might be willing to help. Over several visits for scabies treatment, they chatted amiably, before the inevitable subject arose. Might the doctor be able to help Paterson escape, he wondered, especially since he was very likely slated for execution?

The doctor confirmed that he might, but only if he could get Paterson transferred to the prison infirmary. To do that, Paterson would need to have a serious illness. The doctor offered to give him some pills that would turn him yellow, so he could fake jaundice – a potentially fatal condition that causes yellowing of the skin.

Paterson returned to his cell with his hopes lifted, and his thoughts turned to Switzerland and his beloved Karen. Sure enough, over the next few days the pills started to turn his skin an unhealthy shade of yellow. But before his transformation was complete, he had an unexpected visitor: Sergeant Major Franz. Beaming, Franz announced that the Gestapo were done with Paterson, which meant he would be transferred to the Wehrmacht – the military – wing of the prison, to await court-martial.

On hearing this, Paterson's spirits plummeted to an all-time low. He also suspected he knew why Franz had allowed him extra rations. The brute of San Vittore was sure to know the Allies were drawing closer, and that he would be in the firing line if he were found to be responsible for the Canadian's death. But either way, his escape plan lay in tatters.

In the Wehrmacht wing, food proved to be in precious short supply. On a near-starvation diet, Paterson became gaunt and weak. The winter months of late 1944 proved cold and icy, and Paterson was left to shiver under thin blankets. Although most of the warders were less sadistic than their Gestapo counterparts, one took great delight in forcing some of the most emaciated and weak to carry out hard physical exercise.

The months dragged by. Still there was no trial for Paterson, nor any death sentence. Towards the end of April 1945, he was woken by the sound of distant gunfire. His spirits momentarily soared. Perhaps the partisans were rising in Milan, with the Allies advancing just behind them. But no one seemed certain.

Later that day the prisoners were ordered to pack themselves into the cells on one floor, and some feared this signified that they were being readied for transport to Germany.

Paterson decided it was time for action, come what may. Encouraging others to join him, he hatched a desperate plan of escape. The very next morning, when the orderlies brought around the rations, the first person who could do so should overpower a guard, fling open the cell doors, at which point the prisoners should surge forth and create as much pandemonium as possible, in an effort to break free.

The following morning Paterson's nerves were on edge. He strained to listen as the orderlies passed down the cells. Suddenly the corridor erupted with yelling and shrieking, as the first prisoners burst forth from their cells. With tension rising, Paterson yelled: 'All right, everyone, let's make some noise!' At the same time he started kicking and hammering on his bars. Moments later Paterson heard the key turn in his cell door, and he joined the crush flooding into the corridor. Confronted by an angry mob, the sergeant on guard raised his hands with the keys above his head, in surrender.

Inserting the key into the final lock, the gate swung open, the crowd roaring in triumph as figures charged into the open streets. At their vanguard was George Paterson, executing his second miraculous escape from San Vittore. Outside, it was clear that the partisans had indeed risen up. Groups of locals with rifles and pistols were laughing and singing. Someone informed Paterson that a great battle had been won. The Germans were leaving Milan and the city was theirs.

An hour later, Paterson found himself outside Maria Resta's front door once again. Upon spying him she flung her arms around him, kissing him delightedly, before inviting him in to join the celebrations. Among many others, Milan's new Chief of Police was present. He declared himself so grateful for all the work that Paterson had done in the cause of Italy. Later that day, Paterson was driven in a limousine with a police escort into the hills, where he was given a grand reception as an important 'partisan chieftain'.

Amid the celebrations, Paterson received word that British paratroopers had landed at Milan airport, after which they had taken over the villa of one of Mussolini's henchmen, as their headquarters. Paterson made his way there, so he could be re-united with his fellow paratroopers, the force with which he had originally deployed to Italy, on Operation Colossus, over four years ago.

Paterson's epic tale constituted a four-year odyssey, one of repeated capture and escape, which encompassed almost the entire length of Italy and spanned much of the duration of the war. In the coming days he would sadly learn that his fiancée, Karen, had met somebody else, after she had concluded that Paterson was dead, and she had broken off their engagement. Some years later, Paterson would meet another soul mate and they would live a long and happy life together.

In due course, Paterson was promoted to captain and awarded the Military Cross with two bars – the equivalent of the Military Cross three times – for his extraordinary exploits in Italy, his operations with the partisans, his work for SOE and his repeated escapes. He was also made a Freeman of the City of Milan on 31 July 1945, the proclamation reading: 'The Mayor, interpreting also . . . the deep feelings of the patriots who were his compan-ions . . . in the fight against the common enemy, confers on

Captain George Robert Paterson the honorary citizenship of Milan.' He would remain in that city and environs for more than a year, assisting the Allied authorities in the post-war period.

Incredibly, like George Paterson, our next great escapee would also be awarded the Military Cross three times (MC and two bars). The first of two such decorations was earned as a result of the heroic circumstances in which he was captured, and for his breathtaking escape from enemy custody.

His was a tale that would rival that of Paterson, in terms of scope and sheer daring.

Great Escape Two

MUTINY AND MAROONED AT SEA

Lying prone on the roof of the POW hospital and clad only in a pair of shorts, Captain Roy Farran appeared to be innocently enjoying the hot August sun. To any guard – and there were scores manning the machine-gun towers and barbed-wire fences that enclosed the camp – he looked as relaxed as any prisoner working on his tan. But in truth, Farran's 'sunbathing' was all part of a carefully crafted escape plan. And come hell or high water, Farran was determined he *would* escape.

Blessed with striking Irish good looks – piercing blue eyes, blond hair, fair skin, fine features; his ancestors hailed from County Donegal – Farran knew his pallor would give him away very quickly on the far side of the wire. Unless he could tan, and tan quickly, he stood little chance of passing as a local. In Nikaia, a suburb of Athens, where he was incarcerated, the local Greeks were typically darker-skinned, with olive complexions and tousled black hair.

Ever since his arrival, almost three months earlier, Farran had memorised every detail of the POW hospital and adjoining camp. Opened on 9 May 1941 to deal with the increasing numbers of wounded Allied prisoners, the hospital was a 'modern structure built in the shape of a Cross of Lorraine', Farran recalled. A 'large white building', it boasted a high wire fence woven from 'close vertical and horizontal strands', connected to rolls of concertina wire. In addition to this formidable barrier, the perimeter was watched day and night by a rotation of guards.

Despite the fortifications, Farran was far from alone in being preoccupied with thoughts of escape. Shortly after his arrival he had made contact with a small band of men who were determined to break out. Farran described their leader, Robin Savage, as 'a regular soldier of the Queen's Guard' turned 'Commando officer'. Then there was veteran Commando Ken Maxwell, plus a Commando lieutenant from New Zealand named Robin Sinclair. Together, they formed an escape committee dedicated to finding a way to break free and rejoin Allied forces.

They had proven relentless in their efforts. Many of the more successful breakouts had shown real ingenuity and daring: two New Zealanders had hidden in the hospital's dirty laundry and were carried out of the gates by unwitting German guards; some Australians had sneaked beneath the wire, even as another prisoner – a Brit blessed with considerable artistic talent – distracted a sentry by drawing his portrait; and, most audacious of all, two men had pole-vaulted the fence and managed to survive the hail of bullets that came after them. The escape committee were supposed to coordinate all such efforts, ensuring no two escape attempts clashed, inadvertently jeopardising each other.

Farran, Savage, Maxwell and Sinclair spent their time studying the condition and temperament of the sentries and gathering supplies to aid their endeavours once they were over the wall. They dreamed up schemes for escaping from Nazi-occupied Greece, the most unlikely of which involved hijacking an enemy sea-plane – which they had little idea how to fly – and speeding back to friendly lines. Most of their ideas, however, were more firmly rooted in reality.

As far as Farran saw it, they had two options once over the wire: head to the Greek coast to try to get away by boat or attempt the trek some six hundred miles overland to neutral Turkey. Many of the would-be escapees were wounded and battle-weary, and such an epic march was doubtless beyond them, especially as they were certain to be hounded by the enemy. The escape committee favoured mass breakouts, aiming to free as many Allied POWs as possible, but for many the only viable option was to try to make their getaway by sea.

It would be all but impossible to get out of the prison and onto a boat without support on the outside. Farran had heard reports of a resistance movement in Athens, one that was prepared to 'help escaped prisoners', but he had little idea what form that help might take. At first all efforts to make contact with such a group were frustrated, but in early August Savage approached Farran with exciting news: via a shadowy go-between, he'd managed to make contact with members of the local Greek resistance.

That night, by chance, there was a terrible storm. Forked lighting speared the mountains ringing the Attica Basin, which cradles the city of Athens. Farran recalled how a deafening wind blew up, and 'the rain came down in torrents'. The following morning he awoke to discover that, unbeknown to him there had been a mass breakout. Thirteen officers and thirteen men – Savage, Maxwell and Sinclair among them – had seized the chance to slip under the wire, using the chaos of the storm as cover. Farran was thrilled that they had made it, but he was also bitterly disappointed that he had been left behind, and at a loss as to why.

'I felt deserted in a way, for . . . now I was all alone in the hospital,' Farran remarked of the moment.

In truth, Savage and his fellows had excluded Farran from their escape bid for one simple reason: they feared that he was too badly injured to make it. Farran needed ongoing medical attention, and fearing that he wouldn't listen to their arguments they'd kept him in the dark. When pushed, Farran himself admitted that he was only 'just able to walk with the aid of a pair of crutches' and was really in no condition to make a bid for freedom.

Months earlier Farran had been wounded during the battle of Crete, while commanding a force of light tanks – 'battered ancient hulks', as he described them. On 28 April 1941, British Prime Minister Winston Churchill had cabled the then Commander-in-Chief of the Middle East, General Archibald Wavell, warning him that 'a heavy air-borne attack by German troops' was to be expected on Crete. To this Churchill added: 'It ought to be a fine opportunity for killing the parachute troops.' Churchill saw the coming confrontation as a 'heaven sent opportunity of dealing [the] enemy a heavy blow'.

Crete's defences were duly stiffened. Farran, in command of thirty men, sailed from Alexandria as part of the reinforcements, landing at Crete's Souda Bay. His actions on the Greek island over the coming days would earn him a Military Cross for outstanding bravery – the first of three MCs he was awarded during the war.

Just after dawn on 20 May 1941 the enemy began their attack. As hordes of enemy paratroopers darkened the skies, the Luftwaffe bombed Farran's position and raked with long bursts of machine-gun fire the olive groves in which he and his men had taken cover. Thousands of elite German *Fallschirmjäger* – paratroopers – had dropped, aiming to take the key British positions, thus allowing the main invasion force to seize overall control.

Farran's medal citation recorded that he was 'sent to mop up parachutists', first using his .45 Smith & Wesson pistol on one stricken German paratrooper, before opening fire with the tank's Vickers machine gun. When all the enemy he could find had been suitably despatched, he spied 'a party of Germans escorting about 30 or 40 of our [men] who had been taken prisoner'. Farran led the attack, killing the German guards and freeing all the captives. Altogether, some 3,500 enemy parachutists had dropped from the skies and messages despatched to the War Office in London declared how 'practically the whole of these were accounted for, the greater proportion being killed'.

Churchill had been right – they had dealt the enemy a heavy blow – and he sent further telegrams, urging that 'the Crete battle must be won'. The island was a vital stronghold in the Mediterranean, constituting a refuelling point for Allied ships and aircraft. But it was also a potential stepping-stone from which the forces of Nazi Germany could do real damage – for Crete's capital, Heraklion, was less than four hundred miles by sea from the Suez Canal, in Egypt, a crucial Allied shipping route.

The following day, 21 May 1941, Farran led his men to seize the high ground at Cemetery Hill, in an effort to drive off the enemy. He was acutely aware that he and his troops 'had been in action almost non-stop for forty-eight hours' and he felt that to go on 'was almost certain suicide'. But with Allied forces vastly outnumbered, and despite extreme battle fatigue, Farran's actions were 'largely instrumental in the attack being successful'.

Incredibly, Farran – then a second lieutenant – led his men through three further days of intense combat, culminating in the battle for Galatos village, the control of which was bitterly contested. At dusk, he experienced 'a blinding flash inside the tank' in which he was riding, an enemy round from an anti-tank rifle punching through the thin armoured skin, sending shrapnel tearing apart the vehicle's innards. The driver, gunner and Farran himself were wounded, the tank careering into a ditch.

They remained there trapped in the turret, while the anti-tank rifle 'carved big chunks out of the top,' Farran recalled. 'I was hit twice more – in both legs and in the right arm.' Despite being badly wounded, Farran managed to drag his two fellows free of the burning vehicle before collapsing from his injuries. Shortly, Crete fell to the enemy, and Farran, unable to walk and wrapped in bloodied, dirty bandages, was taken captive.

A German doctor duly examined Farran's wounds, announcing that his leg was riven with gangrene – a bacterial infection that damages the blood supply, causing the affected limbs to die. He would need to be evacuated to a hospital on mainland Greece. The diagnosis 'accounted for the stink', Farran remarked, drily. He was loaded into a Junkers Ju 52 transport aircraft, together with others who needed urgent medical attention, and flown directly to Athens.

There, a German surgeon removed the gangrenous necrotic tissue from the most severe wound in his thigh, and gradually it began to heal, though Farran still described it as a gaping hole. That was how he'd ended up incarcerated in the Athens POW hospital, making a painfully slow recovery and scheming daily about how he might break out. Bearing in mind the severity of his injuries, Savage and his fellow escapees doubtless had been right to leave Farran out of things, on the night of their storm-lashed breakout.

But after that escape, camp security was stiffened, the perimeter wire being strengthened and the camp commandant imposing harsh rigours on those who remained. In protest, the POWs embarked upon 'a programme of passive disobedience', Farran recalled. They would let down the tyres of the prison guards' bicycles, drop rotten fruit and rubble onto passing sentries from the roof, and confuse the roll-call by answering to different names.

Farran, possessed of a fiercely rebellious streak, claimed famously: 'I did not care for orders when it suited me.' He typified the POW's spirit of resistance, setting a pile of packing cases ablaze in the camp courtyard. But despite such subversive activities, life remained grim, and Farran was desperate to break free. He watched the camp perimeter intensely, scanning the nearest houses, wondering how the inhabitants might respond to an Allied POW turning up on their doorstep. Those dwellings offered the first potential sanctuary for anyone who made it through the wire, but they were also the places most likely to be searched. With the locals under threat of savage reprisals if caught harbouring Allied fugitives, Farran wondered which – if any – might offer refuge.

One house in particular stood out. Every evening at roughly the same time a woman's voice could be heard singing from the rooftop. She would croon 'South of the Border, Down Mexico Way' – a syrupy love song made famous in the popular 1939 movie *South of the Border*, by the 'singing cowboy', American songster Gene Autry. Over time Farran became convinced that whoever the mystery singer was, she must know the POW camp was full of Allied prisoners and that singing that iconic 'all-American' song had to signal solidarity with those inside.

Surely that house, if any, had to be friendly. Farran scrutinised it more closely. Once he fancied he saw a flash of bright red hair inside, which he figured might belong to one of the New Zealand escapees. Determined to break free, Farran gathered a DIY 'escape kit'. It was paltry enough: a map of Greece traced onto a few sheets of toilet paper, some local currency – the drachma – plus a little surplus food, all stashed in an old pillowcase. But even with such kit, he was in no physical state to outrun the guards with his leg not yet fully healed – hence guile and cunning would be needed, if he were to slip away.

His best chance lay in adopting a convincing disguise. Farran managed to dye some pyjamas dark blue using the 'gelatine violet ointment used for [treating] sprained ankles'. He swapped an overcoat he'd had since the Battle of Crete for a 'pair of Australian brown boots' and stole a 'panama hat' from a Greek plumber who was repairing a pipe in the hospital. He added all this to his pillowcase of escape kit and stashed the lot under his bed. That done, he resolved to work on the last, vital part of his disguise – his tan.

Lying there in the hot August sun, Farran may have appeared relaxed, but he never stopped scanning his surroundings, waiting for some kind of an opportunity. One day he spied a group of local women sifting through a refuse heap set to one side of the camp, searching for anything vaguely edible. Their shapely forms had caught the attention of the gate guard, whom Farran knew from months of observation to be in charge of the western side of the wire.

Farran's pulse quickened. With the sentry distracted by ogling the ladies, might he seize his chance? Moving as swiftly as he could while still on crutches, he came down from the roof and headed for the ward, grabbing his pillowcase escape gear and slinging it over one shoulder. He hastened out of the back door, but there he stopped short. Hurrying – hobbling as rapidly as possible – would be unwise, he reasoned. Any frenzied movement would only serve to attract unwelcome attention. He needed to blend in, allowing nothing to draw the guard's focus away from the women at the refuse heap.

He took several deep breaths, getting his pulse back to something like normal, and, adopting a seemingly relaxed gait, did his best to stroll away from the building. Bit by bit, he strayed ever closer to the wire. He kept one eye on the guard, the other on his route to freedom. Somehow, he remained undetected, even as he stepped up to the fence. The time for pretence was gone. Any man seen at the camp's perimeter was clearly an escapee, so this next part was all about speed. He dropped to the dirt and began to wriggle under the strands of barbed wire.

'Something had snapped in my brain,' Farran would remark of this moment.

He had no memory of fighting his way through the cruel tangle of barbs, failing to notice how they ripped the dressings from his wounds. The bandages were left hanging – bloodied and dirtied – on the strands of wire. Having made it to the far side, he scrambled to his feet and limped out into the open, studying the terrain in front of him. Just as the guard's gaze finally strayed from the women, he dived for a shallow undulation in the ground, landing face-down in the dirt. He hugged the earth, hoping that this dry gully was deep enough to conceal his half-naked form – for he was still dressed only in the shorts he had been wearing to sunbathe.

As he lay there unmoving, the stony ground bit into his bare skin. Dry summer dust filled his nostrils. But one move, one choked breath, and he was bound to be detected and drilled with a burst of machine-gun fire. Farran's eyes followed the guard's visual sweep until his gaze moved across his very hiding place and then . . . nothing. The sentry, clearly feeling he had done his duty, returned to studying the women at the refuse heap. Farran sensed he could breathe once more.

He felt overjoyed that he had stolen out of the camp, but he still had to reach the cover of the nearest houses, and before the guard glanced his way again. Farran hobbled forwards as fast as his injured leg would carry him, but once he reached the shadows beside the first Greek house his mind was plagued with uncertainties. He was deep inside enemy territory in a suburb of occupied Athens, and in the midst of a populace that might prefer to sell him out for a fistful of drachmae, rather than help him.

He turned briefly to scan the camp wire. Had his flight been noticed? He caught a brief glimpse of a figure waving a handkerchief in his direction. A fellow POW had watched his dash to freedom and was signalling good luck. Spirits stiffened, Farran risked a brief wave in return – something to encourage others to follow. To Farran, who hailed from a well-known military family, it seemed only natural that a prisoner would go to any lengths to break out from captivity and return to the fight.

Just twenty years old at the time of his escape, Roy Alexander Farran was born into a devout Roman Catholic family. He was educated in India, where his father had served in the military.

Sent to the Bishop Cotton's School, in Shimla – the capital of Himachal Pradesh, nestled in the foothills of the Himalayas – he had benefited from a tough martial education, for Bishop Cotton's was famous for turning out senior military commanders. At the age of eighteen, he'd moved to the Sandhurst Academy in the south of England, to complete his officer's training.

War broke out three months later and shortly Farran was commissioned as a second lieutenant and sent to fight. He would go on to become one of the most renowned commanders of the Special Air Service in the Second World War, but little did he know that the skills he would develop during this escape – adopting disguises, travelling clandestinely deep inside enemy territory, linking up with underground resistance movements, keeping on the move despite the almost constant risk of capture – would serve him admirably during his time with the SAS.

Turning his back on the POW hospital/camp, Farran – still clad only in shorts – hurried into a narrow, unpaved alleyway. He was spotted by a group of local women gathered at a fruit barrow. They regarded him with undisguised curiosity. Ignoring their quizzical stares, he decided this was as good a place as any to change into his 'Greek' costume. Much to the surprise of the locals, this scantily dressed stranger reached into his pillowcase and began to pull on a new set of clothes in the middle of their street.

Halfway through his brazen performance, a woman approached Farran and beckoned him into her house. Might it be a trap? He had no way of knowing. He reckoned he had little choice but to place his trust in her. So, with trousers in hand he followed her into the shadowed interior. Once inside, Farran finished dressing, before managing to communicate that he was an escaped POW and that he hadn't been spotted by the camp guards. By way of response the mystery woman handed Farran over to a little girl, who grabbed him by the hand and set out, leading him through a maze of twisting streets.

Soon they reached the house of another woman, who introduced herself as Maria. She was busy painting the ceiling of her simple, two-room cottage, and minding some children, but exhibited little surprise at the escaped British officer's unexpected arrival. Calmly she ushered him into a back room, closed and bolted the front door and drew the curtains. She gestured for Farran to take a seat, in a room which seemed as if it doubled as the local crèche. So it was that he found himself amid an utterly surreal scene – an escaped British officer, 'still panting with the excitement' of his daring breakout, surrounded by 'babies of all ages'.

Edgy and nervous, he reasoned that either he had been scooped up by some form of resistance-cum-escape network, or he was about to be handed over to the Gestapo. Despite the homely domesticity of the scene, every noise from outside made him jump. The sound of a truck engine rumbled down the street, the vehicle drawing ever closer to his place of hiding, Farran imagining it crammed full of enemy troops. He feared the sudden crunch of tyres on gravel as it came to a halt; the thud of boots hitting the ground and rifles being made-ready; the crack of butts smashing open the door, as grey-uniformed figures burst in, only to drag him back to the camp and to solitary confinement or worse. But finally, the truck rumbled by without stopping.

An hour passed. Farran's suspicions gradually dissipated, especially as the woman's husband – an orange seller – plus her entire family and several members of the village came to gawp at this novelty: a British escapee. Some greeted him with kisses and brought small presents, mostly cigarettes. One, a widow, made him an immediate proposition of marriage, and before long Farran was in no doubt that the locals were utterly genuine.

'We would have received the same help in nine Greek houses out of ten,' Farran would later remark, concluding that the Greek people were 'the kindest and most hospitable race in the world'.

While he was incredibly grateful for them taking him in, Farran was far too close to the camp to remain safe for long. He described to Maria and her husband the house adjacent to the prison camp, from where he had heard the woman singing her cowboy songs. He felt drawn to that place, sensing that it must be connected to the Greek underground somehow. Maria's husband led Farran back outside, for be believed he could navigate his way to the house of the singing lady.

They set off. Nikaia district was crammed with fruit stalls and flower markets, but as the two men entered a square, they came upon cafés full of German soldiers supping frothing glasses of lager. Farran pulled his Panama hat lower, attempting to look casual, as they edged past the noisy bars, his senses on high alert.

They darted down a side street, and suddenly Farran found himself face to face with the perimeter of the very POW camp from which he had escaped. Doing their best to keep their cool they slipped past the nearest guard tower. Farran could barely believe it when no harsh words of challenge rang out. His leg wounds were beginning to cause him real pain, but he forced himself to keep moving. Finally, they found it: they had reached the singing lady's house.

They made their way to the rear of the building. Gritting his teeth against the agony of his injuries, Farran clambered over the garden wall, together with his escort. The two figures lowered themselves silently onto the far side, only to find the homeowner busy in his garden. For a moment the man stared at the two strangers, seemingly petrified. Farran could hardly blame him. They had materialised silent as wraiths. Farran crept closer, whispering 'English' in the man's ear. Moments later they had been hurried inside, as the householder explained that there were neighbours thereabouts who would happily sell them out to the Germans.

Once inside the small cottage, Farran was struck by one thing most powerfully: standing in the kitchen was a striking-looking woman. Dressed all in white and with bare feet, she was utterly arresting. Farran described her later as being 'the most beautiful woman' ever. He figured she had to be the householder's daughter and he wondered if it had been her voice that he had heard singing from the prison camp. At first, she eyed Farran with undisguised suspicion, but her attitude seemed to soften as he popped his first question, asking if by chance she'd seen Ken Maxwell, one of the POW camp's original escape committee.

By way of response, the woman-in-white stepped forward and kissed Farran full on the lips. 'I blushed scarlet like a self-conscious schoolboy,' Farran recalled of the moment.

Swapping Farran's Panama hat for a Greek fisherman's-style flat cloth cap, she explained that it was time to reunite Farran with his fellow escapees – for, sure enough, Maxwell, Savage, Sinclair and the others had passed through this house. Within moments they set forth into the night to link up with the others, who were apparently billeted near by.

Along with the woman-in-white came her mother and her brother, who pushed on a few paces ahead, scouting out the

route. Farran realised what a cunning disguise their party constituted: Farran was the woman-in-white's beau, and the mother the
ever-present chaperone – it was customary for courting Greek
couples to be accompanied by a family member at all times.

They flitted through a maze of streets. A moment of real panic
came as they approached what Farran knew to be the Italian
military barracks. His fears deepened, as the guard standing gate
duty seemed to scrutinise them far too closely. But of course, it
was the woman on his arm who was drawing the sentry's eye, for
beside her magnetic beauty Farran was all but invisible.

Once past the barracks, the brother – who had dashed off
in front – returned, bringing a mystery figure with him. That
man – a Greek using the *nom de guerre* 'Sorties' – started delving
further into Farran's story, exploring who he was, where he had
been captured and what unit he hailed from. If his story didn't
add up, Farran sensed Sorties might just as easily kill him as
a suspected Gestapo agent. With his blond hair and blue eyes,
Farran could easily have passed for a classic Aryan.

On the spur of the moment, Farran decided to lie about where
he really hailed from, choosing Birmingham as an English city
Sorties was sure to have heard of. Thankfully, his story seemed to
pass muster. Interrogations done, he turned to thank his guides –
the mysterious woman-in-white first and foremost – but she and
her family had quietly slipped away, leaving Farran in the hands
of his new protector.

Sorties ushered him up the stairs of a nearby house, where he
found four Greek men gathered around a kitchen table. Upon
seeing Farran, one jumped to his feet and threw his arms around
him, enthusiastically hugging him as if they were old friends. It
took a moment for Farran to realise that this was fellow escapee

Ken Maxwell, for the man had been utterly transformed. With his hair dyed black, newly grown sideburns and thick moustache, Maxwell would have drawn the ire of any parade ground sergeant.

'It was a perfect disguise,' Farran remarked, who was 'staggered' by Maxwell's transformation. He figured that soon he too would be adopting the look, in order to pass for a man of Athens.

Overjoyed at meeting up with Maxwell again, Farran quizzed him on the details of their mass escape. Maxwell told how they had used the cover of that wild storm – for when it rained in Athens, the heavens truly opened – to slither beneath the wire. Even so, a guard had flashed his torch along the perimeter, pinning one of the escapees in its glare. But for whatever reason – the rain or maybe shock – he had failed to bring his weapon to bear, and they had made their getaway. Ever since then they had been hiding with members of the Greek underground – Maxwell in this house, Savage in the home of a jeweller a few miles south, and Sinclair at another location close to the docks.

It was approaching a month since his friends had escaped, and they 'exchanged reminiscences far into the night', Farran recalled, while their Greek hosts kept them well fed and watered. Maxwell explained that Sorties was the leader of the local resistance. Publicly, Sorties was a simple fruit seller from Nikaia, but secretly he had gathered a group of friends 'to aid escaped British prisoners'. Exhausted from his breakout and the excitement of seeing his friend again, eventually Farran was shown to a bed by a plump and respectable-looking dentist named Tino, who turned out to be the owner of the house.

Sometime later he was awoken with worrying news. German troops were carrying out house-to-house searches. Farran feared it was his escape that had prompted the combing of the city, for his breakout was bound to have caused a considerable hue and cry. But Tino, their host, appeared disarmingly calm and collected. In an extraordinary show of sangfroid, he told Farran and Maxwell to go and sit on the balcony so they could watch the unfolding spectacle, as grey-clad troops dashed around the streets. Somewhat dumbfounded, they took up their positions, as locals were accosted and dragged this way and that, and their ID cards demanded. Those who couldn't produce their papers were thrown into the backs of waiting trucks.

The closer the troops got, the more apprehensive Farran and Maxwell became, until, with the enemy only two houses away, it looked certain they would be captured. Unable to speak more than a few garbled words of Greek and with no papers, they seemed to stand not the slightest chance. At this point Tino ordered them inside and gestured to a drainpipe: if the situation demanded it, they were to shin down that and slip away. He then ushered them into a false compartment hidden beneath the floorboards. They crawled inside and waited. Concealed in the darkness, Farran wondered how fast his injuries would allow him to shin down the drainpipe, should they need to.

From downstairs came the crash of rifle butts on the front door: jack-booted troopers demanding entry. Tino opened up. Thankfully, he was a man of some substance in this part of Athens. Indeed, the enemy believed him to be a 'good Greek' firmly on the side of the Nazi occupiers. It was a dangerous game that Tino was playing, but one that he managed with remarkable aplomb. So convincing was he that the German soldiers did not even venture across his threshold.

For now, at least, Farran and his fellows were safe. But their luck couldn't last. That evening, Sorties, the resistance leader, came, bringing dire news. His brother, Elias, had been arrested. Elias was a fellow member of the resistance; the Gestapo were sure to make him talk. Names would be divulged and with them addresses. There was little time to lose. Farran and Maxwell would need to be moved, as soon as it was dark. The next few hours seemed interminable, a horrible psychological torture. If Elias failed to hold out, capture and worse were bound to follow. As dusk cloaked the city, none could wait to get on the move.

There was a sudden rapping on the door. Farran felt his heart lurch. Was it the enemy at the gates? Tino opened up to find a young woman standing there. He introduced her to all as 'Dolly'. Already a legend in the Greek resistance, Dolly would prove a key ally for the next and most dangerous leg of Farran's journey. She was renowned among the Greeks as being a lioness in the face of the enemy. Her favourite trick was to drop 'V for Victory' signs onto the seats of unoccupied German staff cars, to strike fear into their senior officers.

Farran and Maxwell split up, for it was safer for each to make their own way across the city. Farran's guide was to be Dolly. She would lead Farran a wild dance through the Nikaia streets, as everywhere German troops hurried this way and that. At first, he tried his best to keep his distance from them, but Dolly knew better: that would only arouse suspicion. Linking arms, she led Farran through the heart of the threat, acting as if they had every right to be there, their shoulders brushing against those of the enemy. They were hiding in plain sight, and for Farran this was to prove a nerve-racking and unforgettable experience.

Eventually they boarded a bus, Dolly steering Farran to a window seat. He concentrated on gazing out over the crowds, apparently unconcerned. But a man in a seat near him couldn't help but catch Farran's eye. Dressed in a white gabardine trench-coat, there was something about him that was oddly sinister. He appeared to find Farran of unusual interest, regarding him with piercing blue eyes. When Dolly realised that Farran was staring, she jabbed him in the ribs. He averted his gaze.

Finally, the bus pulled out of Nikaia, making its laborious way towards Piraeus, the city's port. Though the journey was less than three miles, that was still plenty of time for the stranger in the trenchcoat to take an unhealthy interest in Farran. They got out at the port, but so too did their mystery watcher. By now Farran felt certain he was a Gestapo tail. If he could follow one Allied escapee – Farran – he might find his way to a whole group of them, so boosting his haul.

As Dolly led Farran along a series of winding alleyways, the mystery figure tracked their every move. Farran pointed out that the man was still in hot pursuit. Dolly told him not to worry. Asking him to continue walking, she slipped away into the shelter of a shop window. Farran pressed ahead, trying not to allow his tension to show, for he was alone in a strange place with a mystery man in pursuit, and he was at a loss as to what direction the harbour might lie.

Fear and tension rising, he was relieved to see Dolly again. With a few whispered words, she reassured Farran that all was fine. The sinister man in white had been dealt with, she explained. Farran had no idea what that might mean. Had he been wrong about the identity of their tail? Or was that mystery figure now a corpse slumped in a doorway, bloodstains blooming across his white coat? Farran didn't dare enquire further as to what exactly

Dolly might have done, 'for she was quite capable of sticking a knife in his ribs'. Either way, this was war.

Dolly led him to a safe house, set deep within the maze of narrow streets around the port. This, it turned out, was where Kazarsis, the jeweller, had been hiding Robin Savage since his escape. Farran and Savage were reunited, the latter apologising for having left Farran behind on the night of the mass breakout. Praising his host, Kazarsis, for his fearlessness and hospitality, he advised Farran that the area was 'getting too hot to be safe', especially as the captured Elias would be facing horrendous torture to make him talk. Word was that the net was closing.

Shortly Farran had to move again. 'It was a long walk,' he recalled of the journey to the next safe house, and by the time they had got there the wound in his leg was 'bleeding profusely'.

It took days for Farran's leg to fully recover, during which time Dolly taught him to ride the Athens trams like any local: they might well have need of them, if they had to make a swift getaway. Dolly's inventiveness and sheer courage never ceased to amaze him. On one tram excursion, she employed a crowd of ragged street urchins to act as their 'family'. Farran opened a newspaper, making a pretence as if he were reading it. A Greek man sat next to him tapped him on the knee and fired off a question. Farran froze. He had no idea what the man had said.

The man repeated what he'd asked. At that moment one of Dolly's urchins intervened, causing a diversion that drew the focus away from Farran. But a second man, this one seated opposite him, still seemed curious. He eyed Farran searchingly. Farran turned bright red under the stranger's gaze. He wondered whether it would be possible, given the severity of his injuries, to jump from the moving tram. But just as he was feeling increasingly desperate, the stranger rose to his feet and disembarked.

As he climbed off the tram, he 'winked one eye and put up his thumb', Farran recalled. 'So much for my disguise!'

Should Elias break under torture, none of the escapees was safe – that they all knew. But incredibly, Elias never did, despite the savagery that was visited upon him by his Nazi captors. He endured horrific torture at the hands of the Gestapo, Farran remarked, 'but [he] refused to talk'. His act was so convincing that the Gestapo finally had no option but to release him.

Elias was far from an isolated case: there were scores in the Greek resistance who withstood torture, rather than disclose what they knew of the whereabouts of escaped prisoners. But despite such immense fortitude and courage, Farran and his fellows could sense that they were living on borrowed time. Their newest hiding place might be discovered at any moment. They had to complete their escape from Greece and make it back to Allied lines. The challenge was deciding how exactly they should go about it. The streets were crawling with a wrathful and suspicious enemy.

With the noose tightening, only one option seemed open to them: the sea. Egypt lay in British hands and it was a little under seven hundred miles away. If they could navigate a ship across the Mediterranean, they could make their way back to friendly lines. The trouble was finding a vessel to undertake such a journey, for the enemy had requisitioned just about every seaworthy ship. A dozen plans were mooted and just as rapidly abandoned.

Savage's proposal turned out to be the most outlandish. He suggested they load a rowing boat with grenades and machine guns, courtesy of the Greek resistance, and row out into the centre of the harbour, close to the enemy's torpedo-net. That net – a mesh webbing suspended underwater, designed to 'catch' torpedoes before they could do any damage to shipping – was patrolled by German E-boats, fast attack craft similar to British motor torpedo boats or MTBs. Once within yelling range, Savage suggested they remove the cork that plugged the hole in the stern of their boat – used to drain any water from the craft when on dry land – so causing it to sink. As it went down, they would cry for help. Presuming the nearest E-boat would steam to their rescue, they would assault it with guns and grenades, like latter-day pirates. Few craft could catch a German E-boat: they were capable of over forty knots. But they were crewed by thirty-odd sailors, and even if the escapees did manage to kill or overpower her crew, the chances of such a ship being fuelled for a long voyage across the Mediterranean were slim.

A part of Farran thrilled to the wild dash and daring of such a plan. But equally, he remembered how he had almost lost his life aboard a similar vessel, just a few months back. On 18 May 1941 – days before the Battle of Crete – a friend of Farran's in the Royal Navy had taken him out on an MTB for a joyride. Almost immediately, they had come under attack from a squadron of German Stuka dive-bombers. The commander attempted to steer the MTB back to land, while his crew levelled their deck-mounted twin Vickers machine guns at the attacking warplanes. One of the crew was wounded in a blast from a near miss and Farran had to crawl along the boat to help him. As bullets flew and bombs exploded, he bound the sailor's wounds in an attempt to stop the bleeding. Somehow, the MTB had made it back to shore in one piece, but with that memory fresh in his mind Farran deemed the E-boat hijack plan not worth the risk.

The crunch moment came for Farran a few days later, when visiting a local cinema. Spending weeks locked inside was driving him crazy. The trip to the movies was designed as a little light relief. When he was next to his redoubtable Greek minder, Dolly, a German officer suddenly plonked himself down at Farran's side. Farran spent the entire movie torn between fear of discovery and marvelling at the incongruity of it all. But it underscored the desperate need to get away.

After various further twists and turns in their fortunes, a local fisherman made an approach. He offered the escapees his boat, one of the few that hadn't been requisitioned for war work by the Germans, but explained that he would need something to replace his lost livelihood. Farran offered him a 'promissory note' – a signed document which he swore had the backing of His Majesty's Government, and which promised to pay the fisherman a set fee once the escapees had reached British territory. The fisherman finally agreed, but only once the resistance had rustled up an extra fee in cash, to be paid just as soon as Farran signalled that the escape party had reached friendly shores.

Farran's MC citation recorded of this moment: 'Eventually, with the help of money supplied by friendly Greeks, a caïque was hired.' A caïque is a traditional fishing boat used primarily on the Aegean and Ionian seas, featuring a sharply pointed prow, one or more masts and a wooden hull. Robin Sinclair, the tough Commando lieutenant from New Zealand and one of the prison camp's original escape committee, was keen to chance the long journey by sea with Farran. Others demurred. Farran and Sinclair teamed up together and all seemed set.

But shortly before their departure, the plan hit the buffers in spectacular fashion. A member of the Greek resistance named

Lefteris had volunteered to be the caïque's engineer, charged with keeping the engine running on the long journey. Lefteris had set out to procure enough diesel for the voyage – no easy matter, with fuel strictly rationed by the occupying powers. He was promptly arrested by a Greek policeman for dealing on the black market. Now their engineer – and their precious fuel – were both in police custody.

'It seemed that all was lost,' Farran noted despondently.

But the following day Lefteris turned up unexpectedly, and smiling broadly, accompanied by the very policeman who had arrested him. Sensing the man's political leanings, Lefteris had explained that he was buying fuel in order to help some British escapees get back to friendly lines. By luck, the policeman hated the Nazi occupiers just as much as anyone. Not only had he allowed Lefteris to keep the black-market fuel, but he had also managed to procure some extra food to help the escapees on their way.

The Greek policeman had brought the escapees some precious loaves of bread, and, with 'tears running down his face, gave me his pistol', Farran recalled of the highly charged moment. He also promised to start a deception action at the docks, the night of their planned getaway. This was a stroke of real good fortune, for as Farran remarked, with the local police on board it increased the chances that 'there would be no further monkey business . . .' Finally, the gods did indeed seem to be smiling upon them.

At the eleventh hour Farran and Sinclair were joined by two more escapees. One was an Australian Army sergeant who had been a musician in Sydney before the war, a man whom Farran initially assessed as being a real 'tough egg'. The other, Staff Sergeant Charles Wright, was from the Royal Army Service Corps

(RASC), and he had developed terrible sores from drinking bad water while in captivity. In addition to Lefteris, their resourceful engineer-cum-black-marketeer, the escapees were joined by Elias, a local Greek whose role it was to captain the caïque on the long voyage across ahead. There were also a half-a-dozen mystery passengers that the Greek resistance intended to sail on the caïque. One at least appeared to be a Polish Jew, and doubtless they were fleeing from Nazi persecution, their flight – like that of Farran and his fellow escapees – courtesy of the brave Greeks.

The night of their departure, the group of escapees and crew crept along the twisting streets that led to the dockside in ones and twos. It was well after curfew and the last thing they wanted was to draw unwelcome notice. The vessel turned out not only to be a traditional Greek fishing caïque – brightly painted, with a wooden hull around thirty feet long – but it was also positively ancient. Among other things, Farran noted with dismay the 'gaping hole where the mast should have been'. It looked as if they would be relying on the diesel engine for the entire journey.

Two berths away was a much larger vessel, on which German sentries could be seen. They would have to slip anchor as silently as ghosts in order not to disturb them. One by one the escapees flitted aboard, only to discover another problem awaited. The teenage brother of one of their Greek resistance hosts had stowed away. Upon discovery, Spike – thus called due to his tearaway haircut – begged to be allowed to stay. Tearfully he explained that he was just another useless mouth for his mother to feed, in enemy-occupied Athens where food was becoming increasingly hard to come by. But if the escapees would take him with them, he could sign up to the British Army and fight.

At first Farran was adamant: Spike had to go. Provisions were in precious short supply. They couldn't afford another mouth to feed and water. But when they tried to eject Spike from the boat, he held on for dear life and made enough noise to awaken the nearby sentries. There seemed to be no option: Spike would have to become an extra member of the crew. That decided, they cast off silently, allowing the caïque to drift on the tide. Only once they were a good distance from shore did Lefteris dare to start the engine. As the citation for Farran's MC noted, finally: 'Farran and a party of escapees left for Egypt.'

With the engine gently phut-phutting through the quiet of the night, Farran glanced around the crew. There was himself and Sinclair, the New Zealander and Commando; the Aussie and British escapee who'd joined them at the eleventh hour; the two Greek crew-members, who were the only ones who knew anything about seafaring – Elias their captain, plus Lefteris the engineer; Spike, the teenage stowaway, plus the eight mystery passengers – refugees – sheltering in the cramped hold. They were fifteen souls in all. Elias was their sea-captain, but as Farran was the senior rank on board, key decisions were bound to rest squarely with him.

Farran had calculated they had just enough fuel to reach Alexandria, in British-held Egypt. For navigation all they had was a battered compass, plus an old school atlas, 'which showed the shapes of the islands we were to follow' until Crete. After Crete, it should be 'plain sailing due south'. By way of supplies they had the bread the friendly policeman had given them, plus some extra loaves, and a few raw onions. For water, they'd filled an earthenware pot and an old olive oil barrel, which Farran hoped would be enough to last the journey.

Once out of the harbour they hit the full swell of the open sea and almost all were violently sick, due to the pitch and roll of the caïque. They rounded the first island and immediately spotted a German patrol boat. In a hurried scramble fishing nets were cast over the side, and all but Elias and Lefteris hurried below decks. The enemy craft drew closer, but their bluff seemed to hold and, satisfied with the caïque's apparent legitimacy, the E-boat roared away, seeking other quarry.

On day two of their voyage, the distinctive form of a Dornier DO17 – a twin-engine German fighter-bomber – swooped low over the craft. The aircrews' faces were clearly visible gazing down at them, the would-be fishermen gesturing at their nets. As no bursts of heavy cannon fire raked the length of the fragile craft, Farran and party guessed the ruse must have held good. In their disguises, tanned under the Greek sun and crewing a genuine Greek caïque, they seemed to be able to pass muster.

Farran was initially delighted at how well the voyage progressed. But during their second night at sea one of the crew misread the shape of an island, turning them way off course to the west, instead of keeping on a south-easterly bearing. Some hours passed before Farran noticed that the islands they were passing didn't match those shown on the atlas. He awoke Elias, who had been catching some much-needed sleep, but at first the ship's captain refused to believe the atlas, trusting instead to his instinct that they were on the right bearing. Farran knew from first-hand experience how easy it was to stray off course if you failed to place complete trust in your maps and navigational aids.

Before Crete, he'd seen action during Operation Compass, in the Western Desert campaign of the winter of 1940, forming part of a reconnaissance unit guiding a squadron of heavy armour.

As a young and relatively inexperienced officer, Farran had had to lead the convoy through the desert south of Mersa Matruh, from the cab of an eight-hundredweight pick-up. He'd been put through a desert navigation course in Cairo, learning the method of 'dead reckoning' – calculating his position by taking a series of compass bearings and carefully measuring distance travelled. But as the convoy chugged through the desert Farran had allowed his intuition to take over. It told him they had strayed too far north, and so he had altered course to compensate.

It proved a near-fatal error, for it resulted in the convoy becoming lost in the desert as night fell. Farran described himself as 'panic-stricken' at the time. He had driven around in the pitch darkness, hoping he might spot the lights of a camp, the convoy following doggedly after him. When he did finally lead the column to their proper destination, the following morning, he was severely reprimanded. From that experience he had learned a crucial lesson: 'The only way to navigate is to have complete faith in your instruments.'

Now, in the caïque, faced with the compass readings and the atlas, Elias finally had to concede that Farran was right: they had strayed far from their course. With dusk upon them and visibility dropping, the only option was to anchor and wait for morning, when they could get a better sense of their location. But with nightfall, someone noticed what appeared to be the form of another boat steaming out of the darkness. This late at night and so far off a bonafide Greek fisherman's course, it would be hard to convince anyone that they were an innocent fishing party.

But as time passed, the silhouette of the 'boat' seemed to come no nearer. At dawn, they realised their mistake: what they'd mistaken for the outline of a ship was actually a rocky crag rearing from the ocean depths. From plotting its position, Farran confirmed they were well out of their way. 'It was a serious business this loss of course,' he remarked, 'since our fuel supply left no margin of safety.' Taking stock of their precious diesel, to their utter consternation they realised that someone had pilfered three jerrycans from the hold. Somehow, the black-market fuel that had been so carefully purloined by Lefteris had been plundered at the docks, just prior to their departure.

It was a dire predicament, landfall in Egypt now lying well beyond their much-depleted diesel supplies. But equally, it was too late to turn back. As escaped POWs with so much accumulated knowledge of the Greek resistance, all would doubtless face torture at the hands of the Gestapo should they be recaptured. Their only option was to press on and hope that on the far side of Crete a passing British warship might find them. Farran was the senior rank, and to a man they agreed that come what may, they had to continue.

They set off once more, the rhythmic phut-phut of the small diesel engine providing the only beat to the passing hours. Shortly, they neared the chokepoint and real danger – the eighty-mile-wide sliver of water that separates Rhodes and Crete, two fortress-islands recently wrested from Allied hands by the Germans. Heavy enemy patrols were known to quarter the waters that lay ahead, known as 'the Sea of Crete'. The escapees had planned to enter these straits at dusk, hoping to make it through under the cover of darkness. But having discovered their lack of fuel there was no time to delay: they would have to attempt to slip past in full daylight.

A journey scheduled to last only four days was already creeping into its fourth with no end in sight. Farran's MC citation described how 'food and water were running short'. If they failed to brave the Sea of Crete and reach the open waters beyond, they had little chance of making the run south to Egypt. Farran decided they would have to risk putting ashore on Santorini, a nearby island, in search of extra provisions.

They landed at what they thought was a deserted and unguarded stretch of shoreline, where the famished escapees were able to scavenge the discarded ears of corn from recently harvested fields. But it was precious little to keep body and soul together. Acting on instinct, Farran decided to approach a small church. A devout Catholic by upbringing, he stepped inside, said a prayer to grant them safe passage, and left the remainder of his drachmae in the collection box.

His prayers seemed to be answered: one of the Greeks gave a shout that he had found a cistern of fresh water. Every man slaked his thirst with sweet, delicious water. They refilled their containers, and then a shout went up from further down the cliffs. On the beach, the fugitives had discovered what seemed like manna from heaven: fishing boats could be seen bobbing in the distance, and the fishermen had left baskets of fruit hidden in the shade of some rocks. Farran was up for taking it all, but Elias was adamant they should only take the one basket, lest they bring ill-fortune by 'violating some unwritten law of the sea'.

Farran relented, for here on the shores of the Aegean, home to legendary gods, goddesses, sirens and sea monsters, he had no wish to push their luck. Leaving whatever money they could spare as some recompense, they hurried back to their boat, where Farran decided to take charge of rationing their meagre supplies, with Wright – the RASC staff sergeant – assisting him. Over time, Farran was becoming increasingly impressed by Wright, who struck him as being an utterly reliable and resourceful individual. Indeed, Wright would turn out to be the real 'tough egg' among the escapees, as opposed to the Australian Army sergeant.

The men aboard that boat – famished and fearful – sailed into the gauntlet of the Sea of Crete, Farran sensing it would take iron will to brave what lay ahead. As dusk fell, the powerful beam of a nearby lighthouse swept the waters. Sooner or later, they would have to venture into its pulse of light and the caïque was likely to be spotted. German warplanes could be seen, taking off and landing over Heraklion airfield. It would be a simple enough task to call them in to investigate the mystery vessel.

But miraculously, just as they were about to nose into that beam of illumination, a ghostly bank of sea mist rolled across the waters, enveloping all. Giving thanks to the gods, Elias steered the caïque into its embrace, and they chugged onwards towards the open Mediterranean. Yet their relief was to be short-lived. In this part of the world, thick night fog invariably heralded a storm. Farran noticed the sea getting progressively rougher. Soon the 'slight choppiness' had been transformed into 'a boiling cauldron'. In no time the wooden caïque was being tossed from one forty-foot crest to another, as it lurched and groaned its way up and down the towering swell.

For two full days they braved the terrible storm – Elias, holding tight to the tiller and steering the boat into the wind, for if one of those waves caught them broadside on they would be smashed to matchwood. Countless times, it was only their skilled Greek captain's use of rudder and engine that kept them from being dragged to the depths. As Elias battled the storm, the others desperately bailed water from the craft, hanging on grimly as each wave threatened to pluck them from the boat and hurl them into the sea.

Battling the storm threatened to exhaust their meagre fuel supplies, but they couldn't risk shutting down the engine – the one thing that enabled the boat to make headway and keep position in the terrible conditions. Finally, the tempest subsided, and – exhausted but elated – Elias steered them into relatively placid waters. Farran was hugely impressed by their captain's seamanship, single-mindedness and stamina, noting that 'only an expert sailor could have brought us through . . . such a sea'.

Having braved the storm, it was a case of being out of the proverbial frying pan and into the fire. As soon as they reached calmer waters, 'the engine gave out'. They had run out of their diesel. Worse still, Farran discovered that all their food had somehow disappeared, and there was precious little water remaining. It turned out that even as the storm had raged, some of the crew had 'mutinied', polishing off what remained of their supplies. Farran's response was to take up position beside their last remaining jerrycan of water, the Greek policeman's pistol laid across his knees. If anyone tried to get any more than their meagre daily water ration, he would shoot them dead.

This was no idle threat. Farran was only at the beginning of what he would go on to describe as a 'long career of violence' in the military elite, and he had already shown what he was capable of when his temper was roused. During the Battle of Crete, he had ordered his men to shoot a group of German parachutists who were attempting to surrender. While he did not think he 'would make a practice of shooting prisoners', Farran noted that 'in the heat of the moment', he had had 'no time to think' during the bloody and bitter fighting on Crete.

Together with Sinclair, Farran would now maintain a permanent armed watch on what remained of their precious water supplies. Even so, on the morning of their sixth day at sea the 'tough egg' of an Australian sergeant seemed to lose it completely, yelling wildly that he had not received his fair share. Driven half-mad by thirst, he punched Farran in the face in an effort to get at the jerrycan. Farran made short work of subduing the man, after which the crew had to be talked out of throwing him overboard.

Morale among the escapees plummeted. Most were in a state of 'collapse, in resignation to their fate' or were 'staring moodily out to sea', Farran noted. But he commanded a rump who were determined not to give up. They managed to cobble together a mast of sorts, using planks ripped from the deck, and hoisted their blankets lashed together as a makeshift sail. With that providing a little leeway, they tore-up more planking to fashion crude oars. It proved too hot and debilitating rowing by day – Farran's MC citation described how most 'were too weak to paddle' – but during the relative cool of night they could make a little headway.

As they limped southwards, Farran was ever more struck by Wright's indomitable spirit and resourcefulness. He noticed how Wright began to time 'how long it took for a cigarette packet to pass from the bows to the stern'. From that he figured the boat was making around one and a half knots' headway. Wright also managed to make a rough estimate of their position, using a right-angle fashioned from two sticks. By studying the shadows so cast, he judged them to lie around a hundred miles off the North African coast.

Despite the huge distance they had covered since leaving Athens – they had travelled many miles out of their way, and figured they were closer to Benghazi in Libya than to Alexandria in Egypt – there was little chance of making landfall before running out of fresh water. Sure enough, by the seventh day the final jerrycan – though rigorously policed – had run bone dry. Men lay helpless on the deck, dousing themselves in seawater to try to keep cool and wrapping wet rags around their heads. One or two lost it completely and tried to drink from the sea. Of course, it only served to make them violently sick.

By the dawn of day eight Farran noted that all were 'far gone with thirst and exhaustion'. With lips chapped and tongues swollen to twice their normal size they lay motionless. But as the sky above turned pink with the rays of the rising sun, Farran heard the thrum of an aircraft. Figures sprang into a frenzy of activity, shouting and waving handkerchiefs in the air. One scrawled 'NO WATER' on a blanket with some old engine oil. Suddenly, the aircraft banked over. Not knowing if it were friendly or hostile, Farran could barely believe the sense of joy and relief he felt at spotting its distinctive RAF roundels.

It was actually a seaplane, and for a blessed moment it looked as if it were about to alight on the water. But the pilot's test-run showed the sea to be too rough: it would rip the floats from under his wings. Instead, he soared aloft again, waggled his wings and sped away. It could only be a matter of hours now, Farran reasoned, before a destroyer steamed into view, intent on their rescue. But by the morning of their ninth day at sea, there was still no sign of any Allied vessel. The escapees' spirits 'sank from the heights of joy to the depths of despair', Farran noted. They were so weak by now that they could only move by crawling and even that seemed to take superhuman effort.

Earlier in the voyage Farran had suggested they build a mechanism to distil sea water, but the idea had been rejected by the others as unfeasible. Now, with death from thirst staring them in the face, it seemed their only chance. With Farran's help, Wright began scavenging parts from the dead engine, as he set about creating a basic still. 'We hacked a petrol tin in half and punctured it with holes,' Farran recalled, forming a rough-and-ready stove. A second tin was filled with seawater to make the boiler, from which a copper pipe ripped from the engine fed into an earthenware pot, which was cooled by wrapping a wet shirt around it, the junctions being sealed with scraps of rag. Around the outside of the pipe Wright fashioned a cooling jacket, using a component scavenged from the bilge pump.

That done, they stuffed fragments of wood and oily rag into the DIY stove and set it aflame. Farran and Wright watched, hardly daring to breathe, as steam began to escape from chinks in the mechanism and slowly, wondrous beads of moisture began to run down the pipe and into the earthenware pot. Encouraged by those first faint trickles, they set about finding anything that could feed the fire. Within an hour they had distilled enough water to give every member of the crew a few precious mouthfuls.

'We were saved,' Farran remarked of this moment. 'No doubt about it, we were saved.'

With death by thirst defeated – at least for as long as they had fuel to fire the stove – their primary goal had to be to get rescued by a ship – any ship. By now the importance of slipping the enemy's clutches had dwindled into insignificance, when faced by their own mortality. They had noticed aircraft passing overhead at night, which they assumed were Luftwaffe bombers on their way to hit targets in Egypt. They decided that if they heard them again, they would do all they could to alert the aircrew. They tied oily rags around some planks, fashioning basic signal flares, and awaited nightfall.

Farran was roused in the small hours by one of the Greeks, who had detected the thrum of engines. He listened hard and soon he could hear it too. Taking it to be aircraft, he gave orders that they light the first of their makeshift flares. It was only when the engine noise grew louder, drifting across to them on the open sea, that Farran realised this was no aircraft: it was the rumble of a ship's engine.

He could barely believe it as he spied 'two long black shapes coming towards us out of the darkness'. The crew, forgetting momentarily their utter exhaustion, scrambled to light the remaining flares, waving them in the direction of the ships, which they could now make out to be men o' war of the Royal Navy. But they were forced to watch in agonised frustration as the vessels stuck to their course, ignoring the boatload of desperate escapees.

'We screamed and wept to see them pay so little heed to us,' Farran recalled of this dark moment, when even he began to lose all hope. But it was then that the second ship altered course and headed back towards them. That vessel was a sleek J-Class destroyer, some 350 feet in length, with the number 'F22' emblazoned on its side. No sight had ever been more welcome to Farran's parched, cracked and painful eyes.

The ship hove to. A voice carried across the waters: 'Ahoy there, who are you?'

Through cracked lips Farran yelled a reply that they were British POWs hailing from Greece. 'Who are you?'

'The *Jackal*,' the voice replied, adding that they were about to board the caïque.

Farran's MC citation recorded that 'some 40 miles out of Alexandria they were sighted by a destroyer and picked up.' He and his emaciated crew were carried aboard HMS *Jackal*, all barring Lefteris, who opted to man the caïque as it was towed into port. In an epic of sheer determination and superhuman endurance, they had made it 1,300 miles across the Mediterranean, and were just a few dozen miles short of friendly shores.

For his action during the Battle for Cemetery Hill, Farran earned his first Military Cross. For his incredible escape from Greece he would be awarded a bar to that medal. The citation would praise his 'inspirational leadership, inventiveness and daring in escaping from enemy captivity and piloting a local vessel hundreds of miles through hostile seas', adding that 'it is largely due to his perseverance that this party eventually reached safety.' Farran's citation continued that 'this officer has shown courage, resource and initiative. He has set a very fine example of determination and leadership to the men under his command.'

The story of Roy Farran's epic getaway offered many vital lessons to those tasked to ensure would-be escapees stood the best chance of making it back to Allied lines. MI9 – Britain's so-called 'Escape Factory', a top-secret branch of military intelligence, whose mission was to aid Allied escapees across all theatres of the war – worked closely with men like Farran, to perfect the most ingenious and usable escape aids. First and foremost, they needed kits including cleverly disguised maps and compasses, which could be secreted in Red Cross and other charity food parcels, so escapees wouldn't have to rely on loo-roll maps, school atlases or the like.

As the boffins at MI9 got busy perfecting such equipment, Farran would go on to earn a legendary reputation in the SAS, commanding many daring missions. During those later operations, the lessons learned in his long weeks on the run would be put to good use: self-reliance, bluff, disguise, resourcefulness and nurturing the unbreakable spirit. Official reports would write of Farran how, 'commanding a Special Air Service Squadron, he directed his officers and men in parachuting behind enemy lines . . . and was conspicuously successful in supplying their needs for sustained harassing operations'.

Farran would end the war as one of the most highly decorated members of the SAS, for in addition to his Military Cross and two bars he would be awarded the Distinguished Service Order, as well as the Legion of Honour and Croix de Guerre for his services in France, plus a Legion of Merit from the USA. Indeed, his final big mission of the war – the March 1945 raid on a German Army headquarters in northern Italy – would be hailed as 'one of the most dangerous and effective attacks ever undertaken by this Regiment against the enemy'.

The recruits that David Stirling – the founder of the SAS – had assembled embodied Farran's maverick, do-or-die spirit. It was just such men that Stirling sought, to enable the SAS to rise from the obscurity of their earliest desert operations and to revolutionise warfare. Stirling was not interested in those who would blindly follow orders; he wanted independent spirits and self-starters, individuals who could think for themselves. Almost by chance, he created in the SAS a band of men who were naturally more inclined to escape and evasion than your average soldier.

Our next great escapee's story embodies just the spirit that Stirling sought.

Great Escape Three

FROM THE AFRICAN DESERT TO THE FROZEN NORTH

Two raiders moved cat-like through the darkness along the perimeter of Berka Satellite Airfield, pausing every few feet to insert their explosive charges into the ammunition dump. Their primary objective had been to destroy enemy aircraft. But when the mission's commander, Lieutenant Blair 'Paddy' Mayne, discovered stores of munitions stashed in tarpaulin-covered dugouts spaced around the airfield's limits, he saw an opportunity to create extra chaos and mayhem.

Mayne – a legendary figure who had a reputation for knowing exactly how to exploit surprise – had split his team of raiders into two parties, instructing Corporal Jack Byrne and Lance Corporal Johnny Rose to lay explosives in the bomb dumps, while he himself, accompanied by Corporal Bob Bennett, would hit the warplanes lined up on the runway. It was well after 0300 hours on the morning of 21 March 1942, and the men moved quickly, for they knew they were running out of time.

This raid was one of several planned that night. All across the Benghazi Plain, deep in enemy-occupied Libya, small SAS units four or five strong were targeting key German and Italian military bases. The raiders had traversed over five hundred miles of sun-baked Sahara to get here, advancing from their desert base camp at Siwa Oasis, just beyond the Egyptian border far to the east. They had been guided across this vast sea of sand by another band of Special Forces operatives – the Long Range Desert Group, known as the LRDG.

The LRDG were primarily an intelligence gathering unit, undertaking reconnaissance missions and gleaning information on enemy activities, all the while honing their desert survival and navigation skills. They had been operating across the vast sun-blasted interiors of Egypt, Libya and Tunisia for almost two years now, travelling in convoys of heavily adapted Willys Jeeps and Chevrolet light trucks, with .30-calibre Brownings and Lewis Guns mounted on pivots. The modifications and weaponry made the LRDG a superlative fighting unit.

The former Commander-in-Chief of the Middle East, General Archibald Wavell, had written of the LRDG: 'In conditions of indescribable hardship these patrols constantly scoured the desert, shooting up convoys, destroying petrol dumps and generally har-assing Italian desert garrisons,' adding, with great admiration, 'for obvious reasons patrols were unable to use recognised tracks and have found their own ways over sand, seas, uncharted desert, outcrops of rock and other difficulties previously considered . . . to be totally impassable.'

Despite their wild appearance – skin tanned russet-brown by the sun, beards bushy and unkempt, heads wrapped in tradi-tional Arab *keffiyeh* headwear to keep off the flies – the LRDG were the 'supreme professionals of the desert', averred the SAS's founder, David Stirling. Able to find their way through seem-ingly impossible terrain with pin-point accuracy, the LRDG had been enlisted by Stirling to 'taxi' his raiders to and from their objectives.

For the 21 March raids, an LRDG patrol had 'dropped off' Mayne and his men five miles east of the target, but they had been hampered by unexpectedly rough terrain, delaying their progress by several hours. But despite this, none had considered abandoning the operation. Paddy Mayne hailed from Newtownards, in Northern Ireland, and had played rugby at international level prior to the war, representing both Ireland and the British Lions. A born fighter, tough as nails, he possessed an unrivalled ability to lead from the front, forging ahead in situations where others might consider the risks too great. Bennett believed that Mayne could take on anything, and that with him in command his men seemed to have no fear at all, following their 'ruthless' commander into even the most impossible situations.

The wider strategic importance of tonight's mission was not lost on the raiders. If they could blast apart the aerodrome and warplanes, it would hamper the enemy's aerial bombardment of the British stronghold of Malta. The island fortress's fate hung in the balance, as German aircraft pummelled it unrelentingly, using the full advantage of their air superiority to hit convoys shipping in desperately needed supplies. Malta constituted a vital British base in the Mediterranean, providing harbours from which Allied warships could attack the enemy's supply lines. If it fell, General Erwin Rommel, the formidable commander of the Afrika Korps – the German expeditionary force in Africa – would be free to bring in more troops and weaponry.

Under siege as it was, Malta would not hold out without desperately needed food and ammunition. Many of the aircraft that bombarded the Allied supply ships flew out of Libyan airbases, so if the SAS could destroy those warplanes on the ground, the convoys would have a greater chance of reaching Malta and breaking the siege. To fulfil that aim, Mayne and his men had travelled for days across the desert. Turning tail was never going to be an option, no matter how far behind schedule they might find themselves.

As they stole onto the enemy airbase and set their fuses, Mayne's raiding party knew they were running out of time to make it back to their pre-arranged rendezvous with the LRDG, waiting in the foothills of a rocky escarpment lying to the east. With every minute that passed, it became more and more likely that they would be left behind, stranded deep inside enemy-held territory.

Just as Byrne and Rose reached the last of the airfield's bomb dumps, the silence of the desert night erupted in a rush of light and heat: the first dugout full of munitions had ignited with spectacular ferocity. Byrne recalled a 'terrific continuous roar', with 'dump after dump belching out flames and smoke', as one after the other they blew themselves to pieces. Moments later, there followed another series of blasts towards the centre of the aerodrome, confirming that Mayne and Bennett had also found their targets: they would destroy fifteen aircraft that night.

With their mission complete, the raiders' thoughts turned now to escape. Over the roar of the flames they could make out the cries of their enemies. Byrne and Rose, their position illuminated by the burning carcasses of warplanes and ammo stores, dashed from the airfield into an adjacent petrol dump, where they paused to dispose of the last of their bombs. Then they threw themselves behind the cover of a low wall to consider their options.

One thing was clear: there was no way they could make the rendezvous with the LRDG. But as the Berka Airfield ammo dumps threw out massive clouds of thick, oily smoke, Byrne and

Rose congratulated themselves on taking out a sizeable chunk of the munitions being used to bomb the Maltese convoys. Even so, in the absence of their iconic commanding officer, they couldn't seem to reach a decision on what to do next. Rose was keen to head to the LRDG rendezvous, on the chance that the patrol was still there, waiting. Byrne figured that to be a waste of time, for those desert warriors had a ruthlessly pragmatic attitude. So too did the SAS: every man knew when he signed up to the unit that they were not above leaving their own men behind if they had to.

Byrne argued they should head for a second set of coordinates issued by the LRDG, a point roughly thirty miles east, where the vehicles were scheduled to regroup before returning to Allied lines. This was the back-up plan. But neither man could be persuaded of the wisdom of the other's viewpoint, and so they decided to separate – Rose hurrying off towards the original rendezvous, while Byrne took a different route at a far steadier pace.

John Vincent 'Jack' Byrne thought little of striking out on his own. Born in Preston in April 1921, he had spent his childhood in 'a tough Lancashire orphanage' where he had quickly learned to take care of himself. From there he had attended the Army Apprentices College, in Chepstow, Wales, an institution created to train the next generation of soldiers, to replace those lost in the First World War. He'd learned a mix of practical skills – carpentry, metalwork and electronics – plus warcraft, including 'leadership', 'adventure training' and 'character development'.

In February 1939, Byrne had lied about his age in order to join the Scottish regiment the Gordon Highlanders. He was only seventeen. 'I couldn't get a job. That's why I joined the army,' he remarked later, to explain the subterfuge.

The Gordon Highlanders deployed to France the following year, forming part of the spirited yet ill-fated British Expeditionary Force, which battled the forces of Nazi Germany as their *Blitzkrieg* – lightning war – ripped through the French countryside. Byrne fought courageously, being wounded twice, first by shrapnel and then at close quarters, during savage hand-to-hand combat with a German soldier, in the defence of the Dunkirk beaches. Wounded in the right hip by a bayonet thrust, he'd been left for dead. Incredibly, he was discovered in a state of semi-consciousness by some French civilians. Realising Byrne was still alive, they hurried him to the beachhead, from where he was evacuated to the UK.

Just as soon as his wounds were healed, Byrne volunteered for the Commandos, joining Number 11 (Scottish) Commando. Promoted to the rank of corporal in France, he was accepted into the Commandos on the condition that he revert to private. Byrne was fine with that, having little interest in moving up through the ranks. After five months of intense training, 11 Commando was despatched to the eastern Mediterranean, along with several other Commando units. Under the command of Colonel Robert Laycock, they were known collectively as 'Layforce'.

Deployed to Vichy-occupied Syria, 11 Commando 'stormed the beaches north of the Litani River', Byrne's brave actions quickly earning him promotion back to the rank of corporal. But the Syrian campaign would prove a rare triumph. The Commandos spent most of their time in the Middle East in a frustrating state of limbo, waiting for assignments that were called off at the last moment. When the decision was made to disband Layforce, it left a glut of elite warriors with little to do.

Many of them, Byrne included, hungered for the action that Commando life had failed to provide. From among those remnants of the Middle East Commandos, Stirling selected many of the original members of 'L-Detachment, the first Special Air Service Brigade', Byrne recalled, 'myself among them'.

Founding a new kind of elite unit in the desert, Stirling's selection process was uncompromising, remaining resolutely firm in rejecting those who were 'unable to reach that standard' that was required. Stirling cherry-picked the best and brightest, selecting those who were truly 'first class material', all of whom had 'considerable operational experience'. He sought men with 'courage, fitness and determination in the highest degree', but equally important were 'skill, intelligence, and training'.

Reverting to the rank of private once more, Byrne was accepted into the SAS, arriving at their camp in Kabrit on 4 September 1941. In this remote set-up, situated on the shores of the Great Bitter Lake in north-eastern Egypt, he started four months of gruelling training. These earliest SAS recruits underwent some of the most intense and ground-breaking instruction in the history of warfare. They jumped from the back of fast-moving trucks to simulate parachute landings; they marched for hundreds of miles through the desert; they learned to get by on the most meagre of rations of food and water – all under the eagle eye of the SAS's relentless training officer, Lieutenant John Steel 'Jock' Lewes.

Lewes was the very finest of training officers, early recruits recalled, one who led from the front by example. Formerly of 8 Commando, Lewes was second only to Stirling in terms of his influence upon the SAS at this time. His nerves, stamina and discipline were seemingly without parallel. The aim of Lewes' training was to make it 'as hard as humanly possible' for all recruits. That way, when his men found themselves on real operations they would be ready for anything.

Lewes trained the recruits in parachuting, explosives, sabotage, guile and all the elements of 'ungentlemanly warfare', plus desert survival skills. He wanted his trainees to be so familiar with these qualities that they became innate, the subconscious brain knowing automatically what was required in a given situation, so the trooper's conscious brain was free to deal with any dangers and opportunities for wreaking havoc and mayhem that arose. Such training would be tested to its very limits by Byrne, as he attempted to escape and evade capture and get back to friendly lines, following the Berka raid.

Byrne marched at a constant pace all that first day, reaching the foothills of the escarpment at dusk. He skirted the edge of the hills until he found the distinctive tyre tracks of the LRDG. From there he turned east-south-east, navigating using his compass and the positions of the stars. Keeping a steady course was challenging, particularly at night, but by dawn he could see where the hills gave way to the vast desert beyond. The LRDG had planned to converge at the point where the foothills met the flat expanse of sand, before beginning the long drive back to base. Byrne settled down to wait. Although he could not be sure of his precise location, he had a good view from his vantage point and felt certain he would be able to see the LRDG column arriving.

Noon came with no sign of the LRDG. Alone in the wilderness, Byrne's thoughts turned to his 'long walk back from the Marble Arch airfield' the previous December. 'Marble Arch' was the rascally nickname given by Allied troops to the Arch of the Philaeni, a high stone monument that straddled the Libyan coastal highway, marking the border between the Italian colonial provinces of Cyrenaica and Tripolitania. Mussolini revered Caesar Augustus, who had reputedly 'found Rome a city of brick and left it a city of marble'. He indulged similar grandiose visions for Italy's colonies, erecting the lavish edifice of the Arch of the Philaeni a few years earlier, to celebrate Italian mastery over Libya. The British, ever eager to poke fun at such delusions of grandeur, likened it to London's Marble Arch, which stands at the top of Oxford Street.

On 30 December 1941, Byrne had been part of a five-man raiding party that had journeyed to an enemy airbase situated not far from the Arch of the Philaeni. On arrival they had discovered there was nothing much there: the airfield appeared to be little more than a landing strip hewn out of the desert, devoid of any warplanes. Disheartened, the team had returned to their rendezvous point to wait for the LRDG. But the patrol tasked to collect them had come under fire from enemy aircraft in a ferocious eight-hour attack, the survivors were forced to limp back to base in their one remaining truck.

Official reports noted that Byrne's party waited seven days to be picked up, during which time they consumed most of their food rations and almost all of their water. As time passed it became evident that the normally reliable LRDG were not coming. Byrne described this realisation as 'every desert soldier's nightmare coming true'. After a week of such waiting, they finally started the long trek back with very little by way of supplies. Thus began a desperate, nine-day slog through the desert.

They covered 150 miles in total, scavenging water wherever they could: draining the radiators of enemy vehicles, drinking their own urine and even trying the brackish water from polluted salt marshes. They trudged through fields of battle littered with burned-out tanks; they ate lizards and snails; and they came under fire repeatedly from enemy patrols. Worst of all, on the last night of their epic march Byrne recalled how they came upon a mass grave, where the stench of death hung thick in the air, and the 'arms, legs, heads and feet' of British soldiers 'protruded from the sand at odd angles'. The party were finally picked up by a patrol of the King's Dragoon Guards, who delivered them back to their base camp.

Unavoidably, that ordeal was at the forefront of Byrne's mind, as he contemplated the unending desert before him now. It had been a near-fatal mistake to remain so long at the Arch of the Philaeni, one that Byrne had no wish to repeat. He estimated that it was over two hundred miles to the closest friendly out-post now – the French-held fort at Bir Hakeim, which marked the southernmost point of the Allied frontline. While he had yet to sip from the two-pint bottle of water he carried, he knew it would not last long if he tarried in the desert heat. He told himself that he would wait until dawn and not a moment longer.

Byrne killed time by taking stock of his supplies. In addition to his two pints of water, the only rations he had were a tin of emergency chocolate and half a pint of brandy in a silver flask. He had been delighted to receive the liquor as a gift from his commander during an earlier SAS operation, after being pro-moted back to the rank of Corporal. But now, he badly wished it were full of water instead. He also carried a Webley revolver, a Thompson submachine gun – commonly known as a 'Tommy gun' – binoculars and the iconic Commando fighting knife.

With dawn, there was still no sign of the LRDG, and Byrne felt his resolve begin to falter. Summoning all of his willpower, he forced himself to get to his feet and, with reluctance, stepped out into the vast wilderness. He headed south-east over the featureless and empty desert and did not rest until the sun had risen high enough to really warm the sands. While thirst was a constant companion, Byrne recalled, he was 'determined not to drink until dusk'.

Byrne had an iron will when it came to water discipline, something that had been drilled into the SAS recruits remorselessly. During training at Kabrit, maintaining iron-tight water discipline had been sacrosanct. Jock Lewes had marched for days on no water, and all were expected to follow his example. There was good reason behind this, as another renowned SAS desert survivor, Jack Sillito, explained: 'The basic thing was never drink during the heat of the day because you'd just perspire and it would all come out of you again.'

During training each man was permitted, under observation, to swig from his bottle, wash the fluid around his mouth to dispel the terrible dryness, and then spit the water back into the bottle. Recruits would be sent out on exercises in the morning with a full water bottle and expected to return with it a day later. In this way they trained their minds to ignore the water they carried, leaving it alone in spite of their thirst.

Ignoring the burning heat, Byrne marched until twilight, when he took his first drink. 'The first mouthful evaporated as it passed down my throat,' he remembered, though he did sense the second reaching his stomach. As night fell, he tried to sleep, but was beset by worry. He reckoned he'd covered around thirty miles that day. If he turned around now he could make it back to the rendezvous before dawn, in the hope of meeting the LRDG patrol. Perhaps they had arrived after he'd left and were even now making efforts to find him. He lay awake until the cold night air forced him to make a move.

With a heavy heart he took up a bearing for Bir Hakeim, so abandoning the possibility of turning back. For better or worse, he was now committed to the long march. He would just have to keep walking: 'Day or night, it did not matter now.'

Byrne pushed on a further twenty miles that night, and after a brief rest continued at a good pace. The following day a vicious sandstorm blew up, leaving him little choice but to curl up on the ground and wait for the worst to pass. He must have drifted into sleep, for he awoke stiff and shivering, his eyes, ears and nose caked with sand. It was the depths of the night. He swigged some brandy to warm himself. Surprisingly, the gift had actually come in handy, after all . . . Forcing himself to his feet, he decided to press on, using the stars to find his way. Byrne's pace only slowed with the return of the burning heat, come dawn. He rinsed his mouth occasionally with what remained of his water, spitting the liquid back into the bottle.

Byrne staggered on, but by the morning of his fourth day he was feeling horribly weakened. After much agonising, he decided to abandon his Thompson submachine gun, first rendering it useless by scattering the parts across a wide area of sand. Relieved of that extra weight he set off once more. Come noon he went to swish a sip of water around his mouth, only to find that the remaining liquid had congealed into a 'lukewarm slime, having become nothing more than spittle'. Byrne gagged and vomited on the warm sludge, sinking to the ground. He lay there, face in the sand, 'unable or unwilling to go on'.

His mind turned to the friends and comrades he had lost, for the early days of the SAS had been marred by tragedy. In November 1941, the desert had claimed around half of the men of L-Detachment during their first ever mission, codenamed Operation Squatter. For Squatter, Middle East Command had defined their primary task as being 'to raid both aerodromes at Timimi and Gazala', taking out the enemy warplanes based there. This was in preparation for Operation Crusader, the Eighth Army offensive designed to relieve the coastal city of Tobruk, which was besieged by Afrika Korps forces.

David Stirling had reported that the operation involved dropping teams of parachutists 'at night without moon, thus preserving surprise to the upmost'. But as the time for Squatter had approached, the weather deteriorated. Unseasonable wind and rain swept the desert, until the raiders faced the worst weather seen in the area for thirty years. But in spite of the terrible conditions, everybody wanted to jump. The SAS troopers, keen for action, insisted that the mission go ahead regardless.

Thrown off course by strong gusts and appalling visibility, the pilots had faced horrendous conditions in which to drop the troops. Some of Stirling's men were knocked unconscious by the impact of landing; others were killed outright or injured so badly they had to be left behind; and those who did make it to ground in one piece struggled to get out of their parachute harnesses in the ferocious wind. A number were swept along and, unable to free themselves from their 'chutes, were 'dragged to death'. Still more had been dropped so far off course they ended up falling into enemy hands while wandering through the dunes.

Of the fifty-odd men who had taken off from Kabrit, only twenty-one made it back alive. Byrne was one of the survivors, though he could hardly bear to recall the trauma of that night, when so many of the men that he had trained alongside had been killed. Thinking now of his fallen comrades, their remains lost for ever in the sand, Byrne stubbornly refused to join their number. Summoning his last vestiges of strength, he pulled himself into a sitting position, scrabbled together a couple of cigarette packets and some blank pages from his diary and lit a fire, warming the viscous sludge in his water bottle until it liquified. He mixed this with some brandy from his hip flask and, grimacing, swallowed the lot in one.

With that, he struggled to his feet and by sheer effort of will he marched on. It was dark now, and he staggered ahead by the light of the stars alone. He continued through the dawn, finally taking a break in the late afternoon and falling into an exhausted sleep. He came to his senses sometime later. Once more, it was dark. His mouth was dry and his head throbbed painfully. He figured it was the night of his sixth day alone in the desert, but he was no longer entirely sure. The last twenty-four hours had left him in a state close to delirium and he was losing track of time.

Byrne struggled to his feet and 'plodded on slowly and uncertainly', he recalled, barely able to keep moving. Then, suddenly, quite 'without thinking about it', Byrne decided to try a spell at running. He forced himself to walk and run for hours on end until, finally feeling the need to rest, he dropped to the sand once more. He had no way of knowing how long he lay asleep – his watch had stopped some days ago. But when he awoke it was daylight. Doubting whether he had the energy even to stand, Byrne pulled out his binoculars and surveyed the scene. Then he noticed, standing motionless no more than a hundred yards away, the unmistakable figure of a man. He was dressed in the flowing robes of the local Bedouin – desert nomads who live a wandering existence across North Africa, thriving in the desert as their ancestors had before them.

The stranger stood very still, shading his eyes against the glare, regarding Byrne with interest. Byrne tried to call out, but his parched throat could only croak out a hoarse rasp. He waved his hands and threw clouds of sand into the air, trying desperately to get the man to comprehend his dire condition. Finally, the Bedou hurried forward, dragged Byrne to his feet and helped him towards a pair of goatskin tents, concealed in a depression in the desert.

Byrne's would-be saviour settled him in the shade of the largest of the two tents, making him comfortable with pillows, before holding a large enamel bowl of goat's milk to his lips. Byrne drank deeply, finding the liquid 'delicious and cool', slowly finding his strength and clarity of mind returning. He was joined in the tent by more Bedouin. Though he feared he must be 'a revolting sight, not having washed or shaved' for more than two weeks, they treated him with kindness and respect, sharing a meal of goat meat in thick gravy and coarse Arab bread.

Using a mixture of English, Arabic and Italian, the Bedouin explained to Byrne that they were heading across the desert, to take camels to Mechili, a remote village 170 miles east of Benghazi. Byrne felt 'very lucky to come across them', for it was by sheer chance that they happened to have chosen this spot to break their journey. After thanking them for the meal, which he recognised had been 'especially laid on' for his benefit, Byrne announced that he would have to leave. His hosts were shocked. They invited him to accompany them to Mechili, or at least to spend the night in their tent to regain his strength.

Now that Byrne 'had fallen in with friendly Arabs', as the SAS war diary from the time noted, he would have been forgiven for opting to remain in their care until he was fully recovered. Yet he remained resolute: he must keep going and return to his unit. He checked with the Bedouin the direction in which Bir Hakeim lay. They indicated it was around eighty miles due east. Before departure, an elderly Bedouin woman refilled Byrne's water bottle, pressing a parcel of food into his hands. Inside lay more of the coarse bread and some dates. Byrne felt deeply touched by their generosity. The war had been hard on these nomadic people and they were often hungry.

With final words of thanks and farewell, Byrne set out east into the desert night, walking with renewed energy and spirit. At this pace he guessed he would reach his destination in a little over two days, depending on the terrain. The next night he was still 'too excited to sleep much', and he set out again before daybreak. Feeling fit and confident, he covered the ground rapidly, figuring he had less than forty miles to go now.

The following morning, he began what he reckoned would be the last leg of his journey. He walked at a slower pace, taking care to rake the shimmering horizon with his binoculars, searching for any sign of Bir Hakeim. The ground sloped upwards and Byrne increased his pace, hoping to be able to spot an Allied outpost from the higher ground. He crested the top of the rise and the distinctive form of a Chevrolet truck hove into view, the kind favoured by the British military here in the desert – none more so than the LRDG.

Byrne felt his heart leap. 'I thought that I was by now in the British lines, and walked towards the truck,' he noted in his escape report. But as he stepped forwards, the sand around him erupted under the impact of heavy machine-gun fire. The firing only stopped when Byrne found himself surrounded by a patrol of Afrika Korps soldiers. Just ahead, beyond the rise of the hill, a pair of tanks squatted in the valley, camouflaged against the desert. The turret of one of these flew open and a young German officer sprang out, sprinting towards Byrne.

'Hand over your weapon!' he yelled. 'Get your hands up!' The figure did not stop running until he was mere feet away, his pistol pointed directly at the SAS trooper. 'Get your hands up!'

Reluctantly, Byrne pulled his Webley from its holster. Dropping it to the sand, he refused to raise his hands. Sensing his defiance, the German officer made to strike Byrne in the face with his pistol, but instead unleashed a shot at point blank range.

Byrne collapsed to the ground. Blood leaked into the sand, staining it scarlet. Figures rushed to help Byrne, turning him onto his back. Shortly, he realised how incredibly lucky he had been. The bullet had taken a slice out of his nose and his eyebrow but had miraculously caused no more serious damage than that. The gashes were bleeding badly, as was his lip, which, already painfully blistered, had been split open by a rock when he fell.

The German officer seemed badly shaken. He explained to Byrne in broken English that he had not meant to shoot him, only hit him with the pistol when Byrne had failed to raise his hands. He had pulled the trigger by accident. For his part, Byrne was caked in blood and sand, and unable to believe that he had survived a journey of almost two hundred miles across the desert, only to be captured by the enemy at the final hurdle.

The German soldiers fussed about, brushing the sand from his uniform and trying to persuade him to lie on a stretcher, but Byrne shook his head. He was damned if he would let them carry him! As he allowed himself to be led in the direction of the tanks, he realised that amid the shock and drama of his capture the German officer had failed to search him. He still had his fighting knife and compass.

Byrne was led past the tanks and over a further rise, where he regarded the scene before him in astonishment. There 'were hundreds of armoured fighting vehicles' parked up amid the featureless terrain. 'The whole of the German Afrika Korps' seemed to be gathered there, Byrne noted. Indeed, the Chevrolet that he had spotted was nothing more than a captured British vehicle.

Before long they reached a vehicle that Byrne described as being like a mobile library, with 'the whole of one side covered in maps'. There, he was brought before a group of senior commanders. The young officer who had shot Byrne began recounting the story, until a senior officer cut him off by barking out some orders. Figures stepped forward, grabbing Byrne roughly by the arms. He resisted violently, startling them and causing one to drop his rifle. Despite their nervousness and apparent inexperience, the German soldiers persevered, attempting to drag Byrne forwards, but they were no match for his brute strength and stubborn, unyielding nature.

Finally, the German commander shouted another order and the soldiers stepped away from Byrne. When he was no longer being forcibly restrained, Byrne approached of his own accord. Byrne's attitude represented more than just wayward obstinacy – it embodied the spirit of the SAS. Self-possessed, despite the gravity of the situation, Byrne refused to compromise on being treated respectfully, no matter the difference in rank between himself, a corporal, and those before him. The appreciation of merit above rank was actively encouraged in the SAS, being the bedrock of the unit.

Of the men he had recruited, David Stirling once remarked, 'they weren't really controllable. They were harnessable.'

Despite his bloodied face, unkempt beard, dirty uniform and swollen lip, Byrne stood bolt upright as he met the enemy commander's gaze. He held his head high as the German examined the emblem stitched over his breast pocket. That badge – depicting the open wings of a desert beetle and a stylised parachute in two shades of blue – had been bestowed upon Byrne when he completed seven successful parachute jumps. All SAS troopers wore their 'wings' with pride. Initially, they were sewn onto the man's sleeve, but when a trooper had carried out three raids, or had otherwise distinguished himself, he was granted the privilege of wearing his wings above his breast pocket. That was where Byrne – a seasoned and distinguished raider – wore this iconic emblem.

After thoroughly inspecting the insignia, the German commander spoke some words to the young officer, who escorted Byrne to a medic. The German doctor carefully cleaned the congealed mess of blood and sand from Byrne's face. He stitched closed the gashes on his nose and eyebrow, and extracted two of Byrne's teeth, which had been damaged when he had fallen heavily on the ground. The doctor explained that some shards of tooth were still embedded in Byrne's lip, but there was not much he could do about that. Byrne's face was bandaged all over, leaving only one eye visible, and breathing holes for his nose and mouth. He was given water and instructed to sit in the shade.

The young officer outlined to Byrne that he was to be sent to a prisoner-of-war camp for Allied airmen, in Germany. Byrne protested that he was a soldier, not an airman. The general had ordered that he 'be classified as a flier', the German officer explained, glancing at the parachutists' wings gracing Byrne's chest.

He escorted Byrne to a nearby infantry camp, where he was briefly patted down. To his relief, the rudimentary search didn't unearth his fighting knife, nor the various items of escape equipment concealed in his specially modified uniform. MI9, the Allied 'Escape Factory', had taken to inserting hidden items into the tunics of all flying officers and parachutists, to aid the escape of any who might be shot down or on the run in enemy territory. Byrne's concealed a rubber-coated hacksaw blade secreted in the breast pocket, a silk map of North Africa sewn into the lining, plus a map of Europe printed on high-strength, weather-resistant tissue paper hidden in his belt.

After the search, Byrne was handed over to an elderly German officer for interrogation. He offered the man his name, rank and service number, nothing more. At that his interrogator scoffed, declaring that he knew very well that Byrne was a member of the Special Air Service. He added that he knew that his overall commander was David Stirling, while urging Byrne to try to recall other details of the unit with which he served.

By now, the SAS had acquired a legendary status among members of the Afrika Korps. Byrne's reputation and that of his fellow troopers – a team of hardened raiders who came stealing out of the sand dunes and disappeared like cats in the night, seemingly striking *anywhere* along the North African coastline – went before them. The presence of these desert warriors and their enigmatic leader – already known as 'The Phantom Major' to the Germans – brought an element of British romantic heroism and eccentric derring-do to this otherwise savage and bloody conflict.

After his initial interrogation, Byrne was treated to both threats and promises, his captors seeming desperate to discover 'the nature of the operation on which [he] had been engaged'. While held at an Italian police station in Benghazi, Byrne was locked inside a bare cell. Finding himself finally alone, he took out his fighting knife and stuck it between two of the joints of the bed frame, for he knew it would not go well for him if the enemy discovered he was still carrying a weapon. With that safely stashed, he climbed onto the bed and gratefully slept.

His first sleep in a real bed for many weeks was prematurely interrupted, when two men entered the room. One spoke reasonably good English and was dressed in the uniform of an officer in the British Fleet Air Arm. The other was apparently a sergeant in a British Anti-tank Battery. They were friendly to Byrne, perhaps overly so, particularly the Fleet Air Arm officer, who had a bandage wrapped round his head, which he claimed to be the result of recent fighting. The three men talked and smoked for a while, until the Fleet Air Arm officer left the room.

The moment he was gone, the sergeant leaned closer to Byrne. 'I think that bastard's an informer,' he whispered. 'Be careful.'

When the man returned, he kept up the pretence of friendliness, asking Byrne about the unit with which he served and offering to send a message home to his family. At that, Byrne slipped from his uniform his concealed hacksaw blade, warning that he knew full well how the Italians employed stool pigeons. If ever he met one, Byrne announced, with quiet menace, 'I would like nothing better than to use this on his throat.'

Most often, such 'stool pigeons' were German or Italian intelligence officers who had spent time in Britain, America or other English-speaking countries before the war, as students or on business. Now, serving as agents of the Reich, they used their British or American accents to deceive POWs into dropping their guard. At Byrne's words the suspected stool pigeon blanched. He hammered on the door and was released by the guards, after which Byrne never saw him again. Sometime later the sergeant was also taken away, along with Byrne's SAS uniform. An old Italian tunic was tossed into the cell instead.

For two days Byrne was kept in solitary confinement and deprived of any food. Then, on 5 April 1942 he was taken to the main transit camp for Allied POWs, where he was finally allowed to mix freely with other prisoners. At first, many of them treated him with outright suspicion. Byrne could hardly blame them. His appearance was wild beyond measure. He was thickly bearded, had 'hair sprouting through bandages', was 'filthy' and dressed mostly in scraps of Italian uniform. Even so, he took comfort from being around his own people, after so long alone in the desert and then in the hands of his enemies.

But his relief was to be short-lived. The next day four Italian soldiers appeared, pulled Byrne roughly away and shoved him into the back of a vehicle. As they hurtled along the Libyan roads at breakneck speed the tension in that car was palpable, and Byrne could hazard a guess at the cause of the soldiers' ire. They must have found the fighting knife that he had hidden in the bedstead.

The car arrived at its destination. The soldiers used Byrne's bandaged face to smash open the door of an interrogation room and they manhandled him inside. They stripped him of the Italian tunic, one of them holding his old SAS uniform before him, tauntingly. Grinning, he proceeded to wrap the fabric around his fist, before slamming it directly into Byrne's damaged nose. His stitches burst open, blood pouring from the freshly opened wound.

They held Byrne by his arms, as a thuggish-looking Italian officer carrying a long black cane entered. He raised it threateningly, before bringing the full force of it down upon the crown of Byrne's head. Using all his strength, the officer 'continued to strike at my face, knees, shins and ankles', Byrne recalled. The man lashed out anywhere and everywhere, as Byrne did his best to escape the savage blows, twisting and turning, flinging himself from side to side, stamping on the feet of the men holding him and kicking out at the figure at his front. But all resistance proved fruitless. The pain was close to unendurable, and Byrne started to retch and vomit with agony.

Byrne's suspicions were confirmed when the officer finally laid down his cane and picked up the fighting knife that Byrne had left hidden in the bedpost. With that in hand, the officer sliced open the pockets of Byrne's SAS tunic, revealing where M19 had hidden the rubber-covered hacksaw blade. He removed it theatrically, before slashing at the tunic some more. He continued to cut and slice, revealing both the tissue paper and silk maps. It later transpired that the Germans had discovered the secrets of M19's escape-adapted tunics, and all Axis forces were now aware of what they concealed.

By the time the Italian officer was finished, Byrne's tunic hung in tatters, where the knife had sliced through the fabric. Byrne stood there, cowed and panting when, without warning, one of his captors kicked out his legs from under him and he went crashing to the floor. All four of them unleashed upon his prone form.

Having kicked him all over and ripped apart his clothing, they finished off by jumping on Byrne's stomach and stamping on his bare hands. Byrne lay there, pretending to be unconscious, until finally his assailants decided he'd had enough. Naked except for his boots, his entire body was bruised and bleeding, and what remained of his bandages hung in shreds around his neck. His hands and knees were swelling badly and one of his fingers jutted out at an unnatural angle.

One of the Italians threw a pair of shorts and a shirt in Byrne's direction. He did his best to pull them on, though his hands were too swollen to do up the flies. From there he was taken to a square building, which looked like a disused stable. The Italians shoved him roughly through the door, locking it shut behind him, leaving Byrne in solitary confinement for several days.

On 12 April Byrne was taken to an airport under escort and flown to Crete, and from there to Athens. By now he was dressed as a Greek airman, for that was the only Allied uniform his captors had been able to lay their hands on. He was under the guard of two German soldiers who were heading home on leave. They treated him with respect and even, at times, with kindness.

From Athens the three caught a train towards Berlin, and then onwards three hundred miles or so, to the Dulag Luft transit camp, near Frankfurt, where captured Allied airmen were detained before being sent to more permanent places of incarceration. Rumours of torturous Nazi interrogation techniques were rife at Dulag Luft, but luckily for Byrne, the officer who interviewed him seemed to have very little interest in his story, after it was confirmed that he was not an airman after all, but a soldier.

From Dulag Luft Byrne was transferred to Stalag Luft III, a prisoner-of-war camp in the town of Sagan (modern-day Żagań), situated around one hundred miles south-east of Berlin, close to the border with German-occupied Poland. He reached the camp on 23 April and was quickly informed that a Lieutenant

Charles Bonington of L-Detachment SAS was being held in the officers' section of the camp. Byrne's spirits leapt: Bonington had been one of those they had lost on Operation Squatter, the SAS's disastrous first mission. His fate had been unknown, but, like so many others, they'd feared him dead.

Stalag Luft III was divided into separate compounds – including an eastern block, where Byrne was held, containing British NCOs, and a western one containing British and American officers. At a pre-arranged time, Byrne walked down the fence separating the two and was able to speak through the wire to Bonington. From him he learned that Captain Thompson, another SAS man believed lost, was also in the camp. Byrne was hugely heartened to know they had survived. For their part, they were keen to hear news of the fortunes of the SAS. Byrne related their numerous successes in the Western Desert, regaling Bonington with tales of the SAS's growing infamy, interspersed with the sad news of comrades who had been killed in the line of duty.

Byrne learned that the Germans considered Stalag Luft III to be escape-proof. It was surrounded by dense barbed-wire fences, and had watchtowers set at regular intervals around the perimeter that were manned by guards 'armed with machine guns and equipped with searchlights'. The huts themselves were supposedly tunnel-proof, and were regularly searched by the camp guards. The unrivalled security of the camp made it the ideal place to incarcerate those who had tried to escape before – the so-called bad boys. Though disappointed that he had ended up in such a high-security establishment, Byrne was heartened to be surrounded by fellow escapees – men with keen brains, opportunistic natures and the bravery and guts to attempt a breakout.

In their company, he became obsessed with escaping, spending his days mooching around the perimeter 'trying to find a loophole in the system', and his 'evenings and nights scheming'. He made contact with the group of officers who formed the camp's escape committee, those who played a vital part in overseeing breakouts. Each escape plan had to be submitted to the committee, to make sure it was feasible and that it did not clash with existing schemes. The escape committee would organise various ruses and diversions to keep the guards busy during such attempts, and would cover up the evidence of any escapes for as long as possible, to give the prisoners the best chance of getting away.

The committee also kept in touch with M19 via doctored letters and clandestine radio sets, and could request maps, fake identity papers, local currency and other vital escape aids. These were smuggled in by ingenious methods, including being loaded into parcels sent to non-existent prisoners, concealed inside the covers of books donated by fictitious charities, or secreted inside food packages and shaving supplies.

Byrne learned about all sorts of incredible escape attempts, noting how many 'individual tunnel schemes' were being excavated, using tools fashioned from the powdered milk tins included in their Red Cross parcels. Inspired by such ingenuity, he fashioned himself a compass from a broken wristwatch, using a needle made from a magnetised razorblade. With the inner mechanism removed it was possible to get a north–south reading by 'balancing the needle on a tiny post in the centre of the casing'. He kept the components for the compass with him at all times – the broken watch strapped to his wrist and the razorblade concealed inside a cigarette – and waited for his chance.

Byrne's tenacious desire for freedom would go on to win him a Distinguished Service Order. His medal citation describes how, despite his dislike of rank and hierarchy, 'he volunteered to act as an officer's batman as he thought this would give him a better opportunity of escaping.' Stalag Luft III was becoming overcrowded and he hoped that as an 'officer's servant' he might be transferred elsewhere. Five months after arriving in Germany, in September 1942, his wish came true. Along with around a hundred officers, fifteen NCOs were transferred to Oflag XXI-B, an officer's camp in occupied Poland, which Byrne described roguishly as 'an escaper's dream'.

At Oflag XXI-B Byrne volunteered to help in the kitchens, hoping that might provide him with the chance to sneak past the perimeter. The perfect opportunity soon presented itself. Food was scarce in wartime Poland and the kitchen workers kept a handful of pigs, fattened up on camp leftovers. Byrne noted how every day, one POW would head down to the camp pigsties with a cartload of swill, escorted by a German guard. That guard was quite old and carried his rifle 'bandolier fashion' across his back, as he pushed a bicycle along. Byrne reckoned that if he could get onto the pigswill duty, he might steal the guard's bike and be off and away before he had time to make ready his weapon.

Byrne outlined his plan to the camp's escape committee who gave their approval. With their blessing he began preparing the items he would need, gathering together chocolate, raisins, cheese and cigarettes from the Red Cross parcels. He still had his homemade compass and the escape committee provided him with maps to aid his getaway. They also offered to furnish Byrne with a counterfeit *Ausweis* – a German identity card – but he declined, reasoning that it would be a waste of time, for anyone who got close enough to ask for his identity card would quickly realise he couldn't speak German. Finally, he needed a disguise. He still had the Greek airman's uniform, in which his captors had despatched him into captivity in Germany. He removed the buttons and pockets, to give it a non-military look, and fashioned a civilian-style cap sewn from blankets.

Thus equipped, late in October 1942 – seven months after his capture in the desert – Byrne sallied forth on pigswill duty, accompanied by the guard. Once at the sties, Byrne manhandled the handcart carrying the pigswill so it blocked the entrance, effectively trapping the guard. That done, he sprinted around the corner, seized the guard's bike, jumped aboard and pedalled off at top speed, jamming the 'civilian' cap on his head as he did so.

Elated at the guard's failure to open fire, Byrne turned right onto the main road and followed a sign for the city of Bromberg (modern-day Bydgoszcz), some fifteen miles north-west of the camp. He sped into the first town but was spotted by a local man who immediately seemed suspicious. The man stepped into the road, and when Byrne tried to swerve around him, he lunged and grabbed hold of the front of the bicycle. Byrne tumbled off and was quickly set upon by a crowd. There was no escape. Byrne was marched to the nearest police station and searched, from where he was delivered, feeling foolish and dejected, back to Oflag XXI-B.

Despite his failure, Byrne reasoned all was not lost. 'My maps were hidden inside my belt and my compass inside my wrist-watch,' he reported, and neither had been discovered. Sentencing him to twenty-eight days in the 'punishment block', the camp commandant stipulated that he should be fed a punishment diet of 'bread and water with a bowl of soup every fourth day'. The cell was small and spartan, with a barred window set high in the wall. There was one narrow bunk, which had no mattress, and only a wooden pillow, with a rough depression where he could rest his head.

In solitary, Byrne was allowed no exercise and he spent his days lying on his bunk – fully clothed, for there were no blankets – living in his imagination. Fellow prisoners tried to sneak him extra food, but by the end of his sentence he was half-starved. At this point he was brought before the camp commandant again but ended up being condemned to a further twenty-eight days on the same rations, for 'looking at a German officer with insolence'.

Byrne returned to the punishment block in a state of disbelief. By now, he had been under arrest or punishment more times than he cared to remember. The first had been at the regimental HQ of the Gordon Highlanders, in the Bridge of Don barracks, Aberdeen. There, serving as a young recruit, Byrne had been thrown in the cells for 'refusing to polish the brass cannon on the edge of the barrack square'. His last spell in the cells had been for striking his troop sergeant major! But never had he been confined for so long, alone, and on such pitiful rations.

Towards the end of Byrne's second stretch in solitary, an RAF officer in the next-door cell complained to the guard that his floor was filthy and needed sweeping. Moments later Byrne's door was unlocked and the sentry handed him a broom. Byrne took it and swept out his own cell. The guard gestured towards the RAF officer's, next door, the message being clear. Byrne felt it was wrong that he – an experienced Special Forces raider with an impressive combat history – should face the indignity of clearing out another man's cell, no matter what his rank. He propped the broom against the wall and sat on his bunk, immovable, despite the guard's enraged yells.

For this 'wilful defiance of authority', Byrne was duly given his third twenty-eight days in solitary. At the end of that sentence, the sentry opened Byrne's door, handed him the broom and ordered him to sweep out the whole of the cell block. Byrne, of course, refused – he would not allow them to break his spirit. He was duly punished with a further twenty-eight days, bringing his total sentence to 112 days of solitary confinement: four months trapped in a tiny cell, alone, on starvation rations.

Byrne felt his body withering away. Much more of this, he noted, and he would not be physically capable of escaping, even if he got the opportunity. His thoughts became uncharacteristically dark. As he lay on his wooden bunk, thoughts of 'what if' and 'if only' chased themselves around in his mind: if only he'd waited at the rendezvous for the LRDG; if only he had stuck to crossing the desert under cover of darkness; if only he had accepted the Bedouins' hospitality, staying with them in their tents. He wondered how many of his SAS friends had been killed, and he felt ashamed of himself, locked up and useless, while his comrades soldiered on.

Though his spirits spiralled downwards, somehow, with super-human effort, Byrne endured. When finally he was released back into the main prison – without further comment from the guards – he resolved to redouble his efforts to escape. He scrutinised every possibility, considering any potential, no matter how seemingly marginal. But during his long confinement there had been a mass breakout attempt and the vigilance of the guards was much intensified.

Byrne learned that the only way for a prisoner now to leave the camp was to perform coal fatigues – manhandling coal-sacks into the camp. Despite his emaciated state, he took a place on the coal-carrying parties, during which he spotted a garage lying adjacent to the coal yard that seemed to offer a temporary place of hiding. Once more he approached the escape committee. Outlining his plan, he won their approval. Again, they gave him food supplies, plus detailed maps of the route from the camp north to Danzig (modern-day Gdansk), lying on the Baltic coast, and south-east to Warsaw – furnishing two alternative escape routes. They also devised a ruse that would make it appear as if Byrne were still in the camp days after his breakout, so buying him precious time.

Finally, he tried to put together a more convincing disguise, so this time, if he managed to make it out of the camp, he would not alert any casual observer's attention so swiftly. He duly acquired 'a pair of blue pin-striped trousers, a black morning coat', plus a civilian style cap, all of which had been manufactured ingeniously by the camp's tailors, using blankets stained in dyes made from jam.

Byrne's official escape report took up the story. 'I put on these garments . . . and wore an army overcoat over that. I carried a compass, and stowed my food, some chocolate, a razor and soap, in bags under my arms. On . . . 15th March '43, I went out with a coal party, and managed to slip into the garage . . . The other members of the party and their guard shut the door of the garage, leaving me inside. When they had gone, I immediately got through a window . . . made my way to the pigsties and by luck again found a bicycle . . . I mounted this and rode through the town . . . then turned down a side road and hid my bicycle among some trees.'

Byrne trekked over the marshy Polish countryside, heading for the large railway marshalling yard at Bromberg. The damp conditions caused his feet to swell painfully and he decided he needed to board a train. He found the railway track and followed it to a point where a number of goods trains were parked up. After observing them from a ditch, he climbed into the guards' wagon of an empty train, which was duly shunted into a marshalling yard. There he proceeded to jump between wagons as they were moved back and forth, until he found one full of coal and managed to hide himself amid the blackness.

The following days were 'some of the most miserable I have ever endured', Byrne later remarked, for after the coal train left Bromberg it travelled only a short distance, before halting for several days. Finally, Byrne decided he had to risk swapping trains, but as he sneaked between wagons at a busy station, wild-looking and covered in coal dust, he was spotted by some railway workers. They chased after and seized him, after which Byrne was duly returned to the punishment block at Oflag XXI-B.

Worse still, in the five days that Byrne had been on the run, conditions at the prison camp had changed utterly. There had been a mass tunnel breakout, and while most of the escapees had been recaptured, the Gestapo had seen fit to seize control of Oflag XXI-B. The new camp commandant sentenced Byrne to twenty-eight days' solitary confinement for escaping, but first he was to be sent to Gestapo headquarters for questioning. He was taken to an unmarked vehicle by two silent, black-clad officers. On arrival at their headquarters he was thrown into a four-foot-square cell. The Gestapo kept the lights on, so Byrne had no way of knowing how long he was there, but he figured it to have been five or six days.

When, finally, he was taken out, he was brought before a Gestapo officer. The man gestured to a pile of papers lying on his desk. They were all concerning Byrne, he remarked, and did not make for 'very pleasant reading'. Byrne had proven a real 'nuisance'. He had one question to ask. If Byrne answered truthfully, he would be returned to the prison camp. But if he lied, he would be given into the hands of 'someone who will be more persuasive'. Was that clear, the Gestapo officer demanded?

'Yes,' Byrne replied simply.

'All I want to know is how you escaped from the prison camp.'

Byrne had long been considering how to answer this question. He had heard tell of the Gestapo's torture techniques, and he didn't feel that anyone could endure them for long. He'd decided that his only chance was to lie convincingly.

'I escaped through the tunnel,' Byrne announced abruptly.

The Gestapo officer looked doubtful. According to their records, Byrne was still in the prison camp the day after the tunnel was discovered. The escape committee must have managed to cover up his getaway so convincingly that the guards had still thought him inside the camp, even after the tunnel breakout. By way of answer, Byrne stuck doggedly to his story, insisting that he had slipped away at the same time as all the other tunnel escapees.

He had not, the Gestapo officer countered. He had in fact slipped away the day after the tunnel had been sealed shut. Not only that, once they had taken control of the camp the Gestapo had ensured that the perimeter guards were tripled, the staff inside the camp doubled and general security massively tightened. 'Yet, in spite of all these precautions, *you* succeeded in escaping,' he pointed out accusingly.

Suddenly, Byrne realised what was his interrogator's main concern: it wasn't chiefly for the camp's security, but for the Gestapo's reputation. Playing to the man's fears, Byrne pointed out that no man could have escaped after the Gestapo had imposed such stringent extra security measures. Perhaps amid all the confusion of the mass breakout, there had been a miscount, and Byrne's absence had been missed?

The Gestapo officer considered this for a moment. Following the tunnel breakout, the prisoners had been counted by the old security staff, he mused. Byrne could sense the Gestapo officer was tempted to go with this version of events. If Byrne had slipped away through the tunnel along with all the others, that would let the Gestapo off the hook, for it could be blamed on a counting error by the previous staff. He watched the man sip his coffee, nibble some biscuits, then wander around the room smoking a cigarette, deep in thought. Byrne's head throbbed and his stomach ached, for he had not eaten for days, but he remained silent and still, as the officer made up his mind.

Finally, Byrne's inquisitor perched on the edge of his desk and offered a cigarette. 'You escaped through the tunnel with the others,' he ventured. That was before the Gestapo had taken over responsibility for the camp. The former prison staff had simply miscounted. Byrne felt a surge of relief as he enthusiastically agreed, but then the Gestapo officer added some dark words of warning. If Byrne were to make one further escape attempt, 'we will shoot you'. If by chance he achieved 'the impossible' and reached England, 'we will search you out when we occupy your country and execute you.' Was that clear?

'Yes,' Byrne replied.

The interrogation over, Byrne was returned to Oflag XXI-B where he was again locked up in the punishment block. Before his term of solitary was up, the majority of the camp's inhabitants were transferred to Stalag Luft VI, in the far north-east corner of the Third Reich. Byrne was left behind in the cells, until on 15 July 1943 he began his journey to Stalag Luft VI, along with a handful of other prisoners.

'I was taken under guard to Berlin, and thence to Königsberg [now Kaliningrad] by train, en route for Stalag Luft VI,' Byrne reported. He knew that Stalag Luft VI would likely be escape-proof. So, despite the Gestapo officer's stark warning, he had to look for any chance to break away now. Some twenty-four hours into their journey they arrived at the Königsberg transit camp, where they were given medical treatment by some French POWs.

One of Byrne's fellow prisoners, Flight Sergeant Jock Callander, had served with the French Foreign Legion and spoke fluent French. He and Byrne had already discussed the possibility of escape, and Callander asked one of the Frenchmen for help. From him they learned that the French POWs were free to walk about Königsberg, for they were easily identifiable by their French uni-forms, which sported a special diamond symbol on one arm. The Frenchman told Callander that his countrymen would be sure to assist them in any way they could. He wished them good luck, before giving Callander 10 Reichsmarks and 100 French francs. Byrne and Callander split the money between them, and readied themselves to escape, should the opportunity arise.

A few hours later Byrne was let out of the prison hut to visit the latrines. He noted that on the far side of a wire fence were a number of Russian POWs. They motioned to him that they wanted cigarettes. Throwing a couple of precious packets over the wire, Byrne managed to get a look at their side of the camp. The drain from the latrine ran beneath the fence, and the Russian side seemed less well-guarded than the British and French sections.

He reckoned from there it might be possible to reach the road, out of sight of any guards.

Byrne was about to return to fetch Callander, when a party of French POWs arrived, momentarily distracting the prison guards. He sensed that if he were to make a break for it, it was now or never. 'I dared not wait for Callander to join me,' he recalled. Decision made, he lowered himself into the latrine drain, which was about two feet deep, slid under the wire and crawled across into the Russian sector. Then he scrambled into some thick grass near the perimeter fence, adjacent to the road.

Byrne lay hidden in the grass for a moment, waiting for any sign that he had been spotted, but the noises of the camp continued as usual. The best place to get through the fence appeared to be at the corner, where the wire looked worn, but this was directly beneath the guard tower. Studying the guard above, he became convinced the man was reading a book, for each time he looked around his posture would return to the exact same position, staring intently at something in his lap. Byrne decided to seize the opportunity.

At the point he had chosen the wire turned out to be old and rotten, and he managed to break through with his bare hands. He crawled out onto the road, and, taking a deep breath – taking his very life in his hands – he stole away. 'The road on which I now stood ran parallel to a railway line,' he wrote in his escape report, 'and between the road and the railway there were a large number of rusty metal bins. I lifted one up and got underneath it. Here I remained until dark.'

While thus concealed, Byrne took stock of his supplies. He had ten cigarettes, a box of matches, plus the Reichsmarks that Callander had given him. In addition to his trusty razorblade compass, he had also managed to acquire a map of the area of their proposed transportation route. He was dressed in khaki battle-dress with a blue RAF shirt – so nowhere near as well disguised as he had been on his previous breakout attempts. But crucially, he also had a razor and a bar of soap, which should enable him to maintain an air of clean-shaven respectability, as a stubbly chin would signify to any onlooker that he was on the run.

Hidden inside the metal bin, Byrne's mind strayed to thoughts of Callander. He wished there had been time to alert him to the escape plan. But he remembered that they had agreed that if either 'saw an opportunity to escape' they should 'take it independently'. Either way, once darkness fell he would have little option but to make his way into Königsberg alone and try to enlist the help of the French POWs there.

Come nightfall, Byrne made his way along the railway tracks into the town, trying to work out where the docks must be, for the city lay on the Baltic coast. By a stroke of luck he noticed a discarded sailor's hat, complete with ribbons, gleaming white against the darkness. Might that provide just the disguise he was looking for to bluff his way aboard a ship? Delighted with his find, he slipped the hat inside his tunic. At the docks he found a number of empty goods wagons, one of which was damaged and parked a little way from the others. He climbed inside it and fell into an exhausted but fraught sleep.

If he were caught, he was dead: Byrne knew that. He was over a thousand miles from Britain by now, for his gaolers had kept transporting him eastwards, away from friendly shores. This was his very last chance. Somehow, he had to make it home.

The next morning, 18 July 1943, Byrne, peered out of the wagon, noticing a number of Frenchmen standing in groups near by. They had all the appearance of work gangs, and he waited anxiously for one to draw near, so he could try to attract their attention. None did. He remained hidden all day, unwilling to reveal himself, especially since certain execution at the hands of the Gestapo would follow recapture. Just as dusk was falling, he noticed a gang of prison workers leaving the docks. They appeared to be unguarded, and most were dressed in battledress blouses, with the distinctive diamond badge on their sleeves. Despite the danger, Byrne seized his chance. He jumped from the train, shaking hands with those nearest and furtively explaining that he was an escaped 'English airman'.

Obligingly, they swept up Byrne in their midst, hurrying him along until they reached the hut that was their sleeping quarters. There he learned to his distress that there were no ships of any significant size in Königsberg – just a few small coal barges. It was hopeless to try to escape by sea, and so, together with his new accomplices, he weighed his options. During his long imprisonment Byrne had heard the escape story of Sergeant Wareing, who had become a good friend in Stalag Luft III. Wareing had managed to reach neutral Sweden by stowing away on a ship sailing from Danzig. Danzig lay over a hundred miles to the west of Königsberg, but still Byrne felt it represented his best shot. He asked if his newfound friends would help scavenge some civilian clothes. Obligingly, they gathered together a suit of blue worker's overalls, a beret and a haversack stuffed with food. He accepted it all, but refused to take the money they offered, for he still had cash stitched into the lining of his trousers.

He asked for one more favour. Might they procure for him one of their diamond badges, so that he could more convincingly pass as a French POW? That done, Byrne bade farewell to his accomplices. As they left to report for work duty, Byrne hurried towards Königsberg town centre, searching all the while for an unattended bicycle. He spotted one lying in a gateway, got his hands on it without the alarm being raised and moments later he was pedalling away.

Byrne was little troubled by such acts of thievery. Theft, burglary and larceny had lain at the heart of their SAS training. Anyone who hadn't the stomach for it was weeded out fast. When Byrne and fellow recruits had first arrived at their SAS training camp at Kabrit, all they found was a small board stuck in the ground, with 'L-Detachment' daubed upon it, and with nothing but 'a vast empty space behind it'. When one perplexed recruit had asked David Stirling where the camp was, their leader had replied: 'Well, that's the first job you do – you steal one!'

The British military bureaucracy – which Stirling famously referred to as 'layer upon layer of fossilised shit' – had refused to provide him with the equipment he needed to begin training, or at least not fast enough, hence his exhortation that his men should 'go out and start stealing'. But apart from satisfying their immediate needs, he also wanted to normalise the idea of thieving from civilians and other military units, so that his men would think nothing of resorting to such measures while on operations.

Recruits had been only too happy to oblige. 'We thought *this* was the unit to be with!' one recalled enthusiastically.

Pedalling his stolen bicycle, Byrne headed westwards, following signposts to Elbing (modern-day Elblag), which he knew to be on the route to Danzig. As he approached the town he saw a roadblock up ahead, where travellers were having their papers checked. Luckily, he was just in time to turn down a side path leading into a wood. There, he hid himself until dark, when he shouldered the bike and struck out across country, stumbling around in the inky blackness until he was sure that he had bypassed the danger. That done, he hid the 'bicycle under a hedge, climbed into a tree, and spent the rest of the night among the branches', his escape report noted.

Come dawn, Byrne washed and shaved in a nearby stream before remounting the bike. He passed through Elbing without incident, but in a village on the far side he had a stroke of misfortune. The front tyre burst and, having no pump or puncture repair kit, Byrne was forced to carry the bike on his shoulder. He cursed himself for not being more careful about his choice of bicycle. His previous escape attempts had taught him that as long as he was on a bike, it reduced the risk of anyone stopping him to talk. As Byrne spoke no Polish or German, even something as innocent as a passer-by asking him for directions could reveal his identity as an escaped Allied POW.

Wandering the country roads with a bike on his shoulder, Byrne felt horribly conspicuous. He needed to get off the road. He followed the first track he came to, found a hidden field and sat with his bicycle under a tree. There he painstakingly 'stuffed the punctured tyre with grass', chewing it into a green pulp so he could more easily squash it inside. When he was done the tyre still looked flat and bumpy, and Byrne conceded that he would only be able to ride the bike 'in an emergency', but at least he would be able to wheel it along rather than carry it. He remained in the field that night, sleeping in the branches of a large tree, the bicycle hoisted up alongside him.

The next morning Byrne shaved again, moistening his face a patch at a time with a raw potato he had dug up from the field. Feeling 'rested and renewed', he continued westwards, wheeling his bike. He estimated he was now around fifty miles from Danzig. As he walked he became aware that he was not alone. A small white dog had begun to follow him. It remained at his side the whole day, curling up next to him and his bicycle as he slept through the night under some bushes in a disused quarry.

The following day Byrne pushed on, flanked by his scruffy canine partner, occasionally carrying the small dog on the saddle of the bicycle when he began to lag behind. He had realised that his four-legged companion gave him the appearance of nor-mality whenever they passed through a busy area. Later that morning Byrne reached a pontoon bridge over the River Vistula, the longest in Poland, which empties into the sea at Danzig. It was menaced by a checkpoint. Realising there was no way around this one, Byrne mounted the bicycle and cycled ahead, praying the grass-stuffed tyre would hold out until he was safely across, his little dog scurrying behind.

Luckily the traffic on the bridge was heavy, and by putting a lorry between himself and the checkpoint Byrne was able to cross without attracting any notice. He pressed on and reached the outskirts of Danzig just before dark. On the edge of the city he stowed the bike beside a railway line, hiding himself and his dog in an old signal box. Before long, the mongrel's ears pricked up: someone was approaching along the track. Byrne peered out of the signal box, and to his relief saw that it was a man wearing the kind of French uniform he'd become familiar with in Königsberg.

Byrne managed to attract the man's attention, explaining that he was an escaped English 'airman'. Fortunately, the Frenchman spoke decent English and understood right away. He led Byrne to a nearby station, little more than a hut beside the train tracks. He heated a pot of water to make coffee and Byrne used the rest to wash and shave. Once he was done, Byrne confessed to the Frenchman that he wished to get down to the docks and 'board a Swedish boat'. His new friend cast a critical eye over Byrne's disguise, pointing out that his diamond badge was of little use in Danzig, as the French POWs there sported two crosses and the letter of their prison camp on their sleeve. Byrne removed both the tunic and the badge. The Frenchman outlined the best route to take to the port, and what Byrne could expect to find there. He offered some francs, but Byrne refused the money. Instead, he pressed his haversack and battle-dress on the Frenchman, along with the little dog. Byrne hated leaving the dog, but escape was foremost in his mind now, and his four-legged friend would be better off like this.

It was early on the morning of 21 July when Byrne joined the crowd of workers heading towards the city docks. There, he noted several heaps of coal piled alongside ships flying the Swedish flag. A German guard was busy checking papers, but Byrne quickly realised there were far too many workers to stop and check them all. He took some tobacco and cigarette papers, rolling up as he walked and, spitting in the opposite direction to the guard, he hurried past. The German was too busy and had neither the time nor inclination to stop Byrne.

A little further on there was a second control point, where an elderly guard was checking passes. Those around Byrne held theirs aloft, and Byrne – praying that the guard's sight was not at its best – held up his map in the same way. The old guard ushered him through, along with the others. Using a combination of bluff and trickery, he had managed to smuggle himself onto the dock undetected and without arousing any suspicion.

Byrne strode along 'a cinder track parallel to the wharf where the Swedish ships were berthed', he wrote in his escape report, doing his utmost to appear purposeful, while taking note of his unfamiliar surroundings. Somehow, he managed to maintain an icy calm, even though he was surrounded by enemy guards and in the heart of one of Nazi Germany's key dockyards. Discovery would spell all but certain death, but Byrne was utterly determined he would not be caught. Still, there was no easy way onto any of those vessels. 'Between the track and the ships there was a wire fence with gaps in it opposite each ship,' he noted. 'At each gap a German guard was posted.'

Clearly, he needed to find some cover from where he could observe the comings and goings of the workers and sentries. On the opposite side of the track there was a latrine built from rough-hewn logs. He sneaked inside and discovered he could keep watch through a gap in the wooden planks. Byrne noted a German watchman patrolling in front of the nearest ship – the Swedish merchant vessel the SS *Capella* – with a rifle slung over his shoulder. He was quite elderly and walked slowly back and forth along the length of the vessel, taking a long time to turn around when he came level to the *Capella*'s bow or stern. He was clearly bored, and just then it started to rain, adding to the guard's woefulness.

As the downpour became heavier, Byrne seized his chance. He had no idea how the sentry would react to someone approaching the ship, for nobody had tried to during the time that he had been keeping watch, but he hoped that the rain would make the man less alert. If he was captured, Byrne knew what fate awaited him, but he steeled himself to take his chance.

Summoning all his courage, Byrne swapped his worker's beret for the sailor's cap he had found back in Königsberg, and stepped out into the rain. He strode purposefully towards the *Capella's* gangway, whistling loudly, as if he had absolutely nothing to hide. Once he was sure that he had the guard's full attention, Byrne made a show of combing his hair back with his hand, checking his watch and straightening his sailor's cap, in order to appear as if he was making himself presentable to meet somebody aboard the ship. He strode towards the gangway, his gait full of the confidence of an experienced seaman. The German guard cleared his throat and took his hands out of his pockets, readying himself to challenge Byrne's credentials.

This was the make-or-break moment. Acting like any sailor who'd been carousing ashore, Byrne turned to face the guard, taking up a 'comic boxing stance'. He circled the German, 'punching the air' all around him and grinning inanely. For a long moment the soldier – 'an old man who was not amused' – stared at Byrne in irritation, before turning away wordlessly and stomping off. Hardly daring to believe his own brazenness and luck, Byrne hurried up the gangway and boarded the Swedish vessel.

Finding his way to the boiler room, he checked that it was unoccupied and clambered inside. The only illumination came from a narrow grid in the celling, which opened onto the deck above. Via its dim light Byrne could make out the hulking shapes of the twin boilers, which were stone cold, for the ship had been at berth for some time. Byrne wriggled into the narrow space underneath one, concealing himself in the shadows. As he lay in the dark, he tried his best to keep awake. The escape committee had warned him that all neutral ships were said to be thoroughly searched by the Germans before they were permitted to sail. Often they used German Shepherd dogs to sniff out contraband goods or stowaways, and Byrne was desperate to keep alert.

But despite his best efforts he drifted into slumber. He awoke sometime later soaked with sweat, for the boiler above him had begun to heat up. Byrne gingerly extracted himself from beneath the hot metal. As he'd slept, the ship had become a hive of activity, with deckhands moving around above, shouting to each other in Swedish as they loaded cargo.

It was now that Byrne heard heavy footfalls outside the boiler room: someone was coming. As the heavy door creaked open Byrne noticed, by the dim light from the vent, a metal pipe running horizontally overhead in the space above the boilers. He leapt towards it, hoisting himself onto it and doing his best to lift his feet up – out of the line of sight of whoever was making for the boiler room.

A German guard stepped through the door and began to flash a torch around. Its beam seemed to miss his dangling feet by inches. As the figure bent to check under the boilers, Byrne held his breath, praying that he would not think to shine the torch into the shadows above. After what felt like for ever, the guard seemed satisfied and left the boiler room. Byrne released his grip and dropped to the floor. Hardly daring to believe his good fortune, he curled up in the darkness behind the boilers and fell asleep once more.

He was jolted awake sometime later by the ringing of a loud bell: the ship was ready to depart. Byrne remained in the boiler room until the following evening, sleeping fitfully and longing for daylight, but knowing that he must remain in hiding until the ship was far away from enemy-held waters. Once it was dark, he furtively made his way onto the deck. Finding no one about, he 'dropped into the coal bunker and hid among the coal'.

Byrne remained in that coal store until the afternoon of 24 July – three and a half days after he originally boarded the SS *Capella*. By then, he felt they were far enough from German-controlled waters for Byrne to risk attracting the attention of one of the Swedish crewmen. Informing the sailor that he was an Englishman, Byrne declared that he 'wished to see the captain'. He was led to the bridge, where the Swedish captain regarded the soot-blackened stowaway with undisguised suspicion. He challenged Byrne to prove that he was English. By way of response, Byrne handed over his British Army identity tags, which he had managed to keep secreted on his person ever since his capture in Libya, fifteen months earlier. The captain studied them and finally seemed satisfied.

He shook Byrne's hand, and broke into a smile. 'You ought to be in England in a week.'

Late the following morning the ship arrived at Gothenburg, on the west coast of Sweden. Upon disembarkation, Byrne was handed over to the Swedish police. After interviewing him briefly, they took him to a hospital where he was disinfected, before being despatched to the Swedish capital, Stockholm. There he was met by the British military attaché. Byrne remained in Sweden until 14 August 1943, when he left by air for Britain.

Seventy-three weeks had passed since the raid on Berka Airfield, when Byrne had first become separated from his unit. That raid, together with subsequent operations in support of besieged Malta, were considered to be among the SAS's most effective missions, and Allied convoys were eventually able to bring in vital supplies, effectively breaking the enemy's stranglehold on the island. David Stirling regarded it as a significant success, stating that the SAS had been 'congratulated on making it possible to get those ships in'. The other men who had been tasked with raiding Berka had made it back to their base unharmed, Rose, Bennet and Mayne all managing to link up with the LRDG.

When he reached Britain, Byrne's epic escape was finally over. He had survived days crossing inhospitable desert terrain, near-death by thirst, capture by the Germans, savage beatings at the hands of his captors, three escape attempts, months of solitary confinement and near-starvation, repeated interrogations, a Gestapo death sentence, and finally a sea voyage as a stowaway. He received the Distinguished Conduct Medal for his bravery and determination to escape at any cost. His citation recorded: 'This NCO showed courage, pertinacity and initiative of the very highest order under the most trying circumstances.'

After a brief rest period Byrne joined the 1st Special Service Brigade as part of 6 Commando, for 'one more crack at the Germans'. Alongside those men, whom Byrne considered to be some of the 'most formidable soldiers in the world', unsurpassed in 'courage and skill at arms', he became part of the sharp end of the spear that led the D-Day landings, the largest seaborne operation in history, which began the liberation of France and turned the tide of war on the Western Front.

Likewise, our next great escapee would play a pivotal role in a daring seaborne operation. But unlike the D-Day landings, luck was not on the raiders' side, and what began as an audacious operation deep behind enemy lines would become a desperate battle to escape, and a superhuman test of evasion and endurance.

Great Escape Four

ESCAPE OR DIE

Lieutenant Thomas Bennett Langton pulled hard on the oars as plumes of water erupted on all sides. The small craft was under fire from the enemy's coastal defences. Unless they could get out of range, Langton and his fellow rowers would join the scores of bodies floating in Tobruk harbour. Near by, the hulking shape of HMS *Sikh*, a British Tribal-class Royal Navy destroyer, listed dangerously to stern. Flames spouted from the terrible rents torn in her hull.

A few short hours ago, Langton and his fellow raiders had felt confident in the success of their mission; exhilarated by their sheer audacity. They had managed to penetrate this Axis-held fortress undetected, sneaking in under the very noses of the enemy. But fortune's tide had turned, and now they were fleeing for their lives, massively outnumbered and outgunned. In the depths of enemy territory and over three hundred miles from friendly lines, it was every man for himself.

The objective of their daring strike on the strategic coastal fortress of Tobruk was, as described by General Sir Harold Alexander, Britain's then Commander-in-Chief of the Middle East, 'to hold port for 12 hours, destroy shipping, harbour facilities, petrol and supplies'. The Afrika Korps' supply chain – strung out along the

North African coast – was stretched almost to breaking point, thanks in part to a series of hit-and-run raids undertaken by the SAS, and this daring thrust into Tobruk was supposed to be the *coup de grâce*.

Lieutenant Colonel John Edward Haselden, a charismatic, Egyptian-born British officer who specialised in covert operations, had originally conceived of the mission. He had planned for a team of elite Commandos disguised as Allied prisoners of war to infiltrate Tobruk – arguably the most important port on the North African coast – to plant explosives on the petrol reserves stored there, so preventing vital supplies of ammunition, weaponry and food from reaching Rommel's Afrika Korps.

Tobruk had changed hands many times during the war. It had been wrested from the Italians in January 1941, only to fall back under Axis control in June 1942 after a 241-day siege, in which Rommel's forces had taken thousands of Allied prisoners. If Haselden's unit succeeded in infiltrating Tobruk to target the petrol stores, senior Allied commanders wondered, what more might they achieve? If the munitions and harbour facilities could be destroyed, that would render the port useless to the enemy at a crucial juncture in the war, when the balance of power rested on a knife-edge. The allure of Tobruk was just too tempting.

Rommel had forged a formidable reputation leading his Panzerwaffe – armoured force – across North Africa. But with ever-lengthening supply lines, and the British Eighth Army amassing to his front, the German commander was under pressure. Allied generals wanted to tip the scales decisively in their favour. Accordingly, they'd taken Haselden's bold plan to attack the city's fuel dumps and inflated it into 'a combined land-sea-air operation' involving nearly two hundred aircraft, two

CHAPTER 1: George Patterson's escape

1. Lieutenant George Paterson (left), of 11 Special Air Service Brigade, parachuted into Italy in February 1941, on the first ever airborne operation by Allied forces. Tough, daring and audacious in the extreme, Operation Colossus would end with all being taken captive.

2. Paterson, rear centre of photo, had been nicknamed 'The Big Canadian' for obvious reasons. From the moment of his capture – here shown at Italy's Sulmona POW camp (PG 78), November 1941 – Paterson never ceased his efforts to break out.

3. *Left*: Having escaped, Paterson spent three years in the Italian (and Swiss) mountains, operating alongside the partisans, finally serving as an agent of the Special Operations Executive (SOE).

4. Captain Roy Farran MC (right of photo), on parade with Major E. Scratchley DSO, MC, for an inspection by General Bernard Montgomery. Farran, typically, holds a German MP40 'Schmeisser' submachine gun. Note, military censors have blacked out the SAS cap badges.

5. When German paratroopers landed on Crete, in May 1941, Farran was wounded and taken captive. Flown to a POW hospital in Greece, from day one escape was foremost on his mind.

6. HMS *Jackal*, the Royal Navy destroyer that rescued Farran and his crew, after their epic breakout from Greece, for which – and for his heroic actions during the Battle of Crete – Farran would be awarded a Military Cross and bar.

CHAPTER 3: Jack Byrne's escape

7. and 8. Corporal Jack Byrne, above, a founding member of the SAS, was captured during an epic desert escape and evasion, after a daring raid led by legendary SAS Commander Lieutenant-Colonel Blair 'Paddy' Mayne (right, with dog).

9. *Left*: Byrne's final daring breakout from a German POW camp was one of a string of such escapes, the first of which took place in December 1941, near the Arco dei Fileni – the 'Marble Arch' – in North Africa, pictured here with a column of German armour passing through.

10. and 11. In autumn 1942 the Long Range Desert Group (LRDG), the SAS, the Commandos and the Special Interrogation Group (SIG) set out on one of the most audacious raids of the war. At their vanguard went several men posing as German soldiers, to bluff their way through the supposedly impregnable Tobruk perimeter – fearsome minefields, barbed wire, ditches and machine-gun posts.

12. *Right*: One of those posing as a German soldier was Lieutenant Thomas Langton (right). He would survive the daring bluff and raid that followed, to lead a band of escapees hundreds of miles through the desert, earning a Military Cross in the process.

CHAPTER 5: John Almonds' escape

13. *Left*: When SAS founder David Stirling recruited Sergeant Jim 'Gentleman' Almonds as one of his originals, he landed one of the fittest, most re-sourceful and self-disciplined of recruits, qualities that would prove essential once Almonds was captured by the enemy.

14. *Right*: Almonds, pictured here manning twin Vickers-K machine guns, was awarded a bar to his existing Military Medal for his incredible autumn '43 escape in Italy. As the citation made clear, Almonds had proven unbreakable – whether as a raider, escapee, or operating deep behind enemy lines.

15. During a raid on San Egidio Airbase, in Italy, Lieutenant James 'Jimmy' Hughes was badly wounded and blinded, when their explosives detonated prematurely. Captured and taken to hospital, from the outset he was menaced by the Gestapo, who interrogated him remorselessly.

16. After his daring escape, Hughes reported to SAS intelligence chief Major Eric 'Bill' Barkworth what the Gestapo had told him – that Hitler had issued a 'Commando Order' decreeing that all Allied parachutist-raiders were to be executed if caught.

17. Barkworth would go on to lead the top-secret SAS Nazi-hunting team – pictured, with jeeps – to track down those who committed war crimes under the Commando Order, one of his team being Sgt Peter Drakes, left of photo.

18. Ronald Lewis 'Lew' Fiddick, left of photo, together with twenty-year-old pilot Harold Sherman Peabody (right of photo) and navigator James Harrington Doe, twenty-two (centre), fellow aircrew from the RAF's 622 Squadron.

19. The men of RAF 622 Squadron gathered before one of the four-engine 'heavies'. When Fiddick was forced to bail out of crippled Lancaster L7576 in July '44, he managed to link up with an SAS unit deep in France, and was recruited on the spot.

20. Entranceway to the Natzweiler concentration camp, in the Vosges, where two of Fiddick's crew-mates, pilot Harold Sherman Peabody and navigator James Harrington Doe, were believed to have been taken after their capture and murdered.

21. WWII SAS veteran Jack Mann, with French parachutists, in the Vosges in 2017. Every year a joint Anglo-French memorial service is held to commemorate the sacrifice of those SAS lost on Operation Loyton, plus the hundreds of French civilians who also perished.

Royal Naval destroyers and six hundred troops, all of which were scheduled to converge on Tobruk on the night of 13 September 1942. Their mission was to occupy the port for long enough to free the thousands of Allied POWs held there and to wreck it comprehensively.

For such a mission to stand even a reasonable chance of success, they needed men on the inside, a specialist team that could occupy key positions within Tobruk and make it safe for the seaborne raiders to land. Lieutenant Langton was one of those men. Born into a well-connected, moneyed family hailing from the Isle of Wight, he'd grown up with a love of the sea. The son of a banker, he had attended the exclusive public school of Radley College, in leafy Oxfordshire, where he had excelled at sports – rugby, boxing, swimming and rowing.

But come the war, Langton had outgrown the school's motto: *Sicut Serpentes, Sicut Columbae* – a basic translation of which is 'be wise as serpents, and harmless as doves.' There was little that was 'harmless' or 'dovelike' about this tough Special Forces warrior. Aged twenty-two at the outbreak of war, Langton had enlisted in the Irish Guards, but quickly 'grew restless' and put himself forward for the Commandos. His athleticism, combined with his experience of rowing, swimming and sailing, made him an ideal choice for the Folboat Section, an amphibious unit formed to carry out special missions.

Posted to No. 8 Commando, he'd immediately sailed for the Middle East, along with a young lieutenant named David Archibald Stirling, who would go on to found the SAS. After his experiences with 8 Commando, Stirling recognised the importance of having an amphibious unit attached to the SAS, and was an enthusiastic advocate of forming 1 SBS – the Special Boat

Section, a water-borne raiding party (the forerunner of today's Special Boat Service, or SBS). Langton was one of its earliest recruits, and Stirling's men would go on to form the core of the Tobruk raiders.

On 24 August 1942, seven three-ton trucks had rendezvoused at El Fayyum, a remote base frequented by the Long Range Desert Group, lying just to the south of Cairo. They carried a team of SAS and SBS, plus seventy-seven battle-hardened Commandos. From there the LRDG had guided the force across thousands of miles of wind-blasted sand dunes and sun-baked plains of the Sahara. To most, this journey would have seemed impossible, but as David Stirling had avowed, in the wide-open wastes of the Sahara, 'adventurous men, resourcefully led, could play merry hell with the enemy'.

After weeks journeying over such harsh terrain, they'd reached Kufra, a lush desert oasis situated deep in the desert, six hundred miles south of Tobruk. There, Lieutenant Colonel Haselden, the mastermind behind their coming mission, had outlined the plan. They would drive north, infiltrate Tobruk and disable the key defences, thus enabling the landing of a seaborne force to unleash mayhem. Haselden then played his trump card, introducing the small team of men who would provide the key to the plan's success, leading the strike force through Tobruk's supposedly impregnable defences.

The 'Special Interrogation Group' (or SIG) were described by Stirling as 'consisting mostly of ex-German soldiers who had got out of Germany before the war,' seeking to escape Nazi persecution. They had been recruited into this top-secret unit, charged to pose as bonafide German troops. For months they had been speaking nothing but German, training with German weaponry, wearing German uniforms, and even learning the swearwords and insults then popular among the Afrika Korps. To all appearances they *were* a highly trained Afrika Korps unit, although their loyalties rested staunchly with the Allies.

Langton described their mission as being 'to drive into Tobruk ... disguised as British prisoners of war, with a guard made up of the SIG Party in German uniforms' as their escorts. It was a high-risk strategy and would doubtless mean execution if they were captured, yet it embodied the kind of audacity that characterised the operations of the Special Forces raiders: seemingly impossible missions were an SAS speciality. Nothing could be allowed to jeopardise the secrecy of the raid, for its success hinged upon the SAS's founding principle: 'the fullest exploitation of surprise'.

On the evening of 13 September the Long Range Desert Group parted ways from the raiding party, having spent weeks guiding them across thousands of miles of inhospitable desert, so as to approach enemy lines from the point least expected. It was an emotional farewell for LRDG commander, David Lloyd Owen. 'For a few minutes we stood and watched them go, feeling bare and huge on this naked, scrubby waste,' he wrote. 'I had become particularly attached to John Haselden ... Leaving him alone and unsupported at the moment when he might most want our help ... was the hardest decision I have ever had to take.'

Driving down from the high escarpment where they had parted company with the LRDG, the three army trucks painted in Afrika Korps colours nosed onto the dusk highway. It was thick with enemy traffic making for Tobruk, but the SIGs in their dusty Afrika Korps uniforms blended in perfectly, as did their vehicles. In the trucks' rear, the eighty-odd raiders adopted as cowed a demeanour as possible, their Tommy guns and grenades secreted beneath blankets, their heads bowed in supposed defeat.

Shortly, the empty desert scrub filled with a vast tented encampment, where enemy forces sprawled beyond the outer perimeter of Tobruk's defences. Incredibly, the SIG convoy sped through the heart of the ranks of grey, sun-bleached canvas, seemingly undetected. Dressed in an Afrika Korps greatcoat and cap, Langton kept his weapon trained on the 'captives' in the rear of his truck, playing the part of a 'German' guard, his features suitably hard and merciless. Out of the corner of his eye he spied cookhouses, medical tents, orderly rooms and sleeping quarters, with everywhere enemy soldiers wandering to and fro.

Momentarily, the distinctive form of a German spotter plane soared from the skies, executing a low-level pass over the road. As it did, Langton could see the twin black dots of the pilot's head and that of his navigator peering down. Twice the aircraft seemed to circle their small convoy. For an instant, Langton wondered if the enemy somehow had been forewarned. There was little point worrying about it now: the Tobruk perimeter was fast approaching.

A wall of intertwined fortifications reared out of the gathering darkness. As the trucks decelerated, hands fingered safety catches nervously beneath blankets. In the lead vehicle, a distinctive figure leaned out of the window. Captain Herbert Buck was the commander of the SIG, and he waved about his – forged – papers imperiously. During his time leading the unit, Buck had talked his way through countless enemy checkpoints, at one stage even dining in a German officer's mess deep behind the lines. Though an Englishman through and through, Buck was a fluent German speaker – he had learned the language while living as a child in Germany. He was also blessed with an icy self-possession and was not about to be stopped now.

Straightening his cap – that of a lieutenant in Rommel's Afrika Korps – he eyed the approaching sentries, relief flooding through him as he realised they were Italians. German soldiers tended to look down upon their Axis comrades, often treating them with outright disdain. For their part, the Italian troops often lionised the Afrika Korps forces who had ridden to their rescue in North Africa. Buck intended to use that to the maximum now.

As the Italians called out greetings to their German brothers-in-arms, the figure hunched over the wheel of Buck's truck fired back a string of curses: *'Dummkopf! Schweinhund! Flachwichser!'*

That man, Private Charlie 'Chunky' Hillman, was Austrian by birth and a native German speaker. He had made a close study of the kind of expletives Afrika Korps soldiers were wont to use – hence his firing off a string of them right now. The Italians, suitably cowed, raised the barrier and, with barely a cursory glance at Buck's papers, waved the convoy through. Moments later, the raiders were heading into Rommel's stronghold Tobruk, armed to the teeth and ready to raise merry hell.

There was a momentary panic, as the convoy drew away from the checkpoint. A convoy moving in the opposite direction – no doubt headed for the front – thundered past, and as bad luck would have it the second truck in Buck's convoy struck one of those vehicles a glancing blow, almost veering off the road as a result. Behind them, the enemy column ground to a halt. Enraged voices rang out through the night. Buck urged greater speed, as the SIG operators yelled back in suitably dismissive fashion.

Once inside the Tobruk perimeter the raiders' orders were to seize control of a bridgehead at Marsa Umm Es Sciausc, a small bay surrounded by fortified headlands lying just east of the main harbour. This would allow British motor torpedo boats to land and disgorge the lead troops. It would fall to Langton, plus one other man, to signal from the headlands, calling in the MTBs to land. Swift, sleek and manoeuvrable, they were ideal craft to deliver troops to shore.

That objective, Marsa Umm Es Sciausc bay, was taken in a series of bloody and murderous actions. The defenders turned out to be Italian troops, and the raiders caught them by total surprise – mostly in their barracks and guard rooms – lobbing grenades through doors and down ventilation shafts, killing scores as they slept. The fighting proved fierce but short-lived. At one stage a group of bewildered Italian officers were captured, asking of the wild-looking, bearded raiders: '*Tedeschi? Tedeschi?*' – Germans? Moments later the bitter truth had dawned on them: these were the much-feared, much-dreaded *pattuglia fantasma*, as the Italian troops had nicknamed Britain's desert raiders – the ghost patrol.

Once the bay was taken, Langton had made his way along the darkened coastline to a clifftop position from 'where he was to signal in the MTBs', the citation for the MC that he would later earn stated. From that vantage point, flashing his signal torch out to sea, he was ideally placed to observe the approaching vessels. But they were nowhere to be seen.

Some distance offshore, HMS *Zulu* and HMS *Sikh* – the two Tribal-class destroyers carrying the bulk of the fighting troops – were steaming in to release their landing craft. Spotted by the enemy, the warships had come under fierce fire from Tobruk's coastal defences; it was becoming clear that the raiders had lost the all-important element of surprise. The German and Italian garrisons were now fully alert to the attack.

Finally, Langton succeeded in signalling in the first of the MTBs. He scrambled across the rocks to meet it. The boat disgorged infantrymen of the Royal Northumberland Fusiliers, whose smart uniforms and clean-shaven faces felt almost surreal to Langton, after so many weeks spent in the wilds of the desert. He instructed the new arrivals to unload their weaponry and ammunition and link up with the forces above. He glanced inland and could see Haselden's men exchanging heavy fire with the enemy. Out at sea, searchlights illuminated the waters and fierce gunfire raked the bay.

In an incredible show of do-or-die soldiering, Haselden's force 'remained in possession of the bay area from midnight until after 0600/14th September'. But as the sun rose it was evident that all was lost. From his position at the water's edge, Langton could tell that few of the Allied ships had managed to land their troops. Barring a few dozen reinforcements, Haselden's unit was alone inside an enemy-held fortress hundreds of miles from the nearest friendly lines and surrounded by vengeful German and Italian troops.

Langton noticed that one MTB had become stranded on the beach. If he could refloat it again perhaps some of the unit could escape. He dashed across to where it lay. As he climbed aboard and studied the boat's unfamiliar controls, more men joined him. They had been engaged in a bitter shoot-out with the enemy, but – heavily outnumbered – were forced to withdraw. Private Ronald Walter, another of Haselden's raiders, came to Langton's aid and together they attempted to make sense of the MTB's myriad switches and dials.

'I'm a mechanic,' Walter announced, 'but damned if I can work that lot out!'

Above them on the deck, the second in command of the German-speaking SIG unit, Lieutenant David Russell, brought the MTB's guns into action against the enemy, sweeping the high-ground with heavy rounds from the deck-mounted twin Brownings. He was aided by Commando Lieutenant David Sillito, plus Private Charlie 'Chunky' Hillman – the SIG operator who had talked them through the Tobruk perimeter, and who now 'kept the guns supplied with ammunition until no more could be found'.

When it was clear that little more could be done, the four men clambered into the small craft that had been used to ferry the troops ashore and began to edge away from the battle-torn beach. A natural sportsman, rowing was in Langton's blood. Yet even when he'd competed for Cambridge in the University Boat Race – the annual competition against Oxford, on the River Thames – he'd never pulled as furiously as he did then.

Their intention was to head for the open sea, hoping to be picked up by one the MTBs, but any attempt to do so was met with a fusillade of enemy fire. Instead, they were forced to put ashore a short distance to the east, landing their boat in the mouth of a wadi – a dry ravine that cuts through the desert, but which flows with fierce torrents on the rare occasions it rains.

Langton sought out a place to hide. There they met up with Sergeant Evans, 'a large, tough, Welshman' who was a close friend of Langton's. They had sailed together from England and had served alongside each other in the Commandos. Evans explained that he had been 'sent on ahead with some men' but they had been 'split by enemy fire'. He had just succeeded in making his way through to the wadi in search of reinforcements, when he'd spotted Langton's party.

Together, the five men headed inland. As they crested a hill they saw Tobruk harbour spread out below them. The *Sikh* and the *Zulu* were well in range of Tobruk's coastal guns and one of the destroyers seemed to be trying to take the other in tow. The naval ciphers sent back and forth between the vessels told a bleak tale.

'0526/14 Sept: From Sikh: Force A failed to land SIKH hit aft and disabled am endeavouring to withdraw.'

'0636/14 Sept. From Zulu: Have been hit.'

'0655/14 Sept. From Zulu: Must leave you.'

'Force A' were the hundreds of raiders the destroyers had been supposed to put ashore, to wreck Tobruk's defences. Very few had made it.

Langton and his fellow escapees turned their backs on the stricken warships, hurrying into the next ravine, which turned out to be occupied by more of their number – burly Commando officer Hugh 'Bill' Barlow and battle-hardened New Zealand Lieutenant William 'Mac' MacDonald, plus around twenty men. From them Langton learned that their brave commander, Lieutenant Colonel Haselden, had been killed while leading 'the charge towards the enemy', in an effort to buy time for a truck laden with their wounded to escape.

They talked things over 'quickly and urgently', Langton recalled. Tired and short of ammunition and food as they were, it was clear that they could offer 'little or no resistance'.

They decided to split up. Lieutenants Sillito and MacDonald took their respective sections, hoping to move further down the coast and get picked up by a roving MTB. Langton figured it would be safer to head inland, for enemy forces were bound to be scouring the coastline. So, together with Barlow and Russell – the

SIG's second-in-command – plus eight men, Langton 'decided to take to the hills'.

Langton and Barlow found a small cave and fell into an exhausted sleep. The two men had left Cairo together almost a month earlier, and over time they had become firm friends. They'd enjoyed similar upbringings and shared fond memories of the Henley Regatta and other boating events. Barlow – an artillery officer and a giant of a man – thrived in the harsh wilderness of the desert. He had been stationed in North Africa for two years, engaging in countless skirmishes with the enemy, and he felt at home in the baking heat, blasted by wind and sand. Yet when he awoke a few hours later, he was uncharacteristically downbeat, fearing it was only a matter of time before they were caught and shot.

'It was an awful position,' Langton would later write to his parents. Between them and the frontline lay over 300 miles, most of which was 'waterless desert' and all of which was held by the enemy.

They decided to split into smaller groups to reduce the risk of capture. 'At dusk we disposed of everything we did not require, divided what food we had into three and ourselves into three parties,' Langton recalled. He took with him the Welsh Commando Sergeant Evans, Private Hillman of the SIG and Private MacDonald, a member of the Northumberland Fusiliers who had made it ashore on one of the MTBs.

'We split up and made for the perimeter that night,' Langton recalled. Before long they encountered their first sentry post, a hut set halfway up the side of a deep wadi. They made it down the western side and past the guard post without incident, but the eastern side of the ravine was steeper, and as they climbed it brought them within sight of the hut once more.

Just as Langton drew level with the guard post, a challenge rang out in Italian. Inspired by the success of the SIG the night before, when they had masqueraded as German forces, Langton tried to stall for time, crying out that they were 'Deutsches Mobilische' – Langton's garbled attempt at 'German troops'. The Italians clearly weren't buying it, for they opened fire. Luckily, the shots went wide and Langton made it over the ridge, where he waited for the rest of his men. They all made it, out of breath but unharmed, except for Private Hillman.

When Hillman eventually appeared, he was breathing hard and seemed to be in real trouble. Langton demanded of Hillman why he was finding it so hard to keep up. By way of response, he pointed to his feet. He'd ripped open his boots on some barbed wire, injuring his foot. It was causing him a lot of pain. Langton handed him a handkerchief to bind his wounds, urging him to hurry on as best he could.

Just then they noticed a line of shadowy forms moving up ahead. Fearing an enemy patrol, they went to ground. With Hillman injured, there was little chance they might run or fight their way out of any coming confrontation. It was several tense minutes before they recognised the mystery figures – it was Barlow and his party of escapees. The two forces joined up, pushing on towards the Tobruk perimeter, but shortly the darkness was rent apart by enemy fire. Machine guns roared and grenade blasts echoed through the night, as Langton dived for cover, yelling for the others to follow. By the time the enemy firing had ceased, he noticed that big Bill Barlow was missing.

Langton tried calling 'Bill, Bill!' as loudly as he dared, but after ten minutes they were forced to press on without him. With Barlow missing, Langton was now in command of six men. He would write about them in a letter to his parents, describing the 'practical and down-to-earth' Commando Sergeant Evans, who 'was immensely brave and never complained'. Then there was Private Charlie 'Chunky' Hillman, who had served with the top-secret SIG. Langton would quickly warm to this 'warlike little man' who was struggling with his injured foot.

Hillman, an Austrian of Jewish descent and son of a Viennese storekeeper, had fled to Palestine to escape persecution when Nazi Germany had seized control of his native Austria. At war's outbreak he had enlisted, despite being only seventeen, blagging his way into the Commandos. While serving in their number he had heard about the SIG, a shadowy intelligence unit seeking to recruit fluent German speakers ardently opposed to the Nazi regime. Hillman had volunteered, spending the following months undergoing rigorous training to pass as a member of the Afrika Korps.

During an earlier SIG mission, many of Hillman's comrades had been betrayed by a German turncoat in their midst. Thanks to this treachery, Hillman was sure that the enemy knew every detail about the SIG, including his own name and personal history. He knew that the very worst kind of fate awaited him should he fall into enemy hands and his identity be revealed. To prevent that, Langton and party decided to change Hillman's name there and then to Kennedy. 'He'll always be known as "Ken" to us,' Langton recalled.

Making up the remainder of the party were four Northumberland Fusiliers who had come ashore aboard the MTBs. Corporal Wilson was a twenty-six-year-old Lancastrian who had been a greengrocer before the war, whom Langton described as being charming, but 'somewhat ineffectual'. In fact, in the coming days he would change his view of the man markedly. Private MacDonald was a 'Geordie black sheep', Langton remarked, adding with a sense of foreboding, 'I liked him at first . . .' And then there were the twins – thirty-year-olds from Newcastle – G. Leslie and T. Leslie, who had been miners before the war. Langton confessed that he had some problems in understanding them, because of their accent.

Crawling and scrabbling for hours through the darkness, Langton was able to lead his party of six out through the wire. Miraculously, they had slipped through the Tobruk perimeter, which left their most pressing problem being food and water. Unfortunately, the missing officer, Lieutenant Bill Barlow, had been carrying most of their rations. All told, the six men had one chocolate bar, a handful of Army biscuits, plus three water bottles between them. Langton knew that there were Arabs living in the area who were 'friendly to the British', but he had little idea as to 'where they were exactly, and how many there were'.

In the plans for the Tobruk operation, a British warship was supposed to put into shore at Wadi Scegga, to the east of Tobruk, five days after the raid, to pick up any would-be escapees. With Hillman's injury they would be cutting it fine to reach that rendezvous, but Langton used it as the talisman of hope to spur his party onwards. He had to try to instil in his companions a sense of 'hope and determination' which he hardly felt himself, he wrote of this difficult moment.

So began a deadly game of cat and mouse, as Langton and his men spent the next three nights dodging enemy patrols and the posts of Italian Carabinieri – armed policemen – while making painfully slow progress due to Hillman's wounded foot. They toyed with the 'rather desperate idea of trying to pinch a vehicle', Langton noted, so they might drive along the coast road towards the rendezvous, but the traffic proved too sparse. They pushed ahead on foot, marching in and out of the wadis that cut through the coastline.

In spite of these challenges, Langton tried to remain optimistic. While they were weakening rapidly through lack of food and water, plus the 'constant strain of being "hunted"', seventy-two hours of 'getting away with it' was starting to strengthen his hopes that they might 'get away with it all together'. Though they searched desperately for water, their tongues became painfully dry and by the fourth day their situation was desperate. They had consumed all their rations and had seen no sign of any Arab settlements.

Both hunger and thirst were 'new to me, and I shan't forget them easily', Langton wrote. Thirst dominated hunger. It prompted in his mind fantastic visions of huge, cavernous, icy halls, filled with marble pillars and fountains, and deep pools of 'crystal-clear water'. The more plagued by thirst he became, the more gripping and fantastical became the visions. By the time he reached the stage where his mouth was so dry as to make speaking difficult, he imagined throwing himself into a pool of cool water with his 'mouth wide open'. Langton could only presume that if you died of thirst, in your imagination you would drown.

On the fourth night of their ordeal they witnessed RAF warplanes bombing Tobruk. As gun-blasts turned the sky a fiery orange, Langton was shocked to realise how little ground they had covered. In the harsh glare, it looked as if there was no way they would make it to the Wadi Scegga in time. Langton considered their options. They could hardly continue as they were, stumbling along, close to death from thirst and exposure. With the rendezvous slipping from their grasp, he knew he must find some other way, or they would surely die. He vowed that the following night they would try to steal a vehicle, and if that failed, they would give themselves up to the enemy.

The very thought of being captured was 'most distasteful', Langton recorded, and especially because he would then not know what 'had become of the others'. He had developed a strong bond of loyalty with his fellow warriors, but with no food and water and little hope of rescue he could see no other option. The following night – the fifth of their escape ordeal – he led the way inland 'with a heavy heart'. But even as they moved, he heard something that made him stop in his tracks: the unmistakable sound of a dog barking.

'Could be the first of the Arab villages,' he whispered to the others.

'It's probably only a jackal,' Evans countered.

'That was no jackal,' Hillman averred. 'That was a dog . . . I'm sure of it.'

Hillman – who had the most to lose if they turned themselves in – hastened towards the sound. On cresting a ridge he paused in amazement, before gesturing the others forward. The group of desperate, starving men gazed down to see, cradled in a shallow valley, a shapeless huddle of white tents shining ghostly pale in the light of a thin moon. Their first impulse was to dash down the hillside, but the dog's barking – more sinister now – reminded them that there was no guarantee of a friendly welcome. Fortunately, Hillman was a fluent Arabic speaker, from his time spent in Palestine before the war. They decided that he should approach, while Langton followed behind at a distance with his 'pistol ready', providing cover, should the villagers prove hostile.

Hillman limped forwards, calling out a greeting in Arabic. He was met by a tall figure wrapped in a flowing white robe. Langton watched as the pair stood talking, alert to any signs of danger. With relief he saw them shake hands, before Hillman beckoned him and the others forward. For his actions that night Langton would go on to recommend Hillman for a Military Medal. 'He was entirely responsible for persuading the Arabs to give us food etc,' he would write. 'I have no hesitation in saying that without his example and help we would have had very little chance of escaping . . .'

Hillman told Langton that these were Senussi people, whose national figurehead, Idris of Libya, had formed an alliance with the British, forming the backbone of the Libyan resistance. The Senussi villagers invited Langton and the others into one of the large tents. There they sat in a circle on woven rush carpets, as wide enamel bowls of water were set before them. They drank until their terrible thirsts were slaked, as the Senussi men 'grinned at their obvious pleasure'. Even so, the escapees had been wise to approach with caution. As Hillman spoke Arabic with a Palestinian accent, the Senussi had believed him to be genuine. But they told of how sometimes what was seemingly a group of British escapees would appear, and the Senussi would give them what bread and water they could spare, only for the next day the same party to reappear wearing Italian uniform, to seize those who had proffered help.

The Senussi provided food that they hoped would suit the palate of their unexpected guests – British biscuits and marmalade! 'I don't think I shall ever forget that meal,' Langton recalled.

They set upon it 'like animals, quite unashamedly', and as they ate they could feel the strength returning to their bodies.

The Senussi tent was lit by oil-burning lanterns, and in one corner four goats were tethered. It was supported by poles and while the outer canvas was white to reflect the heat of the desert sun, the inside was covered in colourful appliqué, with fantastical designs in 'soft reds and browns', which Langton thought had to be 'very old'.

His hunger and thirst sated, Hillman gathered what news he could. Their hosts knew all about the Tobruk raid but could not understand how the British troops had managed to make it all the way from Kufra, the oasis deep in the desert from which they had set out. Langton swelled with quiet pride at hearing this, even though all the raiders had been killed, captured or scattered to the four corners of the desert.

Langton had some Italian money and he offered to pay the Senussi for their help. Instead, they asked for a handwritten 'promissory note', which they would show to Allied forces once they had liberated their lands, for they were confident that the British would reward them for their generosity and bravery. Langton readily agreed, scribbling on one of the pages of his precious notebook a personal message addressed to British and Allied troops. The bearer of this note had been of 'the greatest help', Langton wrote. 'Please reward him in every possible way . . .'

With their water bottles filled, pockets stuffed with biscuits and a replacement pair of boots for Hillman, the escapees set out once more. Langton marvelled at their good fortune, for only a few hours earlier they had all been languishing in the 'depths of depression', making for the road and almost certain capture. They decided to make for the Wadi Scegga, for although they were overdue, they hoped that in light of the disastrous outcome of the Tobruk raid, the Royal Navy might be compelled to return several times, to check for stragglers.

They pushed east up the coastline, moving only at night and flitting 'from one Arab encampment to another'. While the Senussi did all they could to help, the villagers had very little for themselves. While no single village had much to give, none turned Langton away, always providing a couple of eggs or a few chapattis. But it was hardly enough for seven men marching through the desert, and in addition the psychological strain was beginning to take a heavy toll.

By the eighth day tempers were starting to fray, the group becoming 'somewhat irritable', Langton wrote. 'I strictly forbade bickering, and made everyone apologise for "snapping"'. He confessed that he had to do 'quite a bit of apologising' himself. Langton found himself clashing with some of his men. They had led vastly differing lives before the war. More to the point, he was used to serving alongside SAS, who were natural survivors and independent thinkers, yet he had landed himself with a troop of war-weary infantrymen deep inside enemy territory.

One of the men proved particularly troublesome. 'The real cause of it all was MacDonald . . .' Langton noted, who 'should never have been sent into an action of this kind . . . was totally unfitted to cope with the hardships and difficulties which we met and this, in time, caused us a great deal of unpleasantness.' With inadequate food, dissension in the ranks and MacDonald's attitude grating, Langton found himself under enormous pressure. The mental strain and worry over their next move 'gnawed at me', he noted, as they pushed on towards Wadi Scegga, and especially since MacDonald seemed to be agitating that they should give themselves up to the enemy.

On the ninth night Langton reckoned that the rendezvous point must be close. They made their way to a Senussi village, seeking directions. After the customary welcome, Hillman asked if there had been any unusual British naval activity in the area. At this one of the Senussi slipped out of the tent, returning minutes later with another man, who wore a dark-coloured *djellaba* – a loose-fitting outer robe – with a navy blue waistcoat over it. That figure introduced himself as Abdul Ahmed, flashing a mouthful of gold teeth as he smiled. He was evidently better off than many of the Senussi and he was considered to be something of an authority in the area.

Ahmed told them of 'boats cruising up and down at night', adding that he 'thought they were British'. He described how 'one had landed a party at night and someone had shouted "any British here?"' Langton's spirits soared. Perhaps they were not too late to be rescued? Ahmed offered to guide them to the Wadi Scegga, explaining that there was 'a large Carabinieri post at the shore end . . . the strength of which had recently been doubled'. They would have to move quickly if they were to avoid discovery by those Italian paramilitaries.

Hillman tried explaining that he had an injured foot that was still very sore and that they were 'all weak and tired', but Ahmed seemed to pay little heed. They set out, following an elaborate route across uneven ground, at one point scaling a thirty-foot cliff to avoid the Italian sentries. The escapees struggled to keep up with Ahmed's lightning pace, but through sheer stubborn willpower they managed to make it to the Wadi Scegga un-detected.

Langton half hoped to find an MTB or submarine lying just offshore. Leaving his men hidden in the wadi, he approached the beach, moving silently between scrubby bushes and keeping low. In sight of the sea, he stopped and observed, but there was no sign of any Royal Navy vessel bobbing on the water. Instead, by the light of the moon he spied something very different – the silhouette of an Italian sentry 'standing motionless' at one end of the beach, a rifle across his shoulder. As Langton watched he saw another guard join the first for a hushed conversation, before they marched away in opposite directions.

Langton returned to his men feeling utterly deflated. The beach, he explained, was closely guarded by the enemy. In an effort to raise their spirits, Ahmed informed them that hiding not so far away were 'an English and an Indian soldier'. Langton wrote a note to these two men, which he gave to Ahmed, before sinking into an exhausted sleep.

Some hours later Ahmed returned, accompanied by a familiar figure. It was Private Ronald Walter, the mechanic who had tried to help Langton start the stranded MTB, back at Tobruk. By his side was an Indian soldier, who he introduced as Corporal Chatta Singh Rowat, from the 3rd/18th Garhwal Rifles. Rowat had escaped from Tobruk earlier and had been living in the wadi for many weeks. Walter explained that after the night of the raid, he had sneaked out through the Tobruk perimeter and walked for a about a week, before linking up with Rowat. They'd set up camp in the nearby Wadi Kattara, which had a fresh water supply and was relatively 'safe' from the Italians. There were sandy caves to shelter in and a friendly Senussi village near by that kept them supplied with food.

On hearing this, Langton noted once more that whenever he had reached his lowest ebb, 'fortune smiled on us again'. Of

Walter he concluded that he was decidedly 'plucky' and would make a fine fellow escapee. Walter and Rowat led Langton and his men to Wadi Kattara. There, Rowat invited Langton – as the senior officer – to share his cave, while the other men bedded down with Walter in a larger cavern. To Langton's surprise, Rowat produced not only a warm blanket but a sheet and pillow. Thus furnished, Langton dug a hole in the sandy floor of the cave to accommodate his prone form and 'slept like a child' for the first time in days.

When he awoke, he and his men took stock of their situation. Despite thirteen days' travel, they were barely seventy miles from Tobruk. It was three times that distance between their present position and that of the Eighth Army, at El Alamein. They had been warned there were no more Senussi settlements heading east, so there would be little chance of finding any food or water. Langton concluded they had no real option but to lie up in the wadi and try to recover their strength.

Wadi Kattara had steep rocky sides some two hundred feet high, ending in a sheer cliff face. At one point a freshwater stream bubbled out of the rocks, providing enough water to sustain a small grove of fig trees, which were tended by the Senussi in the nearby village. At the other end, where the wadi met the sea, it broadened into a sandy beach. This terrain would become Langton's stalking-ground for several weeks.

Each evening the men took turns to accompany Rowat to the Senussi's clifftop settlement, to join the villagers in an evening meal and collect food. 'We were . . . fed by the Arabs as best they could,' Langton reported, for every family gave something each day. As a point of respect Langton insisted that whoever was going must have shaved, for in addition to his blanket and pillows, Rowat also had a shaving kit complete with soap and mirror.

When it was Langton's turn to accompany Rowat, he ate heartily, before listening to 'the rhythmic lilt of the Arabic language' and 'the cheerful laughs' of the men, mixed in with 'the bleating of goats'. Suddenly he sat bolt upright, for a young man dressed in the uniform of a carabiniere had just entered. The villagers roared with laughter at Langton's evident alarm. Rowat explained that this Senussi man was paid by the Italians to inform on his own people but was in fact a staunchly anti-Fascist double-agent. In part, it was his presence in the village that safeguarded the wadi below, for he could give a warning if ever the Italians were planning to search it.

Secure enough in their Wadi Kattara base, Langton ordered Hillman to rest, giving his injured foot time to heal. As the ravine was well obscured from outside view, there was little need to hide, even during daylight hours. He and his men took to bathing in the sea each morning, then dividing their time between beachcombing and fishing. Langton described their catch as being similar to garfish – long and silver with sharp, pointed noses. They scored 'great success' stunning the fish with German stick grenades. Their 'biggest catch was 30', caught with one explosion. They cooked them on the open beach, flavoured with a tin of onion powder that had drifted in on the tide.

Some two weeks after their arrival at Wadi Kattara, the troublesome Private MacDonald went missing. He'd rarely stopped talking about how life in a POW camp had to be better than this and, having checked that he'd not fallen over a cliff, they concluded that he must have given himself up. Langton was not sorry to lose MacDonald, but there was another member of their group who was causing him concern. Sergeant Evans, usually such a strong and steadfast presence, seemed to be becoming increasingly weak. It became clear that he was suffering from dysentery, an infection of the intestines that caused abdominal pain, fever and diarrhoea.

Langton tried desperately to think of a way to get his friend back to friendly lines, before he succumbed to the disease, which can kill. As if by way of answer, a large can of diesel washed up on the shoreline. An experienced naval signaller, Langton devised a way to attract the attention of the RAF warplanes which flew over the wadi almost every night, en route to bomb Tobruk. Using the diesel, they would light fires in the form of a triangle. That had been the aircraft recognition signal for the Tobruk raid, and Langton hoped that if a pilot caught sight of it, headquarters might send a boat to rescue them. In the circumstances, it was the best plan they had.

For four nights they tried it without luck, but on the fifth a low-flying RAF bomber circled around for a second look. The men jumped and waved excitedly. Langton, standing at the water's edge, flashed a frantic 'SOS' in Morse code with his torch. As if in answer the warplane dropped a white flare that lit up the entire beach, followed by a second and a third. Langton was jubilant as he saw the aircraft dive towards them, but his joy turned to horror when an ear-splitting 'whistling, screeching sound' filled the air and the reality of the situation hit him.

'Bombs!' he yelled. 'Dive flat!'

The beach erupted in explosions, as Langton threw himself inside the relative protection of the wadi mouth, along with the others. They stared at each other, panting hard. Miraculously they had suffered no injuries. They began to laugh hysterically at the utter absurdity of their situation, while Rowat stared at the mad Englishmen in disbelief.

With that means of rescue firmly ruled out, Langton considered their options. Only two remained – to go and risk getting through, or to stay and await the coming 'push,' that was if the 'push' – the Allied advance – actually materialised. The only information Langton had was hearsay, passed to them via the Senussi villagers. He was not even certain 'if the Line was still at Alamein'. Perhaps Rommel had pushed the British back still further; at that very moment the Afrika Korps might well be marching on Alexandria or Cairo, for all he knew.

The dysentery-stricken Evans's condition worsened. Finally, Langton advised him that he would have to give himself up, in order to receive life-saving medical treatment. That night, with heavy hearts, Langton and Walter – the plucky mechanic – helped Evans to the road, though he was barely able to put one foot in front of the other. They left him with the hope that he would be picked up by an Italian patrol and receive the care he so gravely needed. While Evans was normally a tall, tough individual, by the time they left him he looked like 'a haggard old man', Langton noted sadly.

In the days after Evans's departure, the North African sky transformed into a boiling mass of storm clouds. Lightning flashed and the heavens opened, the rain pouring down in torrents, uprooting bushes and dragging debris. Their haven was transformed into a raging flood, their sleeping caves swamped. For half a mile out to sea there was a muddy plume, where sand and sediment had been washed into the ocean. That, combined with worrying developments in the nearby Senussi settlement, convinced Langton that they had to leave.

Two of the Senussi had been arrested and were being held prisoner. The villagers feared that the Italians had somehow got wind of the British escapees. They informed Langton that, regretfully, they could no longer provide food. With their very presence in the wadi endangering their Senussi protectors, Langton made the difficult decision to press on. They could not attempt to cross over two hundred miles of open desert without a supply of food and replacement boots, so Langton and the Senussi villagers cut a deal. If the Senussi could provide new boots and supplies, Langton and his party would set out for the Allied lines in five days' time, so ridding the area of their presence.

The escapees began their preparations for the long march, Langton feeling 'most eager to get cracking'. They busied themselves with stockpiling food, gathering anything that could be used to carry water, and walking barefoot over the rough ground to toughen the soles of their feet. Happily, Hillman's injured foot was largely healed. Langton felt huge admiration for the young Austrian, declaring that his courage, endurance and cheerfulness 'was a great example to the rest of us'.

They had set the date of their departure for 20 October 1942. But the very day before, the Leslie twins were struck down with dysentery. Their condition rapidly worsened, until there was no option but for the two men to follow Evans to the road, to give themselves up. After a great deal of indecision, Rowat also decided not to join the escapees on their coming journey. He 'thought little of [their] chances of getting through', and did all he could to persuade Langton to stay. Langton was saddened to part from Rowat, for he had proven to be a good friend and great company. Evidently, Rowat felt similarly, doing his best to hide the 'tears of grief streaming down his face' at their parting.

That evening Langton made one final visit to the village above the wadi, having got Hillman to translate a short speech into Arabic and write it out for him phonetically. To the 'amused delight and with loud encouragement' from the assembled villagers he stumbled through the words, thanking them for all they had done and promising that if he reached safety, he would 'see they were well rewarded'.

As they were readying themselves to leave, fate smiled upon Langton and his party one last time. Rowat appeared from the top of the wadi, with a dead goat slung over his shoulders. It had been killed the night before, most likely by a jackal. Langton decided to delay their departure, so the goat could be properly prepared. Having made a meal of the roasted offal, they boiled the flesh in saltwater to preserve it as provisions for the journey.

With the salted goat meat added to their rations, Langton eyed his much-depleted party. From the group of nine who had come together at the Wadi Kattara weeks earlier, only four remained. There was Private Walter, the Commando mechanic who'd tried to help Langton start the beached MTB; Corporal Wilson, the only soldier not affiliated with Special Forces, but who had survived thus far, proving himself not quite as 'ineffectual' as Langton had first feared; Private Hillman, the Arabic-speaking Austrian-Jewish member of the SIG, a man who had already displayed 'the greatest calmness and courage' in the face of the enemy; plus Langton himself.

Though the way ahead promised to be gruelling in the extreme, three of the four had already spent weeks traversing many hundreds of miles of desert, on the long journey from Cairo to Tobruk. They knew from first-hand experience how veteran members of the LRDG and the SAS not only survived in those sun-blasted wastelands, but thrived there, pursuing a cutthroat campaign against the enemy and striking where they were least expected. Their exploits alone proved that what lay ahead had to be possible.

At nightfall on 26 October – fully six weeks after their ill-fated raid on Tobruk – the four men set out on what the SBS's war diary would later refer to as 'Langton's and Walter's epic march'. They moved south, navigating by the stars and with the help of a compass that Hillman had managed to keep safe thus far. They were only about twenty miles west of the border with Egypt, but the frontier was said to be formidable, bristling with coils of vicious barbed wire. Their objective was to reach the railway line that crossed the border. Once they found the train-tracks they would follow them to the wire, for if a train could pass through, Langton felt convinced they could too.

Having something 'to occupy our minds, and a goal to work for' cheered everyone up mightily, Langton observed. They crossed the coast road and skirted around the city of Bardia, Langton finding the flat desert beyond offering far easier going than the steep wadis of the coast. They made good time and, after spending the first day lying up in a burnt-out armoured car, they reached the railway line the next evening. Then they began to trace the tracks directly east towards the border.

But as they pushed on through the darkness, they 'bumped into a camp and were fired on', which triggered a number of other positions to open fire. Backing away from the railway line, they doubled back around the enemy encampments – a trick they had perfected when dodging Italian positions earlier in their journey. Creeping ahead through sand dunes, they finally reached the border, which consisted of 'coils of barbed wire piled into a pyramid', Langton noted, disappearing into the darkness to left and right.

He crawled forward to take a better look. At close quarters it seemed 'formidable indeed', the tangled strands of wire being almost too thick to see through, let alone prise a way past. Pulse quickening, he inched along the perimeter, searching for any kind of a gap. After some time, he came to a patch where the wire seemed to have been pulled apart and he figured it would be possible, 'given time and patience', to wriggle through.

Lying as flat as possible, Langton took hold of the nearest coil and shook it vigorously. The fence rang as the movement reverberated down its length, but it provoked no other reaction. Convinced there were no enemy in the immediate vicinity, Langton gestured to the others. Though fearful of discovery at any moment, especially as their every move sent 'jangling messages down the wires', eventually they all made it through – clothes shredded and skin torn, but without any serious injuries.

Elated to be out of Libya, the four escapees made their way to an abandoned truck to rest. Though they had made it across the border, there were still well over two hundred miles to El Alamein, the last known location of Allied forces. Somewhere ahead in the vast desert, General Bernard Montgomery's Eighth Army was even then engaged in an epic struggle with Rommel's Panzerwaffe, in the Second Battle of El Alamein. It would leave 13,800 dead, 24,000 wounded and decide the fate of the war in North Africa, though Langton and his three fellows knew nothing about it at the time.

Langton's diary entries in his notebook grew sparse now. He had saved a page torn from a contemporary textbook, with its poetic description of the terrain thereabouts. It read: 'The stony desert, waterless, barren or rocky land, interspersed with patches of sand and a few stunted camelthorn bushes.' Faced with such a wilderness, Langton and his men made the decision to press south, making for the Qattara Depression, a notoriously treacherous expanse of low-lying cliffs, salt pans and sand dunes covering over 7,500 square miles. Though the Qattara Depression was considered to be impassable by most, Langton knew the SAS and LRDG operated there.

In order to get behind Rommel's lines, the SAS and LRDG 'simply went through the No Man's Land of the Qattara Depression', as David Stirling recorded in one of the war diaries from the time. Langton and his fellow escapees hoped to stumble upon one of those patrols, which would spell rescue. Adopting the desert raider's preferred means of navigation, known as 'dead reckoning', Langton used Hillman's compass and 'a small German map' to keep a rough track of where they were, though the map, at 1:5,000,000 scale, gave too little detail to get any real sense of their exact location.

Like this, they walked for eleven days, heading further and further towards the furnace of the Qattara Depression. Finally, they stumbled across what they assumed to be the Siwa Track, one of the main routes via which the SAS and LRDG navigated the supposedly impossible terrain that lay ahead. They took it, heading south-east. Sometime later Langton reported seeing in the distance a convoy that appeared very much like an SAS patrol. But just as quickly as the jeeps had appeared, they vanished into the haze of heat and dust. Later, David Stirling would largely confirm Langton's suspicion that this had been one of his units on the move.

Langton, Walter, Wilson and Hillman had come so very close to being rescued by the SAS, but now they had to push onwards unaided, or perish. Their route skirted the area that General Rommel had nicknamed the 'Devil's Garden', lying immediately west of El Alamein. This vast swathe of desert was peppered with minefields and barbed wire, where the Afrika Korps had dug in their defences. Langton's party stumbled ever onwards, the scars of war all around them – yet it remained eerily, spookily quiet. Other than sighting those distant jeeps, they saw no further sign of any human presence.

'We did not see anyone from the day after we climbed through the frontier wire,' Langton noted. They 'picked up odd tins of bully beef and mouldy biscuits off the ground' – rations discarded by those who had fought across this cursed land. They were able to fill their water bottles, 'twice from rainwater pools and once from the radiator of a [wrecked] German tracked troop carrier', and as a result 'weren't in bad shape for water'. They 'reached the Depression, climbing down into it one evening', continuing eastwards along its treacherous, sunken floor.

By luck, taking a route through the Qattara Depression meant they missed the big retreat, for close by in the desert Rommel's forces – badly mauled by Montgomery's Eighth Army in the Second Battle of El Alamein – were making a hasty withdrawal. As the four escapees picked their way through the alien-seeming terrain, so the Afrika Korps were falling back through the Devil's Garden directly to the north of where they were now.

Langton's diary notes reflected the tortures of their journey: 'Thirst. Water (Petrol. Rat. Salt. Sand.) . . . Gradual change from physical to mental deterioration. Mental strain . . . But our amazing luck relieves . . . Our feast in the tank.' Before long, his scribbles – like their water supply – dried up completely. He, Walter, Wilson and Hillman grew increasingly disorientated, as they wandered this wasteland twisted by heat and warped by shimmering mirages, propelled onwards by sheer force of character and an iron inner will, in what had become a Herculean effort of stamina and endurance.

After an epic twenty-six-day march, the four exhausted, skeletal figures reached Mount Himeimat – a highpoint on the landscape, where distinctive-looking rocks rise from the desert, sculpted over millennia by the bombardment of wind, salt and sand. They arrived there in darkness, and at dawn they spied some distant trucks. Langton forced himself to go on ahead, approaching one of the vehicles, whereupon he was greeted with a friendly wave. It was Friday 13 November 1942, and this turned out to be one of the Eighth Army's frontline positions.

The four escapees rejoined Allied forces exactly two months after the Tobruk raid, having covered over three hundred miles of some of the most inhospitable terrain in the world. Langton was awarded a Military Cross for his superhuman efforts, both during the invasion of Tobruk and during his subsequent escape. His citation, written by the SAS's founder, David Stirling, stated simply: 'Lieut.Langton showed great courage and initiative during the raid itself, while his resource and leadership were chiefly responsible for bringing a party on foot through 350 miles of enemy territory to safety.'

After a short period of rest and recuperation, Langton rejoined the SAS and became commander of the HQ Squadron, where he served throughout the D-Day landings and until war's end. His wartime exploits are perhaps best summed up by his Jesus College Boat Club History entry: 'T. B. Langton, twice Head of the River, twice a rowing blue and President of the CUBC, was the hero of an epic escape across the African Desert to Alamein.'

Hillman was also awarded a Military Cross for his part in the Tobruk raid and subsequent escape. In his MC citation, penned by Langton, he was listed simply as a member of the SAS. The citation ends with a telling note: 'No details of the above operation may be published owing to their secrecy and the fact that Pte Hillman was dressed in German uniform.' Hillman went on to have a long and distinguished career with the SAS, winning a Military Medal on future operations behind enemy lines.

Five days after Langton and Hillman's return to Allied lines, Lieutenant David Russell – second-in-command of the SIG – also stumbled out of the desert, after his own incredible escape. He too was recommended for an immediate Military Cross, the citation stressing how his 'escape was eventually carried out in the face of enemy opposition and under extreme hardship', in 'circumstances of extreme danger and difficulty'.

The commander of the SIG, Captain Herbert Buck, though wounded in the Tobruk raid, had attempted to steal a vehicle and bluff his way out again, along with others of the raiding party. Captured after days on the run, Buck was sent to POW camps in Italy, where, typically, he became a serial escapee. Despatched to a high-security camp in Germany, Buck established a fencing club and ran Highland dancing classes, before being freed upon the camp's liberation by Allied forces. Returning to Britain, Buck was slated for SAS operations in the Far East but was tragically killed when a Liberator aircraft carrying him crashed shortly after take-off from Britain.

At the end of the war Langton and Evans – the dysentery-ridden escapee they had been forced to leave at the roadside – were reunited, when Evans returned to England, his health fully restored, despite the long months spent in POW camps. Lieutenant Barlow – the artillery officer they had lost contact with, while slipping out of the Tobruk defences – was sadly never found and presumed killed in action at Tobruk.

During Langton and party's extraordinary escape march, the tide had turned in the battle for North Africa, and perhaps the wider war. After Rommel's defeat by the Eighth Army at El Alamein, Winston Churchill would remark: 'Before Alamein we never had victory. After Alamein we never had defeat.' As the fighting across Egypt, Libya and Tunisia ended, the SAS's unique abilities, forged in the fires of the Sahara, evolved to suit new theatres of war. The conflict in Europe brought with it fresh challenges, but whenever and wherever the men of the SAS found themselves captured, the burning desire to escape was always at the forefront of their minds.

First and foremost this would be in the soft underbelly of Europe, as Churchill famously christened it – Italy.

Great Escape Five

UNBREAKABLE

To any casual observer, John Edward 'Jim' Almonds appeared like any typical Italian local, with his dark hair and deep brown eyes. Dressed in borrowed black jacket and khaki trousers, he carried himself a little awkwardly as he moved around the streets of Porto San Giorgio, a small town situated on Italy's east coast. Look again, and the clothes were a little too short for his six-foot-three frame. For Almonds it was a challenge to make the ill-fitting garments seem as if they really *were* his clothes.

It was vital that he appear to be just another local labourer going about his business. In reality, of course, he was anything but. In truth, Almonds was a twenty-nine-year-old SAS veteran undertaking a highly sensitive reconnaissance mission. A former sergeant in the Coldstream Guards, he had been recruited as one of the earliest members of the SAS, arriving at their training ground in Kabrit, alongside Private Jack Byrne and others of the 'Originals'. Almonds had since proved his mettle on many a raid, earning a towering reputation and winning a Military Medal in the process.

David Stirling himself would remark to Almonds' daughter, Lorna Almonds-Windmill, years after the war, that her father had been among the fittest and most self-disciplined men he had ever met. The ruse that Almonds was presently employing was not at the behest of Stirling, nor any Allied commander. On the contrary, he was quartering the streets of Porto San Giorgio on the orders of Italian Army Colonel Vincenzo Cione, commander of a nearby *Prigione di Guerra* (PG) or POW camp.

Almonds had been a prisoner of Axis powers for just a few days shy of a year now. Officially, it was Colonel Cione's job to keep Almonds and his ilk securely locked up in conditions that were little short of hellish. Unofficially, Italy was about to announce the signing of an armistice with the Allies, which meant that former friends – the Germans and Italians – were about to become enemies, and former enemies – the British and Italians – were poised to become friends.

It was 8 September 1943, a tumultuous time for Italy. The Fascist leader Mussolini was in gaol, having been ousted from power. Almost two months back, Field Marshal Bernard Montgomery had landed an Allied force on Sicily, and just days ago the first troops of the British Eighth Army had crossed the Strait of Messina to land at Calabria, launching the Allied invasion of mainland Italy. The Armistice of Cassibile agreeing the terms of Italy's capitulation had been signed in secret five days earlier, and the announcement that Italy was swapping sides was to be made later that day.

All of that had made Colonel Cione decidedly uneasy, for his former allies, the Germans, were about to become an occupying power. He needed to get an idea of their troop numbers and positions, the better to gauge what might transpire in the chaotic days to come. Colonel Cione was a staunch supporter of the Italian royal family and had little allegiance to the Italian Fascists.

He spoke excellent English, having spent many a summer in Scotland, and understood the British character well. He had taken good note of Almonds' gift for subterfuge during the long weeks the SAS man had spent as a prisoner in his camp, hence giving him his present cloak-and-dagger mission.

The streets of Porto San Giorgio well and truly scrutinised from end to end, Almonds slipped into a public phone booth. In his rudimentary Italian, picked up during his year as a POW, he asked the operator to put him through to the Commandant of Campo PG 70 at Monte Urano, which lay around ten miles inland from the town. When the Colonel answered, Almonds, as promised, imparted to him the results of his reconnaissance: as far as he could tell, apart from a concentration of troops in the centre of town, there appeared to be few other German forces in Porto San Giorgio.

Colonel Cione thanked Almonds for his report, before ordering him back to the POW camp: 'And now you return.'

By way of answer, Almonds offered an apology that he could not do as the Colonel had asked, for he was about to take leave of him. 'I'm going home.'

As the Colonel began to yell down the phone, Almonds carefully replaced the handset. Not for nothing was he known within the ranks of the SAS as 'Gentleman Jim'. He was always well-mannered and polite, even when escaping from Italian captivity. While Almonds might consider the Colonel to be 'an officer and a gentleman', the conditions he had endured over the past year would have justified a far less courteous farewell.

After being captured during an SAS raid in Libya, Almonds had been shipped to mainland Italy and taken first to Campo PG 51 at Altamura, about thirty miles inland from the port city of Bari in Italy's southern region of Apulia. Conditions in this transit camp were atrocious and they quickly worsened, for the winter of 1942 proved unseasonably harsh. Almonds and his fellow POWs were forced to live under the cover of makeshift tents, constructed from nothing more than ground-sheets strung over basic wooden frames. Campo PG 51 was situated on an expanse of scrubby moorland and the ground was so hard and rocky that it was impossible to 'dig in' to create any semblance of comfort. Almonds had endured weeks of near-ceaseless rain and then snow and was almost always chilled to the bone and damp.

Food was scarce. A British War Office report concluded that there was 'a definite and increasing shortage of foodstuffs' in the camp. Prisoners were given a small bread roll and a piece of cheese at midday, with 'thin soup' in the evening. Even supplementing their rations from Red Cross food parcels, it had become 'a starvation diet', especially as the winter began to bite. Before long, diseases flourished among prisoners weakened by hunger and many failed to last the winter. Worst of all – at least for the POWs' morale – they were frequently reminded that no escape attempt from PG 51 had ever been successful.

When the Allies invaded Sicily in July 1943, the Germans feared that the whole of southern Italy might soon be overrun. Together with hundreds of other POWs, Almonds had been transported some three hundred miles north by train, to Campo PG 70, which was sited in an old weaving mill fenced by barbed wire. With a shortage of water, filthy conditions and few medical supplies, disease was rife. One Red Cross report recorded that POWs suffered from 'malaria, dysentery, pneumonia, nephritis and jaundice'.

Life in PG 70 had proved so unbearable that, despite rumours of Italy's imminent demise, some prisoners had opted to die at their own hands, rather than continue enduring such conditions. Others preferred to make a break for it, come what may. At least one was 'killed on the spot . . . as he was trying to slip under the barbed wire', the Red Cross reported. Hardly surprising, then, that Almonds had decided that he would not be returning to PG 70, and certainly not of his own free will. Once Colonel Cione had allowed him outside the wire, he was making for friendly territory, no matter what solemn reassurances he might have offered the camp commandant.

Of course, Almonds couldn't know for sure exactly *where* the Allied frontline was located, for he had heard only rumours and speculation. Unbeknown to him, at that very moment the Allies were involved in a series of major amphibious operations in the south of Italy, targeting the country's distinctive boot-like southern profile. In a mission codenamed Operation Avalanche, forces had landed near Naples, while further Allied landings were taking place at Taranto – codenamed Operation Slapstick – and at Calabria, in Operation Baytown. All Almonds knew for certain was that he needed to head south.

It would not be an easy journey. It was some 250 miles as the crow flies between Porto San Giorgio and the nearest Allied beachhead that he knew of, at Salerno. Almonds would have to take the greatest care to evade detection by the enemy, for although the Italians were now technically his allies, the country remained rife with danger. In addition to German troops, there were Italian Fascists loyal to Mussolini who would sell out any escaped POWs. Others might do so for fear of reprisals from the German occupying powers.

As the lowlands were likely to be teeming with troops, Almonds' best chance was to make for the high ground. The Apennine Mountains, which run down the Italian peninsula like a craggy backbone, offered relative safety. Adopting the same methods as he would on any behind-the-lines mission, Almonds decided to travel through the low country moving only at night, lying up in hiding during daylight. He had little with him but the clothes on his back, for he could not risk anything that might have alerted Colonel Cione to his plans. The only thing that he had dared take were a few sheets of paper surreptitiously ripped from the Bible of a visiting priest. Almonds – sensitive and contemplative – always strove to keep a diary of his activities, thoughts and feelings, and for him those few sheets of paper represented a great treasure.

Almonds had enjoyed a rugged, outdoors childhood on a small farmstead in the village of Stixwould, close to the rolling green hills of the Lincolnshire Wolds. During winter, he had been wrapped up and sent outside to play. He had soon learned that running around was the best way to keep warm, and to eat heartily of whatever food was on the table. That was the kind of existence that he hoped for now, as he made his way across the cultivated fields of the province of Fermo, towards the purple-tinged foothills of the Apennines.

Encouraged from an early age to make his own amusement, Almonds possessed an innate creativity and a sharp, logical mind. He had learned wood- and metal-working from his father, a farmer and a volunteer churchwarden. As a boy, he was always doing practical things, be it crafting bows and arrows from springy saplings or knocking together rafts from scrap wood, to launch on the nearby river.

At the age of fourteen Almonds had attempted – unsuccess-fully – to sign up to the army. He had to wait until his eighteenth birthday, when he joined the Brigade of Guards. He underwent basic training, before joining the 2nd Battalion, Coldstream Guards – one of the oldest regiments in the British military – where he spent much of his time guarding the various residences of the British royal family. After four years Almonds left the military, becoming a police constable. But then Britain declared war on Germany, Almonds returned to the Coldstream Guards – now with the rank of sergeant – and spent a year teaching new recruits the ropes.

Curious and blessed with an inquiring nature, Almonds had appreciated the need for military discipline, but had always won-dered why personal initiative and individual skills were so little valued or developed in the military. Hungering for something more, he began applying for anything that he thought might offer the kind of challenge he sought. Before long he heard of an opening in the Commandos, who were looking for men with a do-or-die attitude to lead the fight against Nazi Germany. It prom-ised travel to distant frontiers, living off the land, undertaking amphibious assaults and marching over precipitous terrain. In short, it seemed tailor-made for a man like him.

Almonds began his Commando training first at Burnham-on-Crouch in Essex and then at Loch Fyne and the Isle of Arran in Scotland, where his physical fitness and endurance were tested to the maximum. He was unusual among his fellows, for he always kept fieldcraft tools and hunting equipment handy and would often disappear into the wilds to go poaching. During one such expedition he was almost court-martialled for shooting a deer.

As the war progressed into its second year, the likelihood that he would be called to fight became more and more real, and

Almonds begun to wonder if, when the time came, he really would be able to shoot a fellow human being. He had never killed anything bigger than a hare, and so he decided to see how it felt to kill a more man-sized animal. Almonds had felled a young deer with one clear shot from his .303 rifle. In doing so, he had learned his first lesson: he could kill such an animal without flinching. But as he had hoisted the carcass onto his muscular shoulders, a challenge had rung out from behind. Gamekeepers had spied him making his kill.

Attempting to evade capture, Almonds had turned uphill, moving stealthily through the trees, but the valley became a knife-cut gorge the further up he went. Almonds doubted whether he could make the climb up the steep gully before his pursuers caught up with him. So he reversed course, heading back downhill, and thus he was subsequently caught. Almonds cursed himself for taking 'the lazy way'. He felt sure that if he had continued the difficult ascent he would have got away. In this he learned his second lesson: evading capture required the absolute application of all the mental and physical prowess that a man might possess, and unyielding resolution.

Almonds vowed to put those lessons into practice now, on his solo escape through the Italian lowlands. Focusing body and mind on evading capture, he moved silently and under cover of darkness, skirting around the Renaissance town of Ascoli Piceno. From there he traced the course of a river leading into the foothills of the Monti della Laga mountain range, one of the lesser-explored and more sparsely populated regions of the Apennines. Due to its rugged and inaccessible nature, this made the perfect kind of terrain for a seasoned SAS veteran looking to keep out of the enemy's clutches.

Almonds believed he could travel more openly through this area, keeping moving during daylight hours. Traversing the precipitous hills and valleys proved hard going – he was always moving on a steep incline – but it was worth it to stay out of the enemy's way, and after so long in captivity he relished the sense of freedom.

Almonds had been pardoned for the deer-poaching incident, largely because no military tribunal felt like wrestling with the difficult moral issue of how a soldier might best prepare himself for the imminent possibility of having to kill a fellow human being. The case against him had been summarily dismissed. But the reality of life in the Commandos had turned out to be less than Almonds had hoped for, as their operations had been plagued by delays, false starts and cancellations. It was something of a let-down, Almonds felt: men had volunteered for the Commandos 'to *do* something and apparently that was not going to be the case'.

From the very start the SAS had felt different. Almonds, one of its founding members, summed up the attitude thus: 'We knew we were going to go into some exciting things.' He revelled in the companionship of the other SAS men; he appreciated that each had the back of the other; he commended their steely reliability, commenting of the typical SAS recruit that no one was going to 'bow down' because they had hit trouble, but would push onwards, being 'good reliable characters'.

When he had first arrived in the North African desert, Almonds had had to join the other SAS recruits in creating their own camp from scratch. They were intent on making it the finest there was around, and he quickly put his practical skills to good use. Almonds felt that 'any fool could be uncomfortable' and he was determined to make the camp at Kabrit pleasant, as well as practical. He concluded with quiet pride that it had ended up being 'a nice tidy little encampment'.

It wasn't long before Almonds' reputation for being 'a dab hand at making things' had caught the attention of Stirling. As the founder of a new, ground-breaking unit, Stirling was reluctant to ask bureaucratic Middle East Command for anything more than he absolutely had to – the bare minimum of rations, arms and ammunition. He reasoned the less he had to do with them, the less he and his men would have to answer to their authority. Recognising Almonds' considerable talents, Stirling enlisted his creative enterprise and craftsmanship in the production of training equipment for the Kabrit camp.

Almonds built frames for the men to jump from, in order to practise parachute landing techniques. From there he progressed to much taller towers that would allow for the simulation of real parachute jumps. Those towers would need to be 'safe and strong', Almonds wrote in his diary, or else he would be 'responsible for someone being killed'. Stirling's requests became ever more audacious. Almonds recalled being asked: 'Could you make me a boat?' Almonds said he could, if he had enough wood and an engine of some kind to power it. But inwardly he was thinking: 'Oh God, where is this going to end?' His experiences with Stirling forced Almonds to put complete trust in his own practical skills – something that would serve him well now, during his escape attempt.

In addition to his abilities to design and make high-quality training equipment, Almonds had proved himself to be an excellent raider. One of his most important missions was the late December 1941 raid on Nofilia Aerodrome, Libya, for which he had been awarded the Military Medal. The mission war diary described how Almonds' party 'arrived at a point 16 to 17 miles from drome and walked in to find aircraft widely dispersed'. They had 'put bombs in first aircraft', but before they could reach the second, the first bomb 'went off, giving the alarm'. Discovering that the enemy aircrew were sleeping in and around the warplanes, they had 'decided to pull out'.

But on their return journey to the SAS base camp, they were spotted by a twin-engine Messerschmitt Me 110 fighter-bomber, armed with machine guns and cannons. As the full force of this warplane was unleashed upon Almonds and his fellow raiders, he had grabbed a Bren gun and managed to hit the Messerschmitt in the tail section. But no sooner had the stricken plane disappeared than it was replaced by two Junkers Ju 87 dive bombers. The raiders were 'subjected to a very intense strafing and bombed from 10am till 4pm'.

During this sustained onslaught 'four trucks [were] destroyed and another damaged,' but worst of all, Jock Lewes, Stirling's right-hand man and the SAS's veteran training officer, was killed. Almonds took the death of Lewes very hard, for the two men had served alongside each other ever since their time in the Commandos. Despite this, his quick thinking and brave actions helped get the rest of the patrol back to safety. His medal citation noted how Almonds 'took command of his party with only one casualty, although all but one of his trucks had been destroyed'.

Somehow, he managed to evade the enemy warplanes and get the remainder of his men back to base, in just the one damaged vehicle. That night Almonds wrote in his diary, in moving and poignant terms: 'I thought of Jock, one of the bravest men I have ever met, an officer and a gentleman, lying out in the desert barely covered in sand. No one will ever stop by his grave or pay homage to a brave heart that has ceased to beat. Not even a stone marks the spot.'

Lewes' death was a huge blow to the fledgling SAS. Even so, by the end of June 1943, SAS patrols had raided 'all the most important German and Italian aerodromes within 300 miles of the forward area', Stirling would record, and some of them several times over. Almonds had been integral to many of those missions, proving a natural at night operations and a man who thrilled to the open desert wilderness.

During the fateful mission to Nofilia Aerodrome, Almonds' patrol had spent the day before the attack hiding in a large stone water cistern, its moisture long evaporated in the desert heat. He had noticed the skeleton of a desert fox that had fallen into the dry water tank and been unable to get out. Almonds wrote in his diary how he had pondered the animal's last moments and how it made a deep impression on him. It had carried on trying to escape until it was unable to move any more. He felt the 'deepest sympathy', relating closely to the desert fox's burning desire to live and to get out.

It was that same desire that had gripped Almonds when faced with the horrors of prisoner-of-war existence. Throughout his year in captivity, he had striven to maintain his physical fitness, for it was important for the health of both body and mind. He strove to keep thoughts of his wife, Lockie, and their young son, John, foremost in his mind, to bolster his spirits. A dedicated family man, he wrote to his wife constantly, and many of his diary entries were addressed to her personally.

Not once during his imprisonment had he doubted that he would make it home to see her again. It was Lockie and John and the simple joys of home that he pictured in his mind now, as he hurried onwards through the Monti della Laga foothills, such thoughts quickening his pace and boosting his stamina. At times he ran for hours on end during this stretch of his lonely journey, on one day covering fifty miles.

Only when he reached the craggy, towering expanse of Gran Sasso d'Italia – the highest mountain in the Apennines, with an elevation of 9,554 feet – did Almonds take a proper break. He was now some eighty miles south of his point of departure. Here, he finally 'took time off' from his escape and evasion, not to rest as one might have expected, but to explore what he found to be a uniquely beautiful mountain. Almonds had always been enamoured by the natural world and years later, when asked about his time in the SAS, it was his experiences of the physical landscape, not the many daring raids, that he would most often come to mind.

He had felt an enormous affinity with the North African desert, wishing he could have stayed there for a year or more, for he could 'see a lot in the desert'. Almonds noticed far more than simply 'sand and so on', being alert to the rich history of the Sahara, revealed in the shells and fossils that lay hidden among the sand grains and gravel. He was convinced there was 'an awful lot to be learned there', about both the region's past and its present.

Almonds' thoughtful, contemplative nature had helped earn him his nickname in the SAS – 'Gentleman Jim'. He would explain away this unusual moniker in typical, self-deprecating tones, it being all about the fact that he didn't swear or smoke and was 'a quiet person'. Anyone who ever faced uncertainty or was unsure of a situation would tend to seek out Almonds for a chat and some guidance. 'I had a lot of people come and talk to me,' he remarked.

But there was another side to Almonds, who was quite clear about the fact that in war, 'I still had to do my job.' In the SAS, that meant undertaking fearsome missions, often deep behind the lines and at enormous personal risk. In truth, Almonds' 'gentlemanly' exterior masked an iron-willed self-discipline and control, which rendered him calm, unflappable and deadly when under fire. It was her father's wont to run *to* the sound of the guns, Almonds' daughter, Lorna Almonds-Windmill, would point out, something most clearly evidenced by the very raid that had ended in his capture.

Stirling described it as 'the most important and least successful operation' they had ever attempted – a mass raid on 'harbour installations and shipping at Benghazi'. That raid – codenamed, with typical chutzpah, Operation Bigamy – was supposed to take place on the same night as the SAS/SIG raid on Tobruk, over two hundred miles to the east (where Lieutenant Thomas Langton and his crew evaded capture and began their epic bid for freedom). Operation Bigamy was designed to sow confusion among the ranks of the enemy, distracting them from the main strike at Tobruk. But crucially, it was a mission *not* designed by the raiders themselves, but by Middle East Headquarters.

The plan was for Stirling to lead a convoy carrying two hundred men into Benghazi, on a raid designed to wreck its harbour facilities. Almonds – greatly trusted by Stirling – was tasked with his own special responsibility. Once inside the city he and his two accomplices would drive their American-made pick-up truck, loaded to the gunnels with explosives, directly to the main port. There they would hijack a tugboat and use it to tow a larger ship to the entrance of the port, using limpet mines to sink it. With the harbour thus blocked, enemy ships would be unable to exit, leaving them sitting ducks for the raiders.

Almonds feared the Benghazi raid was too ambitious in scope and scale for it to be successful, or for the SAS to maintain the all-important element of surprise. He was proved right. As Stirling's force approached Benghazi, they became delayed, for the trucks – laden with weapons and ammo – had trouble crossing the desert. They were supposed to attack under cover of darkness but, with dawn fast approaching, Stirling ordered Almonds' vehicle to the front of the column, as he had the furthest to travel, making for the harbour mouth. Together with Almonds were two gunners – an Irish Guardsman called Fletcher and a Scotsman, McGinn.

With Almonds now in the vanguard, the lead vehicles advanced, 'whereupon they were met with intense fire at close quarters from concealed MG [machine gun], Breda guns, Mortars and rifles', the official report on Operation Bigamy recorded. The enemy were waiting in well-prepared ambush positions. The lead vehicles 'immediately countered with heavy fire,' the report continued, 'but it remained impossible to locate the exact position of the enemy posts, for they had covered their weapons with blankets, which eliminated the flashes produced when they fired and rendered them almost invisible'. By now, Almonds' vehicle, which was packed full of explosives, was well inside the enemy's defences. To make matters worse, it was under heavy fire, with no space to turn back due to the narrow road.

As Stirling would later learn, the enemy had had forewarning of the attack and had taken all possible steps to prepare for it, evacuating the civilian population, while getting a force of

'200 German machine gunners' into prime defensive positions. Whoever was to blame for the mess-up, by the time Stirling and the main SAS force had managed to withdraw, Almonds and his crew were missing, presumed killed in action, for they were 'last seen vigorously returning enemy fire'.

In fact, Almonds had realised that it was only a matter of time before their heavily laden vehicle exploded. He and his men had leapt from it – McGinn running back down the track after the retreating Stirling, and Almonds and Fletcher diving for cover. Behind them the pick up took a direct hit from an incendiary bullet and burst into flames. Almonds and Fletcher evaded capture for hours, but with the sun rising higher and enemy patrols hunting them everywhere, they had no choice but to give themselves up. Hands raised, they surrendered to a group of Italian soldiers.

Taken to the enemy garrison at Benghazi, they were thrown into shackles, chained in an agonising crouch position, with both wrists attached to one ankle. Simply remaining like that for any extended period of time became torture, but that was nothing compared to the psychological ordeal that was to follow. Almonds and Fletcher were subjected to interrogation by the Italians, and when Almonds refused to divulge any useful information, he was subjected to terrible acts of humiliation, including repeated mock executions, of which he was unable to speak for decades after the war.

The memory of this ordeal in the desert spurred Almonds onwards during his escape through Italy, for he was determined never again to become a captive. After his short excursion around the peak of Gran Sasso d'Italia, he resumed his march southwards. At times he would run steadily, covering around twenty miles a day across rugged terrain. His main challenge was finding enough food to maintain such a level of physical activity, but thankfully his time in the SAS had left him fully prepared to beg, borrow or steal whatever he needed.

Almonds had excelled at this during training, describing how his instructors would set the men a list of things they had to 'bring in', such as 'a lady's bicycle, a cockerel, a hen, a bit of car or bus'. They were permitted to utilise 'any means necessary' to acquire these objects. It was a test of character – to see if they had what it took – and Almonds passed with flying colours. It made for a really 'exciting type of life', he recalled, especially as they were able to pilfer at will and without any fear of any repercussions. Few among them would choose to 'beg or borrow' when they were ordered to go out and steal.

As he pressed onwards through the Abruzzi Apennines, following the route to Campobasso, a mountainous city lying some 150 miles south of his point of departure, Almonds gathered what sustenance he could in the wild, or would 'pinch things' from gardens and vegetable plots. It was not very much, but he was used to marching for miles with nothing but 'a bottle of water and a bag of raisins' from his time under the tuition of Jock Lewes and his intensive training methods.

Prior to joining the SAS, Almonds and Lewes had served together in 8 Commando. There, Lewes had recruited Almonds into an elite reconnaissance unit that had undertaken many clandestine missions on the no-man's-land of the Tobruk perimeter. When Lewes had announced that he was leaving the Commandos to assist in the formation of a new raiding unit, he had invited his best and brightest to go with him, Almonds among them.

Thinking of Lewes, Almonds wondered how many more of his SAS comrades had been killed in action during the year he had spent as a captive. He felt hugely grateful for Lewes's training, not least because that extremely tough regime had done more to prepare Almonds for a long run on minimal rations than anything else might have done.

Almonds also reflected on the members of the camp escape committee that he had left behind, experiencing a pang of guilt for breaking out without them. Ever since his time in the Coldstream Guards, he had cherished the strong bonds formed between fellow soldiers and prided himself on being a team player. Later, Almonds would sum this up by saying that whatever happened, 'You shouldn't let your mates down.' But in his diary, written during the early days of the SAS, he'd been far more forthright and emotional.

Almonds had been stood down for Operation Squatter, the SAS's first ever mission, because his infant son was critically ill back in England. Forced to remain behind, he had fretted as the wind howled and the heavens opened. Less than half of those who had set out would return, and as Almonds waited for them, he lamented bitterly that he had to remain in the 'safety of the camp'. Regarding those brave souls despatched on Operation Squatter, he noted that films and books 'of daring and adventure fall short of the real thing'. For him at that moment, reality really did trump fiction 'for sheer, cold calculating courage'.

Occasionally on his sojourn through the Apennines, Almonds encountered locals hunting and foraging, as he was. Having first taken care to ensure they were unarmed, he would stop and talk with them, for he had little fear of meeting any Italian Fascists in these parts. Mostly, the rural folk were staunchly for the Allies.

More often than not it was the locals who were initially fearful of *him* – a tall, dark, powerfully built stranger, lean, wiry and wild-looking after the long days spent pounding mountain tracks and pathways.

Almonds would first assure them he meant no harm – for, as Stirling declared in a document defining the very essence of the SAS, 'toughness should be reserved entirely for the enemy.' He would strike up a conversation in his rudimentary but workable Italian. Invariably, the locals would offer to share their food, be it only a handful of berries, a portion of charcoal-roasted lamb or a freshly caught trout from a tumbling steam. In the mountains of central Italy, no one, it seemed, had been fond of the Italian Fascist regime.

The *contadini* – the Italian countryfolk of these highlands – were invariably dirt-poor, and led an existence largely isolated from the lowland communities, one bereft of basic healthcare and education. Yet almost without exception they would prove themselves to be warm-hearted and generous towards escaping Allied POWs. Time and again they risked life and home, offering escapees shelter and sustenance and often clothing and footwear that was in precious short supply. Many a British POW would owe the *contadini* his life, and Almonds would be no exception.

Hunting, scavenging and accepting such help as he was offered, Almonds covered hundreds of miles on foot – though far less as the crow flies – before approaching the small town of Civitella Casanova, a historic settlement of pre-Roman origin perched high in the Abruzzo region. Curious as to his surroundings and no doubt feeling encouraged by the warm reception he had received so far, Almonds decided to enter the town. He passed beneath an ancient and gnarled stone archway, only to spy trouble. Parked on the roadside up ahead was a German truck, with grey-uniformed figures busy loading provisions aboard. He figured that if he turned around and backtracked, it would draw immediate attention. The German soldiers had already clocked this lone male of military age who had sauntered into town.

Adopting the slightly stooped posture that had served him so well during his Porto San Giorgio reconnaissance, Almonds strolled ahead, while the enemy soldiers eyed him with suspicion. Surely it was only a matter of seconds before one threw out a challenge. The German troops were bound to ask for papers, which Almonds didn't possess, and then the game would be well and truly up. Projecting an aura of unruffled calm – which he certainly didn't feel – Almonds chose instead to duck into the doorway of the nearest building and hastened further inside.

Heading down the front passage of an ancient-looking but beautiful home, he heard the clink of cutlery on earthenware plates up ahead, plus the murmur of pleasant conversation. Tensing himself for whatever was coming – the cry of alarm from behind, or the cry of terror from the front – Almonds opened the door, which led into a bright, airy kitchen. An Italian family were gathered around the table enjoying a meal of freshly made pasta.

The family stared at him with speechless shock, but it was the woman's expression – the mother of the home? – that most struck Almonds. Her face had turned pale and a hand had gone involuntarily to her mouth: she was about to scream. Smiling in the most unthreatening manner he could manage, Almonds raised a finger to his lips.

'Shhh,' he whispered. 'Shhh . . . Inglesi.'

Somehow, miraculously, it seemed to do the trick. The woman of the house sat there, wide-eyed, hand still at her mouth, but no sound left her lips. Behind her Almonds spied an open window. With a nod of thanks to the awestruck Italian family, he darted for it, dived through and came to his feet in a secluded garden lying on the far side.

Almonds ran down the green slope until he found a narrow, fast-flowing river at the far end. He waded in – apparently still undetected – and began to head uphill towards its source, making his way out of the town and back into the mountains. He moved as quickly and as stealthily as he could, for if the Germans were to knock at the door of the house to enquire about the tall stranger, and could find nothing but a shocked Italian family, he knew the surrounding area would soon be teeming with troops. Following the signing of the Armistice of Cassibile, and the resulting chaos in the POW camps, hundreds of Allied prisoners had seized the opportunity to escape, and the mountains were said to be thick with their number.

Running wherever the terrain allowed, he climbed ever higher into the hills, feeling safer with every step. But as he followed the river he noticed something curious: dead fish floating belly up in the water. That could only mean one thing: there had to be military activity of some kind up ahead. He pressed onwards, moving more cautiously, taking a route south-west deeper into the mountains. Before long he came to a road. From his vantage point he could see that it lay directly across his path and it was bumper-to-bumper with enemy vehicles. He could only presume it to be a main supply route, ferrying men and war material to reinforce the Germans' positions south of Rome.

With General Montgomery driving his British and Commonwealth forces north from the toe of Italy, and US General Mark Clark propelling his American troops and armour in a hard charge towards Rome, the Germans feared a swift and devastating pincer movement. Hitler had warned his senior military commanders that Rome must not be allowed to fall. Much of the traffic that Almonds could see was engaged in a rush south to stiffen the German defences and prevent the Allies from seizing the Italian capital.

Almonds watched the road intently. He noticed there was the occasional gap between the long columns of vehicles. He would need to get closer and carefully pick his moment. Crawling his way through the undergrowth, he headed for a ditch adjacent to the road. From there, he was in a fine position to bolt from one side to the other when there was a break in the traffic. He waited, watching a long column of grey-painted trucks thunder past. Mistime this attempt, and he was bound to be spotted by either a soldier in the back of one truck or a driver in the front of the one following.

Finally, what seemed to be the last vehicle in the lengthy column rumbled by. Bang on cue, Almonds pulled himself out of the ditch and hurled himself forwards. Crashing through the thick undergrowth on the far side, suddenly he found himself face to face with a hapless Italian farmer, who had been tending his field of potatoes. The two figures crouched there, staring at each other in amazement, their confusion mounting. Just then, Almonds detected the sound of another truck approaching. Fearing that he had been spotted on his dash across the road, he dropped to the ground, concealing himself as well as he could between the furrows.

As he hugged the loamy earth, Almonds raised one finger to his lips, giving the universal signal to keep quiet, the farmer eyeing him uncertainly. Then came the most unwelcome sound of all: the growl of the truck's engine dissipating, as the driver eased off on the accelerator. Worse still, it was followed by the noise of squealing brakes. The truck was coming to a halt no more than a dozen metres away, at almost exactly the spot where Almonds had dived through the hedge.

Seconds later he heard the unmistakable sound of boots crunching on gravel. Barely daring to breathe, he kept one eye on the farmer, who had gone back to hoeing his potatoes, but with a tell-tale desperation to his movements. The man was trying to behave as if the strange figure lying prone in his field wasn't actually there, but his eyes kept darting nervously to Almonds' position.

Clearly, both the British escapee and the Italian farmer feared they were for the high jump: Almonds for his escape, and the farmer for not screaming blue murder upon spying the fugitive. Scraps of conversation in guttural German drifted across to them. But then came the sweetest sound of all, which cut through the tension and the fear: the distinctive noise of someone relieving themselves in the bushes.

Relief flooded through Almonds. It seemed that those riding in the truck had not seen anything suspicious. This was simply a rest stop where soldiers could enjoy a brief cigarette or a pee. But for every second that they lingered there, there was always a chance they would spy the farmer and fire a few questions his way. Ten long minutes passed – it felt like a lifetime to Almonds – before the German soldiers finally left the Italian farmer unremarked and unmolested, and climbed back aboard.

To his relief, Almonds heard the truck's engine growl into life as it got underway. Once it was gone, Almonds clambered to his feet, brushing the muck from his civilian clothing. He locked eyes with the farmer. There was a brief look of acknowledgement and understanding: while he did not know exactly who Almonds was, the farmer realised he was no friend to the German occupiers.

Almonds smiled his thanks: '*Grazie.*'

The farmer shrugged: '*Prego*' – You're welcome.

With that, Almonds hurried off across the field, seeking the cover of the woodland on the far side. He made it and headed cross-country, picking up his pace once more and running whenever he could. Before long he became aware of a mass of enemy troops all around him, as convoys of trucks snaked through the landscape. The Germans were readying a series of massive fortifications lying to the south of Rome. These would become known as the Gustav Line, the Bernhardt Line and the none-too-subtly-named Hitler Line. But it was the Volturno Line – which stretched from Termoli on the eastern coast, over the Apennine Mountains to the mouth of the Volturno River on Italy's west coast – that Almonds was fast approaching.

In his diary entry from the time, Almonds estimated that he had walked about 200 miles. But it was clear that he could not press on through terrain crawling with enemy troops. He would have to find a place to hide while he waited for the Germans to pass. He reached the outskirts of the village of San Giuliano del Sannio, and just managed to avoid blundering into a section of enemy troopers manning an 88mm field gun – the superlative German anti-tank and anti-aircraft weapon. Though the Allies owned the skies over Italy, having almost total air superiority, the eighty-eights had proved a menace both on the ground and in the air. The gun could be deployed for action in less than two minutes, which made it far more mobile and versatile than any equivalent Allied weapon.

From his hiding place Almonds heard an aircraft engine and scanned the open sky, hoping to spot the warplane. Ever since he was a child he'd loved aircraft. He had even built one with a friend, using scavenged wood and fabric and attaching an old motorcycle engine as a powerplant. He had savoured every moment of designing, assembling and testing their DIY flying machine, taking huge delight in carving a two-bladed wooden propeller entirely by hand. Sadly for Almonds, neither he nor his friend had had the money to get the plane airborne, but he'd felt certain – if he'd had the funds – that they would have made it fly.

The form of a lone P-47 Thunderbolt, with its unmistakable fat and stocky fuselage, hove into view. The warplane's powerful Pratt & Whitney Double Wasp engine was used in two other American fighters – the Grumman Hellcat and the Vought Corsair – and it made an utterly distinctive, ear-splitting howl. Bulky and bull-like, as opposed to the sleeker German Messerschmitt Me 109 or the Focke-Wulf 190, the P-47 was known as the 'Jug' – short for Juggernaut – and was a veritable flying tank. Boosted by that Pratt & Whitney powerplant, it boasted a top speed in excess of 400 miles per hour, and its guns could unleash a torrent of lead that would tear up anything in its path. A real work horse, it had a hell of a bite.

But worryingly, Almonds could tell that this one was in some kind of trouble. Grey-black smoke billowed from one of its wings, leaving a dirty trail in its wake. He imagined it must have been hit, most likely by shrapnel from a shell fired from the eighty-eight that he had just recently avoided. Almonds watched, transfixed, as the pilot fought a losing battle to maintain altitude. With his heart in his mouth, he saw a tiny figure bail out, the plane still gushing smoke as it went down. Moments later there was a flash of grey-white in the sky and the parachutist's canopy blossomed, as the stricken aircraft plummeted out of view.

For long moments the pilot drifted on the air. In a diary entry, Almonds noted that he watched the man make 'a successful parachute landing', a good distance away. Relieved, he turned back to his journey, pressing onwards with the utmost caution. On the outskirts of San Giuliano village lay a farmstead, built directly into the hillside. It seemed like the perfect place to lie low as the Germans passed, but still Almonds was unsure whether to approach it. The local people so far had proven mostly friendly, but Almonds remembered a time when he had suffered absolute brute savagery at Italian hands.

After his capture in Benghazi, and being shackled hand to foot, Almonds had been taken out at gunpoint and forced to kneel on the flatbed of an open pick up. Three Italians joined him, pointing their loaded rifles at the back of his head. Then the truck had proceeded to drive slowly around the city streets, exhibiting the prisoner for all to see, thus 'proving' his captors' proficiency at keeping the citizens 'safe' from Allied forces. Almonds was pelted with rubbish and spat on by crowds of onlookers. All the while he had no way of knowing if this shameful show of public humiliation would end with his own execution. It had not come to that, but Almonds had been left deeply scarred by the experience.

Despite the vividness of his memories, he decided that he should take a risk on this hillside farmstead. He approached carefully, finally making his presence known to the farmer, an Italian in his forties who introduced himself as Liberato Coapaulo. Coapaulo had a friendly face and Almonds felt instinctively that he was trustworthy. He lived there with his wife and nine-year-old daughter, he explained, tending a small flock of sheep and some chickens.

Coapaulo indicated the hayloft, which was entered via a door set higher in the hillside, offering it to Almonds as a hiding place. There he concealed himself among the bales. From the hayloft, another door led directly into Coapaulo's simple kitchen, and that evening the Italian invited Almonds to join his family for a meal. As the mouthwatering smell of roasted mutton filled the air, Almonds realised – with mixed feelings of guilt and tremendous gratitude – that Coapaulo had slaughtered one of his precious sheep.

It was clearly a considerable sacrifice, for Coapaulo and his family did not have much to feed themselves. Almonds ate heartily, but before he could finish the meal, his host's attention was drawn to something outside. Moments later, Coapaulo signalled that Almonds should return to the hayloft. As he bolted for his hiding place, he glimpsed his host's wife removing any evidence of there ever having been a fourth place at dinner.

His heart pounding, Almonds lay completely still on the hayloft floor. Peeking through the narrow gaps in the boarding, he spied a group of enemy soldiers. As far as he could tell they were not in search of any Allied POWs: it was supper they were after. A squad of tired and hungry German troops were seeking provisions for their journey. They appeared oblivious to the fugitive staring down from above. Almonds watched as the grey-clad figures cut some kind of deal with Coapaulo. Remaining utterly silent and still, he waited for them to finish their haggling, after which he hoped they would be on their way.

Coapaulo, knowing full well the dire penalty for assisting an Allied escapee, figured he would provide something extra to sweeten the deal. He brought the German troop leader a brace of live chickens to add to the parcel of roasted mutton. Watching from above as the German soldiers wrung the necks of the hens, Almonds felt doubly tortured: yet more of the family's precious food supplies had been sacrificed in order to shield him from harm.

The troop leader dug out a fistful of Third Reich 'requisition slips' and handed them to Coapaulo. These 'bank-notes' were issued for soldiers to use in occupied territories, to 'pay' for confiscated goods. But everyone knew they were essentially worthless. Even so, no Italian farmer – no matter how poor he was – could afford to say no to such occupying troops. As for Almonds, he vowed that his presence should not endanger the kind farmer and his family any longer than was absolutely necessary, deciding to press on as soon as he could.

The following day – 10 October 1943, just over a month since Almonds had made his escape – Coapaulo approached him with unexpected news. It appeared that the downed Thunderbolt pilot was also in hiding quite near by. Interest more than a little piqued, Almonds accepted Coapaulo's offer to get a message to the man. For this Almonds used one of his most treasured resources – a page of the paper torn from the priest's Bible – penning a note to the pilot, which Coapaulo would deliver by hand.

As Almonds awaited Coapaulo's return, he used a piece of his precious paper to write a diary entry to his wife Lockie: 'In a hayloft of a little farm . . . hiding from the Germans . . .' Almonds was so near, and yet still so far from reaching the Allied lines, but even so his confidence was steadily growing. He recorded in his diary how 'an American pilot' was in hiding somewhere near by, and pondered if he would make it to friendly lines this time, concluding: 'Yes, I think so . . .'

A while later Coapaulo returned, bearing a reply from the American, signed by 'Captain M. Neilson'. Neilson stated that he was happy to make contact with an ally. He wanted to meet Almonds as soon as possible so they could journey onwards together. Almonds suggested they rendezvous that very night: that way, he could quiz the American pilot – if he truly *was* an American pilot – under cover of darkness, and determine whether or not he could be trusted.

During his time as a POW, Almonds had experienced first-hand the use of 'stool pigeons' – spies pretending to be Allied prisoners, in order to win a POW's trust and so extract valuable information. There was always a chance that the 'American pilot' was not who he claimed to be and was being used to entrap Allied escapees and resistance fighters alike. Either way, Almonds was not inclined to take any chances. Via Coapaulo's efforts he received a reply that Neilson would be happy to meet.

Almonds duly met the pilot – dressed now in civilian clothes – at a midnight rendezvous. After grilling him, Almonds concluded that Captain M. Neilson was genuine, and he accepted the man's offer to press onwards to the Allied lines together. But they would need to leave right away, Almonds insisted, for he was not prepared to intrude on Coapaulo's hospitality any further. Neilson agreed and, after bidding a heartfelt farewell to their host, the two men set off southwards.

For a while, they forged ahead in silence. But as they crept through the blackness of the moonless terrain, they became aware that they might not be alone. They could see very little except ghostly shapes, which were somehow even blacker than the darkness that enveloped them. Suddenly, the eerie quiet was broken by the harsh sound of something metallic striking something hard. Almonds suspected they had stumbled upon a hidden enemy camp. Both men could sense the danger. Almonds remarked that he and Neilson had 'hairs standing up' on the back of their necks. But if there were hostile troops lurking near by, had he and Neilson been detected?

As luck would have it, they managed to slip through whatever perils had lain around them, apparently without being noticed. As the dark night bled slowly into dawn, the two fugitives reached a gravel track running downhill. Neilson made as if to start down it, but Almonds thrust out one arm in an unconscious movement, halting the American in his tracks. Something about the ground ahead had alerted him to danger . . .

Almonds was reminded of a night in August 1941, the day before his twenty-seventh birthday, one that he had almost not lived to see. He had been with Jock Lewes on a Commando reconnaissance mission, in the no-man's-land of the Tobruk perimeter, probing for enemy troops. He, Lewes and three others had stumbled into a freshly laid minefield. The terrifying munitions had been spread out over a large expanse, with trip wires stretched between them. One of their number had caught a wire with his foot, causing a tremendous blast. Though all five had been blown off their feet, miraculously nobody had been injured. Lewes had explained that to make their way out of the minefield, they would have to crawl ahead in single file, the man at the front feeling in the sand before him to locate the mines, or any trigger wires that might be attached to them.

It had made for agonisingly slow progress. When it had come to Almonds' turn to take point, he'd inched forwards tentatively on hands and knees, fingers feeling gently, fearfully, in the sand. Before long he had made contact with the hard, metallic, alien form of a landmine lying just beneath the desert surface. Checking the surrounding area for tripwires, they had carefully circumnavigated the mine. As the sky had begun to lighten, it had become easier to locate the mines, due to the tell-tale lines left around them where the ground had been smoothed flat. But with daylight, the men in the minefield had become more visible. Before long they were spotted, enemy troops taking pot-shots at them with their machine guns.

Incredibly, they had all made it out alive. But ever since, that memory – those scenes – had been etched deeply in Almonds' mind, which was what had somehow alerted him to danger right now: *the track ahead bore all the signs of being sown with mines.* Almonds figured that he and Neilson must be nearing the frontline. The Germans were retreating and, aware that the Allies would be pushing up from the south, they were likely laying minefields in their wake. On closer inspection, it appeared that parts of the gravel track had been disturbed and then replaced, but in a slightly unnatural way.

With utmost care, Almonds knelt at the first obvious disturbance – not so near that it might trigger the device, but close enough so that he could probe carefully with his bare hands. Slowly, gently, sifting the gravel away with his fingers, he grasped the cold metal casing of a German landmine. He paused for an instant, wondering how it was that in the half-light he and his American companion hadn't pressed onwards and blown themselves to pieces. Even if they had not been killed outright, these devices were designed to cause terrible wounds, and they would very likely have bled to death.

Replacing the dirt with the utmost care, Almonds scanned the area, trying to establish the full extent of the minefield – how deep and how far it stretched. He made a detailed mental note of the lie of the land, committing every physical feature to memory with all the skill and practice that SAS training afforded him. He was determined to pass on an accurate picture of the mine-field's location and dimensions to the first Allied troops that they encountered, in the hope that it could be de-mined before claiming any lives.

Skirting around it, he and Neilson took to open country. Before long they came upon another road that they would have to cross. They made several attempts, but each time were forced to retreat for there were enemy troops everywhere. They walked parallel to the road until they came to a point where a bridge forded a shallow river. That bridge, of course, was closely guarded. Come nightfall they edged slowly into the water upstream, trying not to cause the slightest disturbance. Once they were deep enough, Almonds and Neilson lay on their backs, bodies half-submerged and each draping some greenery over his head, to mask the 'glint of a white face' in the moonlight. In that way they allowed themselves to drift silently downstream, propelling themselves along by grasping the stony riverbed below with the tips of their fingers. They passed under the bridge unnoticed, and when they were well out of sight they clambered onto the far bank and con-tinued on their way.

At last, they reached the outskirts of Benevento, an ancient hilltop city around thirty miles north-east of Naples. According to the limited information they had been able to glean, this was the last location of German frontline troops. From his original starting point of Porto San Giorgio, Almonds had covered a distance of some two hundred miles as the crow flies, but con-sidering his route had meandered through the mountains and around countless enemy positions, he'd travelled at least twice as far, over a period of thirty-two days.

The two men approached Benevento with caution, spying a small military force camped in some bivouacs on the city's outskirts. Whether they were friendly or not was impossible to tell. The pair ventured into a nearby village in the hope of gathering some intel. There, via a local intermediary, they were able to make contact with that mystery force: it turned out to be an advance party from the 75th Ranger Regiment, an elite American reconnaissance unit. Almonds and Neilson had reached friendly lines.

Founded in 1942 as the American equivalent of the British Commandos, and modelled along similar lines, the Rangers were a fearsome military outfit. Working in small independent teams, Rangers acted as the spearhead of any American thrust, tasked with testing the ground ahead, just as this small party, no more than a dozen strong, was doing now. Their role was to gather intelligence on the whereabouts and strength of the enemy and report back to headquarters, which is what had brought them to Benevento.

One of the first things Almonds did was to report details of the minefield. A discussion ensued with the Ranger commander as to what to do next. It was imperative to get a warning to Allied commanders of that deadly hazard, one that could otherwise cost many lives. The Ranger commander decided to return to their HQ forthwith, with Almonds and Neilson in their party.

As they set off, Almonds noticed that one of the Rangers was laden with a heavy Bren gun. Struggling under the load, he kept complaining of the distance that he had walked carrying that burden. Ever the gentleman, Almonds politely offered to shoulder the light machine gun. After all, how was the Ranger to know that this SAS veteran had just walked halfway across Italy in a little over a month, after a year spent in captivity?

Once the Ranger unit made it back to their forward head-quarters, Almonds was promptly arrested by the Americans, who could not understand how someone who looked so much like an Italian could speak with such a natural English accent, concluding that he had to be an enemy spy. Eventually, the truth was established and Almonds was released and despatched to England, where he arrived shortly after Christmas day, 1943. He spent a brief rest period at home with his wife and son, before he returned to his parent unit, the Coldstream Guards. There, all his thoughts were of the SAS, longing for the companionship and brotherhood that he had experienced in their ranks.

For his escape, and for his minefield discovery, Almonds was awarded a bar to his existing Military Medal. As the citation made clear, at all times Almonds had been unbreakable, whether as a soldier, raider, escapee, or on any other task put to him. He had beaten the odds by courage, audacity and his willingness to walk through fire in an effort to secure his freedom.

During the period of Almonds' imprisonment, SAS commander David Stirling had been captured on a raid in the Tunisian desert, being imprisoned in Colditz camp in eastern Germany, where he would make many an escape attempt of his own. Unfortunately, none would prove as successful as Almonds', and Stirling was repeatedly thwarted. Almonds learned that during the campaign in the North African desert the actions of the SAS had played a key role in the defeat of Rommel's Afrika Korps. He also learned that the SAS had expanded to become two regiments. William

'Bill' Stirling – David Stirling's brother and a lieutenant colonel in the Scots Guards – had taken command of the second unit, dubbed 2 SAS, while Blair 'Paddy' Mayne remained in command of the original unit, 1 SAS.

Hearing of Almonds' escape, Mayne wrote a letter to one of the SAS's medical officers, Malcom Pleydell, a close friend of Almonds. Almonds had 'got through to our side', Mayne reported, adding that he was 'trying to meet him'. With Mayne's help, Almonds was able to rejoin the SAS in February 1944, whereupon he was promoted to the rank of squadron sergeant major and tasked to help get new recruits up to scratch, in the run-up to the D-Day landings. Almonds himself played a key role in the SAS's subsequent missions in France, for which he was awarded a Croix de Guerre – a French high-valour medal – with silver star. His citation describes how Almonds '*N'a pas cessé durant sa mission d'être un magnifique exemple pour ses hommes*' – that is, throughout the entire mission, Almonds never ceased to be a magnificent example to his men.

Towards the end of the war, Mayne came to Almonds' aid once more, living up to the SAS's wartime claim of the unbreakable spirit and bond forged between officers and men. With no prior warning, Mayne presented Almonds to the foremost British commander, General Bernard L. Montgomery, declaring simply: 'I want this man commissioned.' Despite his distinguished war record, Almonds remained a non-commissioned officer with 'other-ranks' status. There and then, Almonds received his promotion in the field, being given the rank of second lieutenant.

Almonds ended his prestigious military career in 1961, with the rank of major. At this point he found himself in Ghana, where he decided to hand-build a ketch that he named *Kumasi*, this being the two-masted boat that he had designed and committed to memory while in solitary confinement in an Italian POW camp. He proceeded to navigate *Kumasi* all the way back to the UK, a distance of some 4,500 nautical miles, proving once again his incredible ability for exceeding all normal expectations.

Likewise, our next great escapee would demonstrate such qualities par excellence, embodying the SAS motto to 'always go a little further . . .'

Great Escape Six

DEFEATING HITLER'S COMMANDO ORDER

'*Halt! Wer da?*' The harsh challenge rang out into the cold night air.

On hearing it, the six-strong team of Operation Pomegranate scattered, hiding themselves in the shadows between the farm buildings. Three nights earlier, on 12 January 1944, these SAS paratroopers – two officers and four men – had jumped from a C47 Dakota aircraft into the Italian countryside. They had landed under cover of darkness, 'in the valley running eastwards near Magione', the official mission report recorded. Their drop zone lay adjacent to the turquoise waters of Lake Trasimeno, situated a hundred miles due north of Rome.

Since then, they had spent the best part of a week laid up in patches of thick undergrowth amid lonely mountain passes, moving only under cover of darkness. They'd stuck to the wildest terrain, for they were deep within German-occupied Italy and enemy troops were everywhere. 'The going was very difficult,' one member of the team reported, 'as the hillsides were steep and wet,' and they were loaded down with heavy packs, crammed with explosives, fuses and detonators.

In addition, those rucksacks contained 'C-rations, a quantity of dried raisins, sugar, chocolate', one trooper reported, plus special water-purification tablets. Each man also carried an American-made M1 carbine – a weapon favoured by the SAS when they could get their hands on them, due to its light weight and ease of use. Each man also had a .45 Colt pistol.

After traversing Lake Trasimeno via its western shoreline and scaling the 3,000-foot summit of Mount Tezio, they had headed east and approached the River Tiber. British military intelligence had briefed them that the waterway would be fordable at this point, something crucial to their present mission. Yet recent heavy rainfall in the mountains had transformed the otherwise shallow, meandering waterway into a raging torrent. Having reached the river, the six men regarded it with dismay, noticing the swirls of white water, where menacing rocks broke the surface. It would be impossible to wade across.

They'd advanced cautiously downstream, until they had spotted a wire suspended over the water, shining silver in the moonlight. The near end of it disappeared into a small, brick-built hut, and concealed inside they discovered a possible means to cross: a very basic and rickety-looking cable car. The device was hand-operated and 'never devised for a secret crossing', one of the raiders reported. They had hoped the fast-rushing water would mask the noise of their passage, but no such luck. The cable car rattled and the cables thrummed 'as we went across two by two'.

Despite all the racket, the six had made it across seemingly undetected. But they were just moving off, making their way between the darkened buildings, when they heard the sentry's challenge. Though their knowledge of German was rudimentary, there could be no mistaking the meaning: 'Halt! Who goes there?' Hence they all flung themselves into cover.

From his position concealed between two buildings, James 'Jimmy' Quentin Hughes, a young lieutenant, strained to detect any sound that might indicate the size of the force they were facing, but the freezing January night remained stubbornly still and silent. He awaited a steer from their troop commander, Major Antony Widdrington, who lay beside him in the alleyway, as to what they should do next. As all were well aware, the enemy already knew about their presence in the area and would be actively hunting them.

The day after dropping into Italy, they had stumbled upon some woodcutters, deep in the mountains. They had given the SAS men some food and had seemed friendly enough, for, like many Italians, they resented the Nazi occupation of their homeland. Yet they had also brought the alarming news that the Germans had found their SAS team's parachutes and were combing the terrain. Most likely, it was the passage of their lone C47 Dakota that had prompted the enemy to mount a search. As the mission report noted, 'the presence of a single aircraft over enemy territory was liable to arouse the suspicion of parachutist activity.'

It stood to reason that the Germans would have increased their security at every possible crossing point of the Tiber – hence the sentry's challenge. After several minutes' tense silence, Hughes and Widdrington concluded there could be no enemy troops in active pursuit. Perhaps the sentry was alone and, on hearing the approach of several unknown figures, had regretted his temerity in crying out a challenge.

Slipping away in the darkness, Hughes and Widdrington found themselves separated from the other four men of their patrol. They skirted around a cluster of farm buildings, reaching the relative safety of the open land beyond. Their main problem now was finding the rest of their team. Tentatively, Hughes began to imitate the calls of a nocturnal bird. This was the way SAS operators had been trained to locate each other, if separated. Yet other than the steady rush of the nearby river, no response came.

'Where the bloody hell are they?' Hughes whispered under his breath.

The two officers began to probe the surrounding area, alert for any sign of the missing men. Although this was Hughes' first mission with the SAS, he had few problems slipping silently through the night. During a childhood spent at a Welsh boarding school he had been a 'secretive and withdrawn' young boy, teaching himself 'to move about in the dormitory' when everyone else was sleeping, doing so 'in complete silence'. He had been inspired in part by the depictions of Native Americans that he'd seen in Hollywood 'cowboy and Indian' films.

After three-quarters of an hour Hughes and Widdrington were forced to abandon their search. 'We walked on, stopping to whistle at intervals,' Hughes would later report, but there was still no sign of the others. With their force reduced from six to two, there were only two options remaining: abandon their mission, and head south on foot towards Allied lines, or press on to the target, just the two of them.

Their mission, Operation Pomegranate, was no small undertaking, and it represented exactly the kind of task the SAS had been formed for: dropping a specialist team of paratroopers behind enemy lines to support a main military offensive. In this instance that larger mission – codenamed Operation Shingle – aimed to provide the impetus the Allies needed to wrest Italy from German control. Even since first landing on Italian soil in the summer of 1943, Allied troops had met fierce

German resistance, bolstered by massively fortified defensive lines. The British, American and Commonwealth troops were bogged down, unable to punch through the fearsome German defences. Operation Shingle was devised to break the deadlock, by landing Allied infantrymen on Italy's western coast, near the city of Anzio, thereby leap-frogging ahead of the enemy's Gustav Line, a string of defences lying to the south of Rome, which included the ancient hilltop monastery of Monte Cassino Abbey.

Just over a month earlier, in December 1943, British Prime Minister Winston Churchill had met American General Dwight Eisenhower, and other top Allied commanders, to discuss plans for Operation Shingle. The minutes of their meeting noted: 'There seemed to be general agreement among the Commanders-in-Chief that an amphibious landing of no less than two assault divisions behind the enemy's right flank . . . should decide the battle of Rome and possibly achieve the destruction of a substantial part of the enemy's army.' Eisenhower had predicted that such a surprise attack would critically weaken the enemy's defences, thus allowing Allied troops to punch through, stressing that 'there was no likelihood of the Germans suddenly breaking, except under conditions which would be created by a successful Shingle.'

Operation Shingle was scheduled to start on 22 January 1944, just a few days hence. In part, its success hinged on the six-man SAS patrol that had just crossed the Tiber. Their target was the San Egidio Airfield, strategically placed in the dead centre of Italy, where 'all the reconnaissance planes, of the type Junkers 88 and Me 410, were known to be based'. Allied commanders had assessed that one of the primary threats to Operation Shingle was being spotted in open waters by the Luftwaffe, before the assault flotilla made landfall.

The aircraft most likely to detect the Operation Shingle fleet were those that flew out of San Egidio. Hence the SAS raiders getting dropped in tasked with infiltrating the airfield and laying enough explosives to render any reconnaissance flights impossible – 'putting out the eyes of the Germans', as Hughes called it. Without spotter planes to reconnoitre the area, the enemy would be unaware of the approaching Allied fleet until it was too late.

To many, continuing with such a mission when reduced to only two men would have seemed insane. But Widdrington and Hughes were no ordinary soldiers. Major Widdrington, already a decorated veteran at twenty-nine years of age, had had an illustrious military career, being awarded the Military Cross for his brave actions with the Queen's Bays (2nd Dragoon Guards), a cavalry regiment with over two hundred years' history behind it. His medal citation described how, when his 'leading Squadron was held up on an impassable wadi which was covered by enemy HE [high-explosive] and AP [armour-piercing] fire', Widdrington had 'volunteered to carry out a recce on foot [when] he came under heavy mortar and MG [machine-gun] fire'.

With shells and bullets exploding all around, Widdrington had acted 'with great coolness', making his way back 'with full information on enemy dispositions'. Returning to his unit, Widdrington had found his Squadron commander badly wounded. He'd proceeded to take command of the troops and 'led the Squadron forward with great dash and skill and gained the next objective'. Widdrington had gone on to volunteer for 2SAS, where he was considered by all to be a natural leader. His confident attitude and 'cool manner', combined with a tall frame, bristling moustache and steely gaze, helped inspire those who served under him, Hughes included.

Hughes had a somewhat less distinguished military record, and he hungered to prove his worth. Born in Liverpool in 1920, at the outbreak of war he had cut short his university studies at age nineteen to join the Army. Following a year's officer training, in September 1940 he had reported to the 208 Anti-aircraft Training Regiment, in Yeovil, Somerset. Germany had begun its bombing campaign of Britain and the skies overhead were thick with enemy warplanes. Hughes was in Yeovil to learn how to shoot them down.

But longing for something a little more immediate and challenging, he'd volunteered to soldier abroad, stating his preferences for either India, Hong Kong or Singapore. Instead, he had been despatched to join an anti-aircraft battery on besieged Malta, which he described as 'no haven of peace'. When the SAS had been busy raiding aerodromes on the Libyan coast to prevent enemy aircraft from bombing the supply convoys heading for Malta, Hughes had been on the other end of that siege.

He'd remained in Malta for sixteen months, while the island endured a near-constant bombardment. In December 1941, he'd noted in his diary how they had watched dive bombers swooping to attack at night, only to be caught in the searchlights and 'riddled by a Hurricane cannon'. One enemy aircraft burst into flames and went howling towards earth, leaving 'a trail of bright sparks across the sky'. The aerial assault went on for weeks, both 'day and night', the bombs raining down and then 'flash – several flashes – buildings shake and we watch the smoke'.

Finally, in November 1942, the siege of Malta was lifted and the island was left largely unmolested by the enemy. With the battle over, Hughes volunteered for the Special Forces. He was selected to join the newly formed 2 SAS, under the command of David Stirling's older brother, Bill Stirling. Hughes had sailed from Malta to Tunisia, where he stuffed himself with all the good food he could find, after the long years under siege. Then he headed two hundred miles west along the coast, to 2SAS's base in Philippeville (now Skikda), Algeria, where he began his intensive training.

It proved relentless and hugely varied, including explosives use, physical fitness, demolitions, languages, firearms and – most bizarre of all – learning to drive a train. The SAS also continued the long-standing tradition – first thought up by Jock Lewes in Kabrit – of jumping from the back of a moving truck, to learn how to land in the proper way after a parachute jump. With Allied forces moving on from the vast deserts of North Africa to liberate Europe, it would no longer be possible for the SAS simply to drive their jeeps to their targets – they would need to be able to parachute deep behind enemy lines.

Hughes had long found parachuting fascinating, writing in his Maltese diary of how he'd watched, mesmerised, as 'little puffs of white appeared' one by one and 'slowly swayed towards the ground' – Luftwaffe aircrew, bailing out of a stricken warplane. In the SAS, he quickly fell in love with the craft. Of his first jump he noted how the noisy interior of the plane seemed to 'evaporate' as he flung himself through the hatch, after which he felt as though he were 'lying on a feather bed of indescribable softness', experiencing 'a joy so profound that he burst into song'. Hughes would sing at the top of his voice during all of his training descents.

Now, at the age of twenty-three, and sporting a rakish pencil moustache and a newly acquired elite forces mindset, Hughes had been deployed on his first behind-the-lines mission. But, separated as they were from the rest of their party, his and Widdrington's chances of success were rapidly diminishing. Yet if they failed in their mission and a German scout aircraft spotted the Operation Shingle flotilla, the Allied troops might be annihilated on the beaches, rendering the whole operation a failure. On balance, Hughes and Widdrington believed they had no option but to continue with their mission, regardless of their slim chances both of success and survival.

Decision made, they pressed on through terrain thick with German troops, marching only at night and lying up through the hours of daylight. Even with the help of Benzedrine – an amphetamine favoured by the SAS to boost their stamina during long, arduous marches – Hughes struggled to keep up with the seasoned operator, Widdrington. Though he would later describe Benzedrine as 'a wonderful drug', still Hughes was forced to jettison non-essential items from his kitbag to make the going easier.

After sixty hours on the move, the two men finally neared their target. Late on 17 January 1944 – five days before Operation Shingle's zero hour – they set out to recce the airfield, stashing all non-essential gear in a hiding place in the woods, including their American carbines. They also swapped their sturdy boots for tennis shoes, to muffle the noise of their footfalls. The winter light was fading fast by the time Hughes and Widdrington arrived in sight of the airfield, making 'the details and disposition of the aircraft . . . not clearly visible'.

Although they had spent hours memorising every detail of the aerodrome from maps and aerial photographs, it proved hard to get their bearings in the gathering darkness, and they ran the risk of misjudging the attack. Just then they had a stroke of luck. 'While we were watching [the airfield], four Ju 88s came into land,' Hughes reported. 'One of them crashed and caught fire. The flare path and the boundary lights showed the perimeter of the field clearly.'

Having worked out their best route of attack, Hughes and Widdrington rested up for the remainder of the night hidden in some woodland, vowing to strike during the hours of darkness the following day. Sure enough, once it was well and truly dark, they crept towards the northern boundary of the airfield, laden with explosives and timers. Each man carried twelve Lewes bombs, a lightweight incendiary device designed specifically for the SAS by Jock Lewes. Ingenious, practical and comparatively lightweight, the charges were made from a mixture of 'plastic explosive and aluminium and thermite . . . combining the incendiary aspect with the explosive,' recalled David Stirling. The addition of thermite produced a localised exothermic reaction, keeping the burning going long after the initial explosion, thus enabling an aircraft to be blown up *and* set on fire all at once.

Now was the moment to prime their charges. Widdrington and Hughes were using L-delay pencil detonators – a cylindrical brass tube containing a copper wire. Crushing the cap released acid into the tube, which ate away at the wire holding a spring-loaded firing pin at the ready. When the wire snapped, the firing pin would hammer down the tube, striking a percussion cap and so detonating the charge. Varying combinations of acid strength and wire thickness lent the timer pencils their differing durations. The SAS had drawn up charts explaining how, as the outside temperature varied, the detonation time altered accordingly. Widdrington had chosen L-delays that at 18°C would cause the Lewes bombs to explode after one hour. But with the night-time temperature in Italy in January being around freezing, they figured they would have roughly two hours before detonation.

Widdrington and Hughes paused on the airfield's perimeter, where they triggered all their L-delays. In a post-mission report this was described as 'a risky procedure, but a very brave one'. By triggering all the charges before laying them, that should ensure that they would all explode at the same time, giving the enemy no chance to disarm any of them once the first explosion had ripped across the airfield.

With their Lewes bombs thus primed, they crept forwards, using the dim light of a quarter moon to navigate, the perimeter proving surprisingly easy to penetrate. Following the success of the SAS's raids on the airfields of North Africa, the enemy had taken their defence far more seriously in Italy, sometimes assigning a sentry to each individual plane. Hughes had expected San Egidio to be bristling with enemy defences: gun emplacements, pillboxes, barbed-wire fences, minefield and guards. Yet they had spied nothing more worrisome than an occasional sentry patrolling the perimeter – easy enough to identify and avoid. Presumably, the Germans thought San Egidio so far behind their lines that there was little need for tighter security.

'There were four Ju 88s in a row,' Hughes reported. 'Their engines were still warm. At 23.00 hours we prepared our bombs and placed them on the starboard wings . . .'

The Junkers Ju 88 – the so-called *Schnellbomber*, or fast bomber – was a multi-use combat aircraft, serving as a night-fighter, a bomber and in a reconnaissance role. With each standing at 15ft 5in off the ground, Hughes was forced to climb upon Widdrington's broad shoulders, in order to place the charges on the warplanes. He set them adjacent to the fuel tanks, so when they exploded they would ignite the aviation fuel inside. By targeting the same spot on each plane, it made it impossible for the enemy to splice together damaged aircraft using cannibalised parts, so ensuring the maximum number would be kept out of the sky ahead of the Anzio landings.

Hughes and Widdrington 'continued down the east side of the aerodrome and put bombs on two Fieseler Storch co-operation planes and a three-engined Ju 52'. The Fieseler Storch (Stork) 'spotter' planes constituted a particularly important target, for these lightweight, slow-flying aircraft – which Hughes would later describe as 'frail, beautiful creatures looking like elegant gazelles' – were perfect for flying reconnaissance missions. With their task complete, the two raiders headed for the southern side of the airstrip, to slip through the perimeter.

Once they were clear of the aerodrome, Hughes flung himself down and began to deactivate his unused charges. Near by, he could make out Widdrington doing the same to the Lewes bombs that he still carried. Hughes had little idea how long their dash around the airfield had taken. To his adrenaline-flooded senses it had felt like mere minutes, but may have been far longer. Either way, it was well short of the two hours they had allowed for the fuses to detonate. Having stripped the L-delay mechanism from his final bomb, he turned to his commanding officer, but at that very moment there was a flash of blinding white light and heat.

Tragically, one of Widdrington's charges had blown up even as he was deactivating it. Most likely, he had carried the Lewes bombs secreted on his person, and the mere presence of his body heat had served to warm them, shortening the time the detonators would take to trigger. Either way, Widdrington was engulfed in a devastating explosion, Hughes himself being blown off his feet by the blast. Dazed and bloodied, Hughes struggled to stand, checking himself tentatively for any signs of damage, feeling 'the torn flesh and the matting blood'. He touched his face. It was crisscrossed with deep lacerations, and when he felt for his eyes all he could sense was 'a mass of pulp'.

'I was blinded and nearly completely deaf,' Hughes recalled, of the nightmarish moment.

Remembering Widdrington, he sank to his knees, patting the ground ahead of him and shouting his commander's name. Over the ringing in his ears he heard a moan. Following it to its source, he located his friend. As he pawed the man's body, in order to ascertain the extent of the damage, he smelled the scent of burning flesh mingled with the metallic stench of the bomb. Shortly, he realised that the explosion had blown off both of Widdrington's hands. Hughes held the man's shattered body, wondering how on earth he was still alive. He could feel a gaping hole that the blast had ripped in his commander's abdomen, where the 'slimy flesh' spilled out 'like oozing jelly'.

At that instant, the airfield all around them erupted into flames. As aircraft after aircraft exploded, Hughes realised that against all odds, their objective had been achieved. Realising that there was very little chance of saving his commanding officer's life, unless he could be rushed to a hospital, he took his pistol and raised it above his head. Shakily he fired every bullet it held into the air, hoping he could draw the German sentries' attention to himself and to his terribly wounded comrade.

With his eight-round magazine spent, Hughes' SAS training took over. Operational security was paramount now: the enemy could not be allowed to discover the full details of their mission. He needed to destroy all evidence, first and foremost by burning their mission maps – but, of course, the explosion had blinded him. Hughes had always possessed what he described as a 'methodical mind'. He would often draw the 'complicated mechanisms of various guns and weapons' from memory, for fun. Similarly, while blindfolded he could 'strip down a Lewis gun to its many small parts and reassemble them'. Such activities had, unbeknown to Hughes, prepared him for this exact moment.

He groped around trying to locate whatever papers and maps they carried. Finding a pack of matches, he succeeded in kindling a small fire between his legs and there proceeded to incinerate the documents, relishing having a task to focus on and to distract his mind from the terrible reality of the moment. With the job of incineration done, he allowed himself to drift into unconsciousness, all the while hoping that his actions had been enough to save the life of his commanding officer, and to ensure their mission was not compromised.

When eventually Hughes came back to his senses, he found himself in a German military hospital just outside Perugia, an ancient city in central Italy. There he discovered what had transpired in the interim. Sadly, the guards who had found him had been unable to save Widdrington. The distinguished SAS commander had died from his wounds. His conduct during his final raid echoed his original MC citation: 'He carried out his long and dangerous task displaying complete disregard for danger.' Though it was a devastating loss, at least Widdrington's final mission – which Hughes would later claim to be 'the most important SAS operation in Italy' – had been a success. Certainly, the landings at Anzio on 22 January had taken the Germans almost completely by surprise.

With both eyes bandaged and his hearing severely damaged, Hughes was still of great interest to the Gestapo agents who were keen to interrogate him. As if from a great distance, he could hear the arguments in German raging at his bedside. The head doctor was refusing to allow the Gestapo to get near his patient, or at least not before he was well enough to be questioned. Oddly, Hughes found himself reliant on a German now – his physician – to shield him from the worst enemy predations.

The Gestapo had decreed that Hughes, a potentially dangerous paratrooper-raider, not be allowed near any of the other Allied prisoners. Accordingly, he had been moved to a ward reserved for German officers, where he could be isolated from his own kind. Alone, with no one to talk to, Hughes' thoughts switched back and forth from images of the haunting night on the airfield to an uncertain future without the use of his eyes. 'I had been a moody, single child,' he remarked, and during the long, lonely days of his childhood he had developed 'an introspection that was almost unhealthy'. He returned to that state now, wondering if he would survive the war, and if, as a blind man, he would ever know love again.

It was his German military physician, Dr Hansgunger Sontgerath, who offered Hughes some respite from his inner turmoil. In time Hughes would grow to consider Sontgerath a 'kind and generous friend'. Every evening after work, he would come and sit by Hughes' bed and they would talk. In halting English to begin with, but with greater fluency as Sontgerath practised the language, they discussed the various details of their lives before the war. 'We talked of fishing, walking and playing in the woods,' Hughes recalled, as he began to recognise in the doctor a kindred spirit.

As a token of their growing trust and respect, Hughes agreed to give Sontgerath his 'parole'. In military terms, 'offering parole' is a concept that has existed for many centuries. By offering parole to a fellow officer, a prisoner becomes honour-bound not to attempt to escape while in his charge. The practice harked back to a time when a captured soldier could be released under parole and was allowed to return to home and family, as long as he vowed not to take up arms again. If he broke his promise and was recaptured, he could be lawfully executed as a man without honour.

By giving his parole, Hughes had sworn that he would not attempt to escape while under Sontgerath's care. In return, the doctor did everything he could to save Hughes' sight, even calling in a specialist eye surgeon. Gradually, Hughes' vision returned in the one eye, and he found that he was able to see his champion for the first time. Dr Sontgerath had kind, intelligent eyes, which twinkled from behind wire-rimmed glasses. He wore the crumpled uniform of a man whose medical work was all-consuming, and pinned to his chest was the unmistakable form of an Iron Cross Second Class, a German award for bravery in battle. Sontgerath told Hughes that he had won the decoration when serving in the depths of a Russian winter, two years earlier, on the Eastern Front.

With Hughes' sight partially restored, Sontgerath 'brought a book of architectural photographs' for him to peruse, for the Englishman had talked of his hopes of returning to Liverpool after the war was over, to study as an architect. Yet, as the

German surgeon privately feared, the Gestapo had little intention of letting this British saboteur see the end of the war unmolested.

As Hughes' health improved, Sontgerath could no longer legitimately prevent the Gestapo agents from getting access to him. Before long, a softly spoken officer came to his bedside and declared that his sole purpose was to glean as much information about the innermost working of the SAS as possible. Hughes knew that under the Geneva Convention, all a POW was obliged to divulge to an enemy was his name, rank and serial number. Hughes, like any bona fide soldier, should be extended such protections. All he had to do was adhere to that mantra, he reminded himself: name, rank and serial number, no more.

But his German inquisitor would quickly shatter Hughes' illusions that he might be treated properly, shaking his certainties to the core. 'You are not considered a prisoner of war,' the man announced to Hughes, with sinister quiet. A 'Kommando Order' had been issued by the Führer, he added, under which all 'saboteurs, whether wearing uniform or civilian clothes, will be shot'. Hughes' only hope 'for clemency' was if he answered all questions put to him 'entirely and without deceit'.

Hughes was dumbfounded. Certainly, he had never heard of any such 'Kommando Order'. In truth, the order had been issued by Hitler himself, in utmost secrecy, in October 1942. But Hughes, like all in the SAS, had yet to learn of its sinister and deadly intent. Whatever the case, if any of this was true and he was now categorised not as a POW but as some kind of illegal saboteur, his only option was to appear to give his interrogator exactly what he sought, without actually revealing anything that could be used against his SAS comrades.

First off, Hughes decided that he would divulge the location where he and Widdrington had stashed their excess kit the night of the attack – there was nothing much of interest there anyway. Then he regurgitated all he could think to say about his previous posting, in Malta, for the battle had moved on from that once-benighted island many months ago.

Hughes spoke quickly, his inquisitor scribbling on a pad held in front of him, recording his every word 'about a place over which the tide of battle had long since passed'. Finally, the Gestapo officer seemed satisfied, but then he gave the final twist to the knife. He left Hughes with the chilling promise that once he had made a full recovery, the Gestapo would return to execute him, regardless.

Despite his seeming death sentence, over the coming weeks Hughes grew to almost enjoy his time at the hospital. As well as Dr Sontgerath, he forged another highly unlikely alliance. Major Gerhard Schacht was an officer in the *Fallschirmjäger*, the German equivalent of the British Parachute Regiment, and he was also a patient under Sontgerath's care. He introduced himself to Hughes after hearing of the Englishman's daring raid on San Egidio airbase, the two men bonding over their shared experiences as paratroopers.

'He was very friendly and pleasant,' Hughes reflected of Schacht, despite being an elite enemy soldier fighting in 'a bloody, total war'.

As the sole English patient on a German ward, Dr Sontgerath invited Hughes to meet the other German officers, for although 'the war had to be fought', as Hughes noted, 'there was no hate between us'. There were parties, Hughes describing them as 'gay, rambunctious affairs'. They would listen to the wireless – including German and British news programmes – talk, drink and sing together almost as friends. Often these parties would be held in Sontgerath's office, where a detailed map of Italy hung on the wall. Hughes would do his best to memorise it, for although he had given Sontgerath his parole, he hoped that at some point, when no longer beholden to his German doctor, he might find the chance to escape.

'Roy Farran was my hero,' Hughes would later remark, of the SAS commander. Stories of Farran's escape from enemy captivity in Greece were by now the stuff of legend within the ranks of 2SAS, where Farran, now a major, was a seasoned commander. Hughes vowed that when the opportunity arose, he would do his best to emulate Farran and make a break for freedom. But until that moment he had to remain a seemingly benign and harmless guest of the enemy.

His situation was absurd; 'crazy', Hughes would remark of this time. Befriended by these mostly decent German officers, he was being 'nursed back to health', only so that he could be 'taken out and shot by the Gestapo'. It was a time pregnant with paradoxes. During their social gatherings, tongues loosened by German beer, Hughes saw another side of the otherwise kindly Dr Sontgerath. Spurred by the alcohol, the doctor, an 'ideologist and a crazy romantic', as Hughes described him, 'firmly supported the National Socialist [Nazi] line'.

'I'd like to kill every Englishman and American,' Sontgerath declared drunkenly, one evening. It was bizarre, especially since these were the utterings of a man who had spent so many hours 'tenderly nursing a wounded English saboteur'. For Hughes, it only served to highlight the gulf that lay between the two sides of the German doctor's character. Either way, Hughes could not find it in himself to resent the man. He understood the nuanced contradictions men had to accept in order to fight an 'enemy' who in peacetime could well have been a close friend. For his part, Hughes had signed up to join the British Army and had pledged his allegiance to Britain, but his key loyalties lay with himself and with his fellow SAS operators.

'If I was to be faithful, it would be to myself,' he averred.

Before long Major Schacht, the *Fallschirmjäger* officer, recovered and left the hospital. Despatched to join the staff of Field Marshal Albert Kesselring, Germany's commander-in chief in Italy, a short while later Schacht invited his old friends Hughes and Dr Sontgerath to dinner. Over a sumptuous feast, at least by wartime standards, Schacht propositioned Hughes. He wanted the SAS man to desert the Allied cause and join that of the Axis.

'Why don't you work for us?' Schacht asked. Hughes was an elite forces professional, one that Schacht and his ilk could well use. Not against the British or the West, he was quick to add, but on the Eastern Front, against the Russians.

For a moment Hughes was tempted, if only by the quality of friendship that had been bestowed upon him by these men, yet he knew in his heart that he could not do it. He avoided directly answering the question, saying simply that it was a kind offer, one that he'd consider most carefully once fully recovered. But in truth, Hughes would have precious little opportunity to do so, for he was living on borrowed time.

Soon enough, Dr Sontgerath came to his room with a troubled countenance. The Gestapo had requested that Hughes be handed into their custody in a few days' time, he explained. Both knew what that would mean: execution. Hughes sank into a depression, fearing that he would be shot out of hand, nobody at home even knowing the truth of what had befallen him, alone and at the hands of the murderous Gestapo.

But as it turned out Sontgerath and Schacht had different ideas. Together, they worked out that the only way to save Hughes' life would be to somehow engineer the transformation of his status from illegal saboteur to bona fide POW. The one man who possessed the kind of power to orchestrate such a thing was Field Marshal Kesselring himself. Fortunately for Hughes, the Kesselrings and the Schachts were old family friends. That weekend Schacht travelled one hundred miles from Perugia to Kesselring's headquarters in Florence to plead Hughes' case in person.

Come Monday morning, the day set for his handover to the Gestapo, Hughes felt an odd sense of calm. He had recorded himself to his fate and felt 'ready now to face the consequences'. Yet no sinister Gestapo agents appeared. Instead, Dr Sontgerath announced that Schacht had achieved the seemingly impossible: Hughes had been reclassified as a prisoner of war. But there was little time for celebration or delay. The Gestapo were sure to be furious and would be doing everything in their power to get Kesselring's decision overturned. Hughes had to be transferred to a POW camp as quickly as possible – only then might he be safe from the Nazi death squads.

Sontgerath and Schacht had arranged for Hughes to be sent by a hospital train to a Luftwaffe camp in Germany, to avoid the prisoner-of-war collecting centre at nearby Verona. That way he should escape interception by the Gestapo if they were planning to pounce. He would have to leave right away.

Before departure, Hughes turned to the doctor who had saved not only his sight but his very life. 'May I now withdraw my parole?' he ventured.

Dr Sontgerath agreed that he could. His voice thick with emotion, he wished his English friend 'good luck'.

On 10 March 1944, as the hospital train pulled away with Hughes aboard, he considered the unlikeliness of these extraordinary friendships. While he conceded that 'many Germans committed the most appalling atrocities', he understood that some also possessed the capacity for 'great humanity and decency towards their foes'. Without the help of Dr Sontgerath and Major Schacht – who no doubt risked court-martial or worse for their actions – he would doubtless have been murdered in cold blood, under Hitler's secret Kommando Order.

On reaching the next transit point, a POW hospital in Florence, Hughes found himself surrounded by Allied servicemen, all of whom, like him, were recovering from their injuries. Freed from his parole, he hungered to find any who might share a desire to escape. Yet as this was a POW hospital, almost everyone there seemed to have suffered serious injury. Hughes feared that none would be capable of making an escape attempt, let alone of surviving the harsh conditions thereafter, as they tried to make their way through Italy towards Allied lines.

But not so long after his arrival, Hughes was approached by a British soldier named Bill Taylor, 'a small, bright-eyed and sprightly' private from the Signal Corps. Hailing from Newcastle, Taylor had identified Hughes as having the bearing and attitude of a potential co-conspirator.

'Don't you think we ought to try to escape?' Taylor ventured, in his broad Geordie lilt.

Taylor's determination to make a bid for freedom shone through, but Hughes couldn't fail to notice the arm hanging limply in a sling across his body. When he brought up Taylor's injury, the signaller dismissed it almost nonchalantly. He explained that he had received the wound during his previous escape attempt, when he'd been shot in the arm. Taylor was clearly determined to slip the enemy's clutches, no matter the cost, and he knew of another man who might join them.

'There's an American over there, and he's game,' Taylor ventured, gesturing across the ward.

In short order he introduced Hughes to a burly American Airforce sergeant named Jesse Bradburn. Bradburn had been the sole survivor of a B24 Liberator bomber that had been shot down over Italy. He was in the hospital recovering from the *twenty-nine* separate bullet wounds that he'd suffered during the attack. Though Hughes was concerned for the health of his new associates, what they seemed to lack in physical fitness they seemed to more than make up for in toughness and spirit.

If they wanted to join him, he was happy to have them along. Together they settled upon a plan based upon the limited resources they had to hand: they would tie together all the bedsheets they could commandeer from the ward, constructing a makeshift rope with which to descend from the first-floor window, after which they'd seek to lose themselves amid the throng on the streets of Florence.

But on the day of their proposed breakout, luck was not with them. A platoon of German soldiers arrived, charged to escort the prisoners to Florence station for their onward journey. There, they were loaded into metal-sided carriages, Hughes, Taylor and Bradburn doing their best to stick together. The German guards warned any would-be escapees that 'machine guns were placed pointing down the train', and that all tunnels, bridges and stations en route would be closely guarded. Indeed, Hughes had already spotted the fearsome 'Spandau' machine guns mounted atop the train carriages.

It proved swelteringly hot inside the carriage, with the windows locked and the sick and injured POWs crammed together like cattle. As the train picked up speed, Hughes felt his mood darken. With every mile north, they were moving further away from the Allied front, which made his hopes of escape seem ever more fanciful. As the temperature in the carriage crept higher, some of the most severely wounded were struggling to breathe. Hughes cried out, begging for the windows to be opened to provide some air. Finally, the guards relented and the windows were unlocked. With that, the three would-be escapees spied an opportunity and they waited for their moment.

At 0200 hours on 11 March, as the train pulled out of Modena station into the Emilia-Romagna countryside, they took their chance and jostled into position. Before they could pick up too much speed, Hughes and Bradburn 'pushed Taylor through the window feet first', thrusting him onto the running board, while trying to be careful of his broken arm. Despite his injuries, Taylor – the tough little Geordie – threw himself off the train with barely a backward glance. Next to jump was Bradburn, who hefted his huge frame through the window and disappeared after Taylor.

No machine-gun fire followed the first two jumps, but Hughes had no wish to chance his luck. He crossed to the other side of the carriage and clambered out onto the running board, so avoiding the attention of any guards if they had caught a glimpse of the previous jumpers. With no time to waste and still blind in one eye, he leapt, making his bid for freedom.

Thanks in part to his parachute training, Hughes made a fine landing, his hands and knees taking the brunt of the impact.

He guessed the train must have been moving at around thirty miles per hour, but unlike during SAS parachute training he did not roll to take the impact. Instead, he lay motionless on the earth, waiting for the remainder of the carriages to flash past. Every fibre in his body was tense, anticipating the hail of bullets that would come if the German sentries caught sight of him. He stayed there, unmoving, until the sound of the train faded away. Only then did he pick himself up and extract the shards of gravel that had embedded themselves in his palms and knees. Other than that, he was unharmed.

He set off walking back along the single-line train track, searching for Taylor and Bradburn. He found the pair unhurt and exhilarated by their good luck and daring. Together they deliberated over where they might be and which direction to take, for up until this moment they had not considered what to do once they had broken free. Hughes – who had memorised all he could of Italian geography since first being taken captive – reasoned that they had two feasible options: they could head north towards neutral Switzerland, or south for the Allied lines.

During his weeks in hospital, Hughes had seized every opportunity to listen to the wireless in order to piece together a picture of the current state of the war. He knew that the Operation Shingle landings had been successful, yet that still put the Allied lines some three hundred miles away, and on the far side of the Apennine Mountains. Nevertheless, the three escapees decided to head south. As the Apennines ran down the spine of Italy and were said to be a stronghold of the Italian resistance, Hughes figured they might slip through that terrain aided by the partisans, who were ardently anti-Nazi.

Upon his capture the Germans had searched Hughes for escape aids, but they had failed to discover two special buttons. Almost identical in design to all the others, one was made of steel and the other brass. The steel button was magnetised, and the reverse side was marked with tiny luminous orange dots – one dot representing magnetic north and two dots delineating south. Once removed from the uniform, it could be balanced on top of the brass button, which had a tiny spike affixed to its dome for the purpose. Arranged like that, the steel button would rotate until the single compass dot pointed north. These 'button escape compasses', as they were called, had been invented by Captain Clayton Hutton in the M19 'Escape Factory', and were designed to be all but undetectable to the enemy.

Using this tiny compass, Hughes got their bearings and the trio of fugitives set off south. But by the time the sky began to lighten there was little sign of the Apennines, as they had hoped. Instead, a flat plain stretched to the far horizon. Hughes began to feel nervous. He knew that the longer they spent in the low-lands, the greater their risk of recapture. But then the rising sun revealed that what they had taken to be a bank of cloud in the distance was in fact the form of the Tuscan Apennines, rearing steeply from the plain.

It was now that they took their first major gamble, approaching an isolated farmhouse, for without any civilian clothes they stood little chance of making good their getaway. As luck would have it, the elderly Italian farmer was no friend of the occupying forces. All three 'got civilian clothes and were well fed', Hughes recalled. They spent the remainder of that day resting in one of his outhouses, before setting out once more at dusk, reaching the foothills of the Apennines under cover of darkness.

Spirits stiffened, they began to climb. Ahead lay many days trekking on a southerly bearing, moving across a seemingly endless succession of hills, valleys, rivers and ridges. Shortly, Taylor and Bradburn, whose injuries were worse than Hughes', started to find the going hard. They argued for a return to the flatter terrain of the Bologna–Rimini plain, which they could see running parallel to the mountains, a busy road threading along its length. Hughes was certain it would be thronging with enemy traffic. He was adamant they should stick to the high ground, in the hope of securing help from the partisans, or other escaped POWs they might encounter.

After Italy's capitulation, thousands of POWs had broken out of the prison camps. Hughes felt certain that there would be fellow escapees in the mountains, likewise evading the German occupiers and trying to exfiltrate through the lines. But with such a high number of escaped Allied POWs on the loose, the Germans were sure to be taking greater steps to hunt them down. Either way, for now Hughes' argument – to stick to the high ground – won the day.

Hughes noted the locations they passed through: Medelana, Luminasio, Biserna, River Reno, the 'valley at Vado . . . ridge of Manzuno . . . slopes of Monte Visano'. At almost every juncture they were met with kindness from the Italian peasants – a stable or cow shed to sleep in and whatever food they could afford to share. Hughes' escape report told how on 19 March, their eighth day on the trail, the trio 'spent the evening with the priest at San Valentino'. The churchmen tended to form the backbone of the resistance, and this one was no exception, advising the trio to make for the local 'Partisan Brigade HQ, for clothes and boots'.

As the escapees gained altitude, so the early spring weather proved debilitatingly cold. To make matters worse, the weary travellers were engulfed in 'a heavy snowstorm and we had to make our way through', Hughes reported. They had now covered around sixty miles, the lion's share through rugged and difficult terrain. Such a journey would have been daunting for fit and well-fed travellers. For three malnourished POWs, still plagued by their injuries, it constituted a truly Herculean effort. The thick flurries of snow made for almost unbearable conditions, but still they pressed on. Exposed to the icy blasts in their thin civilian clothing, the fugitives were soon chilled to the bone, and at risk of losing fingers or toes to frostbite.

As they kept pushing deeper into the mountains, the drifts grew thicker and more impassable. In each settlement they encountered, the escapees asked where they might find the partisans. The answer they received was always the same: 'No partisans here. Try the next village.' Hughes suspected that the villagers were deliberately refusing to divulge any information, fearing that the three strangers who had wandered into their midst were in truth Gestapo spies, seeking intelligence to help root out the mountain militia.

Half-starved, close to exhaustion and plagued by their injuries, the escapees were beginning to lose all hope when they reached a remote mountainside tavern. Refusing to be daunted, Hughes made his way inside, where he made the usual enquiries about the location of the nearest partisans. He was met with the usual blank-faced response. Just then the door swung open and a young man strode in. He held himself differently from most of the locals that Hughes and his compatriots had encountered so far. He had a rugged, sun-weathered countenance and carried an old rifle slung over one shoulder, the ammunition for which crisscrossed his body in leather bandoliers.

He was followed by a group of similarly attired men. The new arrivals noticed the three strangers at once, and gathered around them, eyeing them with a suspicion bordering on hostility. Hughes had learned a little of the Italian language while stationed in Malta, and he spoke a few words to the man he guessed had to be their leader. That figure stared back for a long moment, before barking out a single inquiry: '*Inglese?*'

'*Sì!* Yes, *Inglese!* English!' Hughes gushed.

He felt a flood of relief, as the mystery gunmen seemed to visibly relax a little. Both groups began talking now, each trying to explain who they were and how they came to be there. As Hughes had desperately hoped, these were members of the elusive Italian resistance. They explained that while they could be of little help – they were heading north, the opposite direction to the escapees' direction of travel – Hughes and his fellows should make for the nearby settlement of Strabatenza. There they would find a partisan leader who could offer every assistance.

Overcome with relief, and fired by a renewed sense of enthusiasm, the three set out for Strabatenza the following morning. By midday they had located the partisan headquarters, which turned out to be a smattering of sturdy-looking houses clustered around a large, elegant church. On arrival they were introduced to the partisan chief, a man whose *nom de guerre* was 'Libero', meaning 'Free' in Italian. After he had double-checked their story, they were welcomed into the fold. Though it appeared unassuming enough, the remote mountain village of Strabatenza turned out to be the nerve centre for the Italian resistance across a vast swathe of the surrounding terrain.

Taylor and Bradburn were taken to the makeshift hospital. The eleven-day march had been terribly punishing on their battle-worn bodies. They had covered some eighty miles as the crow flies, from the point where they'd jumped from the train, but taking into account their circuitous route it was more likely double that distance. As for Hughes, he was immediately put to work, uti-lising his specialist skills to aid the resistance effort. Libero and his men were expecting a resupply of weaponry and ammunition, orchestrated by the Special Operations Executive, better known as Churchill's 'Ministry for Ungentlemanly Warfare'.

Charged with arming resistance forces across Nazi-occupied Europe, SOE were due to make an arms-drop shortly, and Libero wanted Hughes to identify a suitable drop zone to receive the weapons and ammo. Hughes did as he had been asked, and once the drop zone had been selected, with little explanation Libero led Hughes down the mountainside, until they came to a small hamlet straddling a mountain stream. There, Hughes was intro-duced to a seemingly frail-looking elderly gentleman – 'short in stature, thin and wiry' – seated behind a farmhouse table and sipping a glass of wine.

'Good morning,' the mystery figure remarked, in the distinc-tive clipped tones of a senior British Army officer. 'Won't you sit down and join me?'

With 'a disarming air of friendliness and candour', the stranger introduced himself as Brigadier Douglas Arnold 'Pip' Stirling. Though this man was no direct relation to David Stirling, of SAS fame, Hughes certainly knew his name and reputation. He could barely believe that this pinched and tired-looking figure could be the same Brigadier Stirling who had soldiered with distinction since the outbreak of the war, before finally being captured. In the spring of 1940 Stirling had commanded a light cavalry regiment, the 13th/18th Royal Hussars, part of the British Expeditionary Force. Stirling and his men had fought a spirited rearguard action through Belgium, before being evacuated from Dunkirk.

During that time, Pip Stirling had earned a reputation as a brave and indomitable leader who put great trust in his men. At the height of the battle for France, he had remarked, 'I felt certain that whatever might happen, I had human material that would give a good account of itself under any circumstances.' In return his men trusted him absolutely, even after experiencing the nightmare of Dunkirk. Somehow, even under those hellish evacuation conditions, with 'shells and bombs bursting thick and fast', Pip Stirling's force had remained 'a unit with its discipline and morale unimpaired'.

Finally, Brigadier Stirling had been captured in 1941 while commanding the 7th Armoured Division during the defence of the besieged port of Tobruk. Hughes knew only too well the story of that ill-fated defensive effort, for the SAS's earliest raids had been devised to sabotage enemy airfields in the region, to help relieve pressure on Tobruk. It seemed portentous that these two men had found each other months later, in a mountain strong-hold of the Italian resistance, both now fugitives from the enemy.

Since his capture, Stirling had been held at various Italian POW camps, and his time in captivity had clearly been hard on him. That, followed by the months spent hidden in the moun-tains, had aged him well beyond his years: though his vibrant blue eyes still sparkled with boyish charm, his hair had turned entirely white.

He explained how, when the armistice had been signed between the Allies and the Italians, he had joined a group of high-ranking officers who were determined not to allow themselves to be recaptured. They had headed into the Apennines, seeking sanctuary with the resistance. Hughes listened with amazement as he revealed which other senior Allied commanders were concealed among the mountainside villages.

There were four generals, an air vice-marshal, an English lord and an American consul, Hughes noted, plus a number of other VIPs, all of whom were 'awaiting the day of their deliverance'.

According to Stirling, that day was close at hand now. Recently, they had been contacted by A-Force, a clandestine Allied unit formed in August 1943, dedicated to bringing Allied escapees out of Italy. With a network of helpers inserted behind enemy lines and furnished with cash and equipment, A-Force had found itself frantically busy bringing escapees home. Official War Office documentation noted that of the estimated 50,000 Allied POWs who had slipped the enemy's clutches in Italy, some 2,000 had exfiltrated to the Allied lines, and '2,000 more had reached Switzerland', but that left tens of thousands still at large.

According to Stirling, the A-Force agents had already smuggled a number of his party south, and arrangements were underway for the imminent departure of the remainder. Hughes had arrived at just the right moment, for they were about to make their bid for freedom, and it stood to reason that he should join them. The first stage of the escape would involve assuming 'Italian' identities, using counterfeit papers provided by SOE and smuggled to Stirling and his fellows using a back channel at the Vatican. Arrangements would need to be made to procure a 'remarkably convincing identity card' for Hughes, the newest member of their party. Then they would split into smaller groups in order to move less conspicuously, and head for a rendezvous point on the coast some 150 miles to the south-east. There, A-Force had arranged that a Royal Navy Motor Torpedo Boat would be waiting to speed them back to friendly lines.

The march south would be tough, Stirling explained, as many of the top brass were not in the best of health. Like him, they had suffered at the hands of their captors. Nevertheless, these men were still some of Britain's most highly decorated and experienced military commanders, and Hughes felt fortunate to have fallen into step with such men as Stirling and his ilk. Though he held the rank of a brigadier and Hughes was only a lieutenant, in due course the two were to become 'very close friends'.

That seemingly unlikely friendship embodied one of the SAS's founding principles – a disregard for rigid adherence to rank. Rather than those who would blindly follow orders, the regiment sought individuals who could think for themselves and operate outside the strict military hierarchy, with a special status all of their own. With his innate charm and keen, tactical mind, Hughes had flourished in such an environment, and he and Brigadier Pip Stirling would develop a lasting trust and companionship.

After long deliberation, Hughes decided not to tell his two fellow escapees, Taylor and Bradburn, of the A-Force plan. He agonised over the decision. Arguably, they were still too badly injured to manage the long trek to the coast, but in truth, he also had far less altruistic motives for leaving them. 'The truth is . . . we had grown tired of each other's company,' Hughes would remark. He also felt that Taylor and Bradburn would stand better chances when fully recovered, and in any case, he was fully occupied with helping arrange for the VIPs' mass escape attempt.

While Hughes worried that he did not 'come out of this in a very good light' – deserting his fellow escapees – he knew well the SAS had never indulged much sentimentality when forced to leave comrades behind. Theirs was a wholly pragmatic approach driven by necessity. 'You can't sit around thinking about casualties,' remarked Reg Seekings, one of the SAS's founding members. Losing men was a risk you had to accept as a member of such an elite fighting force, and was only as it should be.

On 30 March 1944, Hughes, Brigadier Stirling and a handful of other Allied escapees met the A-Force agent who would act as their guide. War Office reports promised that all A-Force operatives would be 'handpicked and as far as we can make certain . . . reliable'. Hughes and Stirling felt confident that their A-Force agent could be trusted. Indeed, he was putting his own life and liberty on the line by facilitating their rescue.

Together with their A-Force guide, Hughes and his newfound escape party set off moving south through the Apennine Mountains. Though they were leaving the comparative safety of the partisans' stronghold, Hughes felt reasonably optimistic: 'I had congenial companions . . . reliable guides to show me the way,' plus the weather was improving. Yet from the off, the party was plagued by ill fortune. The mild, spring conditions rapidly gave way to unseasonable snow flurries, which slowed the progress of the elderly officers. Without the shelter offered by Italian farmsteads along the way, they were sure to have perished. Even so, time was growing short to make it to the coastal rendezvous, and behind them the enemy was closing in.

As they pushed on through the mountains, they received word from Strabatenza that the Germans had somehow got wind of the planned SOE drop of weaponry – the one that Hughes had helped prepare. German patrols had begun combing the area, searching for the drop zone, determined to crush the rebels once and for all. If any partisans had been captured and forced to talk, the enemy were sure to be hot on the heels of the escaping British officers.

More bad news reached the fugitives, which Hughes found particularly disheartening. German forces 'had taken the village' – Strabatenza – seizing the partisans' makeshift hospital and 'killing those who remained'. Taylor and Bradburn had almost certainly been shot or, if not, recaptured by the enemy. Hughes felt consumed by guilt for leaving them, and to add to his torment he had begun to suffer from a severe fever. Even so, there was little he could do but press on, blanking his mind to the worry and the growing delirium.

Over the next few days he dragged himself along, his world reduced to an agonising haze of undecipherable shapes and sounds. They climbed towards the summit of Monte Nerone, a hulking limestone edifice over 5,000 feet high that lay in their path. Just before they reached the summit, Hughes' fever broke, which lifted his spirits a little. It was a feeling that was intensified when he crested the peak and saw what lay before them: in the near distance was the ancient town of Cagli, the white stucco buildings and terracotta roofs glittering in the sun. Beyond that a plain stretched towards Italy's eastern coastline, where their rendezvous with the Royal Navy ship surely beckoned.

Official advice from the A-Force planners had noted that 'all reports show it is NOT dangerous for them' – the party of POWs – 'as long as they keep moving and do not spend more than one night in the same place'. The key to escape lay in constantly keeping on the move. But barely had they begun to descend the mountain path when they were met by a *poliziotto* – an Italian policeman – coming the other way and armed with a mean-looking carbine. Appearing instantly suspicious, he demanded the party present their identity papers.

Brigadier Stirling gathered Hughes' and the others' forged documents and handed them over. After what felt like a lifetime, the policeman passed the documents back with a few muttered words, before continuing on his way. Once the man was out of earshot, Stirling told Hughes what the *poliziotto* had said.

'He said it was painfully obvious that we were British escapees,' Stirling explained, seeming utterly unperturbed that their cover story had proved so thin. Fortunately, the policeman's loyalties rested with the mountain partisans, and not with 'the Fascists . . . or the Germans . . . We were lucky this time,' noted Hughes.

After a dash across the lowlands, Hughes, Stirling and their party made it to the rendezvous on 14 April 1944, two weeks after they had set out. They gathered near the coastal village of Torre di Palme, a resistance stronghold lying in the Tenna Valley, situated some eighty miles north of the Allied frontline. But things seemed fraught with danger. The party of escapees was split up and kept constantly on the move by their A-Force minders, in an effort to prevent them all from being captured.

Stirling and Hughes fell under the guidance of another A-Force agent, codenamed 'Leo', who brought news of their planned rendezvous. Apparently, the Royal Naval ship would be positioned at the mouth of the River Tenna that very night. Come dusk they hurried to the designated spot, a broad river estuary, and settled down to wait, the smell of sea foam – and freedom – heady in their nostrils. Sure enough, they detected the rumble of a ship's engines echoing across the dark waters. They began to flash their torch in that direction, using the prearranged signal pattern, but the response they received in return made little sense: it was not the combination they had been expecting.

Whoever was crewing that mystery craft, it did not appear to be any Royal Navy rescue party. With sinking spirits, they heard the rhythmic throb of the ship's engine fade into nothing, as the vessel continued on its course. Agent Leo reported later that the 'motor boat' was 'probably German', which explained why it had answered their signal in a way that made no sense at the time. That was how close Hughes, Stirling and the others had come to getting recaptured.

They returned to the beach on the following two evenings, yet 'no boats appeared', agent Leo noted. In fact, the repeated failures were due to a miscommunication between A-Force, the Royal Navy and SOE, all of whom were trying to coordinate the pick up of the stranded escapees. While the A-Force agents persisted in trying to organise a successful rescue, by 3 May – more than two weeks after their initial rendezvous had been scheduled – the escapees were beginning to lose hope.

With 'the weather conditions becoming worse' and the 'loss of the April dark moon period' – both essential prerequisites for a successful Royal Naval operation – Leo and the other agents decided 'to change our plans and try to find some sailing boats'. That way, the escapees could make their way to Allied lines under their own steam. Accordingly, a pair of thirty-foot-long local craft, equipped with no engines but with oars, were acquired from a family in nearby Torre di Palme.

The escape party was split between the two vessels. Hughes and Stirling were to go in agent Leo's boat, together with eight other escapees. They were to be accompanied by two experienced Italian fishermen, to whom 'a reward would be paid for each person safely landed' in Allied territory. The second vessel would carry the remaining escapees, plus another A-Force agent and a pair of local seamen. It was decided by A-Force that both groups should cast off on the first night that offered favourable weather conditions.

It was the night of 9 May – almost four months since Hughes had first parachuted into Italy – when his party headed for the beach and their breakout. They were laden with the boat's mast, oars and sail, a barrel of fresh drinking water, a large white sheet upon which they had daubed the letters 'POW', plus 'one white rabbit to bring good luck'. Rabbits are often reputed to bring bad luck for seafaring journeys, but as Stirling had explained, while he had been interned at Campo PG 12 he 'was given the task of looking after the camp's rabbits', which were one of the POWs' 'main sources of food' – hence the rabbit becoming a symbol of good luck.

As Hughes and his fellow escapees neared the beach, their anxiety levels mounted. In addition to the danger of the coming voyage, the sound of their heavily laden footfalls crunching upon the stones seemed deafening. Hughes feared the noise would echo along the shoreline, broadcasting their escape attempt to every German sentry for miles around.

Having made it to the boat seemingly undetected, they raised the mast and sail under the whispered instructions of their two fishermen guides. At 2300 hours, with supplies and rabbit safely aboard, they lifted the heavy craft, swung her around in an arc so she was prow-on to the waves and began walking her towards the water. Hughes noted that while the sea was calm, 'a heavy swell threw breakers on the beach'. The night was cold and the men of the escape party were keen to avoid getting soaked, for that would mean long hours in wet clothes in the biting sea wind.

Unfortunately, they leapt aboard too soon and the prow of the boat, caught in the breakers, swung around, leaving her wallowing in the shallows and lying parallel to the beach. Before the crew could steer her seaward again, a wave broke over them, swamping the vessel and filling her with water. Every man jumped out and began hauling the boat into deeper water. When they were out of their depth and could walk no more, they dragged their soaking bodies aboard, set the oars in the rowlocks and heaved for the open sea.

By the time they had drawn away from the pull of the waves and began to drift south on the tide, all were soaked to the skin and ready to collapse with exertion. But there was no time to rest or recuperate. Instead of floating buoyantly on the waves, the water level inside the boast was almost 'as high as that of the sea outside'. It looked as if the hull wasn't watertight. If they couldn't bail her out the flooded craft would sink.

The escapees began jettisoning anything they could – including the precious barrel of water – and bailing frantically with whatever came to hand, mostly their hats. With the boat in such a perilous state, at first they tried to stick relatively close to the shoreline, so they could swim to the beach should they need to. But with sunrise, they would be visible to any German guard posts. That was too much to risk. So they hoisted the sail and headed further out to sea, each man silently choosing death by drowning over recapture by the enemy.

When they were 'about 50 miles from the coast', they turned the boat to starboard and set a course south towards freedom. After a few hours they were able to cease bailing. The overlapping wooden planks of the hull had swollen with the seawater and were now mostly watertight. A brisk breeze filled their solitary sail and they began to progress at a tidy pace over the choppy water. They huddled together – thirteen men and one rabbit – freezing and soaked, yet praying that their luck would hold and hopeful for what the morning might bring.

Some hours before dawn Hughes and party were jolted out of a frozen semi-slumber by the sudden violent crack of splintering wood. The pressure of wind in the sail had proven too much for the old mast. It had broken in half, sending their primary means of propulsion tumbling overboard. Casting it aside, they took up the oars, summoning what remaining strength they had and pulling as hard as they could for salvation.

With the horizon to the east beginning to brighten, the strengthening light revealed that the current had carried them back towards the coastline. Among the nearest peaks and foothills they could make out flashes of gunfire, while the crackle of shots echoed across the water. There seemed to be fighting underway, but surely that wasn't possible, Hughes reasoned, for the frontline lay some eighty nautical miles from their point of departure. Surely, they couldn't have sailed that far in the one night.

Before departing Torre di Palme, Agent Leo had been given a sketch of the eastern Italian coastline to help aid their navigation. It showed the mountain ranges as seen from the sea. He and Hughes consulted it and it appeared to confirm that they were abreast of the frontlines. The peak they could see was unmistakable – it was the Gran Sasso d'Italia, the highest point in the Apennines, rising dramatically from the Abruzzo region. It was there that the Allies were locked in fierce combat with the Germans manning their well-prepared positions along the

Gustav Line. Somehow, wind, tide and sheer human grunt – oar-power – had combined to transport the escapees to the very fringes of enemy-occupied territory.

Hughes and crew heard the distinctive rumble of an aircraft high in the heavens. Weary limbs scrabbled to unfurl their POW signal sheet. As they pulled it taut, Hughes hoped the pilot was friendly and that he would spot the message and radio their location to Allied headquarters, or at the very least refrain from attacking their boat. Yet the pilot progressed on his way without seeming to notice them at all.

With the sun now fully up, Hughes and crew were parched from the lack of drinking water. Then they spotted a 'little fishing fleet' coming out from the shore. The escapees pulled on their oars with renewed vigour, for this didn't have the appearance of any hostile force. By 1600 hrs on 10 May they felt the reassuring crunch of their boat's prow making contact with the white sand of a beach, as local fishermen guided them in. They made landfall on a 'stretch of friendly beach' at San Vito Chietino, a coastal village just six miles south of the strategic port of Ortona, which had been wrested from enemy control in December the previous year. The second boat soon followed them into the shore, and all the escapees were greeted by members of the British Army and given mugs of hot, sweet tea.

Hughes' escape had taken him over sixteen weeks, during which time his independent mind, his stamina and his ability to build alliances across nationality, rank and even fiercely held loyalties had won him safe return. He went on to receive the Military Cross and bar, first for his heroic actions on Operation Pomegranate, the two-man raid on the enemy airbase, and second for his die-hard escape and evasion. His citation recorded how

'Hughes displayed throughout high courage, determination and devotion to duty.' Typically, he felt somewhat embarrassed by such recognition. 'I was grossly over decorated,' he would remark later.

After a brief spell at an officer's rest camp set a few miles south-east of Naples, Hughes returned to England, where he was able to rejoin 2SAS. Although his partial loss of sight meant he would never again see action, he became a key figure in recruitment and command, first as a Regimental Training Officer, and then as Brigade Major for the entire 2SAS Squadron. Once the war had ended he returned to Liverpool to complete his studies and went on to become one of that city's most celebrated architects.

Shortly after the war, Hughes learned with deep regret that his friend and saviour, Dr Hansgunger Sontgerath, had been denounced while in the process of trying to organise a party of his men to surrender to the Allies, and had been executed. However, his other German friend and champion, Lieutenant Gerhard Schacht, survived the war. Schacht went on to serve in the post-war German Army, when Britain and Germany were no longer enemies. As for Jesse Bradburn and Bill Taylor, whom Hughes had assumed had been killed during the German sweep of the mountains, evidence suggests that they did in fact survive the war.

As with all Allied escapees, Hughes underwent a full debriefing once in friendly hands. His chilling account of Hitler's Kommando Order – that all captured Allied Special Forces and Commandos should be given no quarter and shot out of hand – was dismissed at his first debriefing as being nothing more than a manipulative Gestapo officer's interrogation technique. It was a hollow threat, in other words. But once he was returned to 2SAS, its long-serving and brilliant intelligence officer, Major Eric 'Bill' Barkworth, didn't take Hughes' account so lightly.

As the SAS were well aware, a shocking number of their own had been lost in action, presumed captured – only never to be heard of again. As far as Barkworth could tell, they had simply disappeared. He didn't doubt that Hughes' testimony was true, and that the missing SAS men had been tortured by the Gestapo and murdered in cold blood, against all the rules of war. Barkworth produced a memorandum entitled 'The Hughes Report' outlining all of this, which was presented to their parent headquarters at 1 Airborne Corps.

Whispers and rumours of the Kommando Order would haunt SAS operations, as the theatre of war transformed once more. Thanks in part to the actions of Hughes and Widdrington, the invasion at Anzio proved the tipping point the Allies had needed to wrest Rome from Nazi control. In due course, the rest of Italy was liberated. Next, the Allies turned their attention north and west, to German-occupied France, where the SAS would once again be in the vanguard. But shadowy reports of brutal executions would dog the regiment's operations, as more and more of their number went missing.

It was to avoid just such a fate that our next great escapee would pull off one of the most daring feats in Special Forces history.

Great Escape Seven

ACROSS ENEMY LINES

While Hitler ordered his commanders to hold the frontlines in France at all costs, Allied forces pushed resolutely onwards from the Normandy beachheads, and the SAS continued to wreak havoc behind the lines. At the same time, the RAF – its ranks swelled with airman brought in from across the Commonwealth – waged a mighty bombing campaign, as did the USAAF. Day and night the skies were darkened by the massed silhouettes of warplanes hitting enemy targets across what remained of occupied France, or flying over Germany itself on raids designed to batter the Third Reich into submission. One of those many thousands of brave Allied bomber crew was twenty-seven-year-old Canadian flying officer Ronald Lewis 'Lew' Fiddick.

On the night of 28 July 1944, Fiddick lay on his belly in the forward nose blister of Lancaster L-7576, bound for Germany. All around him the dark skies were thick with similar-looking Avro Lancasters, the iconic British heavy bomber designed for long-range night raids. The massed ranks of warplanes thundered onwards towards the German frontier, which was soon visible to Fiddick in the eerie glow of a low, bright moon. Their target for tonight was the German city of Stuttgart, situated in the south-west of the country, sixty miles or so on the far side of the border.

A total of 1,142 bombers had left RAF bases across Britain that night, to hit targets the length and breadth of Germany. Their aim was to cause maximum damage to Nazi Germany's infrastructure, thereby preventing the enemy from rushing reinforcements into France and providing Allied land forces the best possible chance of wresting the whole nation from Nazi control. The crew of Lancaster L-7576 were tasked to drop their deadly cargo over Stuttgart's main rail hub.

It had been a late decision to include L-7576, a first-generation Lancaster nicknamed 'K for King', on tonight's mission. K for King had completed ninety-eight sorties and was the oldest aircraft on the squadron's airbase. As the veteran Lancaster – the 'King' of 622 Squadron – tonight would be her ninety-ninth combat flight, a gargantuan achievement considering that such aircraft were typically either decommissioned or lost long before that. Fiddick recalled that 'the wing commander wanted to fly the one hundredth trip', keen for the prestige this 'retirement flight' would bring the squadron, for it was sure to feature on the newsreels. The choice had been made to include the venerable warplane on tonight's raid only because a brand-new Lancaster meant for Fiddick and crew had suffered engine trouble and been grounded.

Fiddick and his six fellow crew members had taken off from RAF Mildenhall at 2200 hours, joining 496 other aircraft at their rallying point over the south of England. From an early age Fiddick had been fascinated by aeroplanes, remembering of his youth that whenever he saw aircraft in the sky, 'I did have a desire to fly.' Yet as the son of a Canadian farmer from the small village of Cedar, on Vancouver Island, and with 'no money to do very much', his hopes of becoming a pilot were limited. That changed with the outbreak of war, when the Royal Canadian Air Force (RCAF) began calling up young men to train as aircrew. Fiddick undertook his flight training in Canada, and soon after qualifying had crossed the Atlantic to the UK. There he underwent a course in 'bomb-aiming' so that he would have the versatility to switch between roles – pilot and bomb-aimer – depending on wherever he could be of most of use. To be 'doing something useful' was Fiddick's primary motivation in the war.

On that 28 July flight he was acting as the bomb-aimer, having the responsibility of ensuring the aircraft's munitions hit their intended target. That was no small task given all the challenges of such a mission, not least of which was the air turbulence caused by so many planes in the sky all heading for the same destination. As the bomb-aimer, he was responsible for spotting the 'primary visual markers' of 'mixed red and green' signal flares, laid out by the pathfinder aircraft which were flying ahead of the main fleet of bombers. Once spotted, he would communicate their positions to his two fellow RCAF officers, seated above him in the cockpit – twenty-year-old pilot Harold Sherman Peabody and twenty-two-year-old navigator James Harrington Doe.

They were all so young, but none gave much thought to that at the time: there was a war to be fought, after all. Fiddick, Peabody and Doe possessed strong bonds of friendship forged in the fires of combat. They had been flying together and billeted in the same hut since February that year, and were based at RAF 622 Squadron's Mildenhall, Suffolk, aerodrome. Doe's diary from the time confirmed how intense the combat sorties had been, but Fiddick also recalled that between missions, they would spend time together in the Suffolk pubs: 'no heavy drinking – just friendly pub-crawling.'

Together with Peabody and Doe in the Lancaster's cockpit were RAF flight engineer George J. Wishart and radio operator Sergeant Arthur Payton. Flight Sergeant Richard Proulx – another Canadian – manned the aircraft's mid-upper gun-turret, boasting formidable Browning 7.62mm machine guns, while Sergeant Percy Buckley – a Brit, and at eighteen, the youngest of the crew – manned the rear turret, defending the Lancaster from an assault from that direction.

Doe had navigated them due south over the English Channel, until they crossed the coast at Le Havre, whereupon they turned south-eastwards, plotting a course towards Stuttgart. As they neared the town of Orléans and the River Loire in north-central France, they had come under attack from the first enemy warplanes. 'Fighters were active in the moonlight,' the official RAF report noted, and before long the formation came under sustained fire.

A twin-engine Junkers Ju 88 dual-purpose fighter-bomber sent a burst of deadly tracer fire slicing into the lead Lancaster's tail section, chunks of shattered debris spiralling backwards in the damaged aircraft's slipstream. The defiant Lancaster's crew managed to hit back at the Ju 88, bursts of machine-gun fire sending it plummeting out of the sky, after which the heavy bomber, though severely damaged, was able to turn for home.

Despite the ever-present danger, Fiddick kept his mind clear and his eyes fixed on the terrain to his front. 'You couldn't afford to be scared up there – you just had to be alert,' he recalled. Before long, they were passing over the dense forests, dark peaks and tight, winding valleys of the Vosges Mountains, which delineated the long-contested border between France and Germany. Soon they would be starting their approach to Stuttgart, if all went well. But at 0130 hours on 29 July, K for King herself became the target.

'Enemy aircraft – corkscrew starboard!' Buckley, the rear gunner, yelled as he spotted a German plane in pursuit.

It was another Junkers Ju 88, part of *Nachtjagdgeschwader-6* – a Luftwaffe night-fighter squadron based near Stuttgart. Peabody immediately banked to forty-five degrees, putting the Lancaster into a right-hand, diving corkscrew turn, the standard manoeuvre taught to Lancaster pilots in order to evade night fighters. 'This meant you threw the airplane over on its side and lost a lot of height immediately to avoid being hit by bullets from the fighter plane and then you pull out and come back up,' Fiddick recalled.

Theoretically, the speed the Lancaster gained in the dive would propel it out of the line of enemy fire. At first it seemed to work, L-7576 seeming to shake-off the pursuing aircraft. But the German fighter pilots had grown familiar with the Lancaster's standard evasive manoeuvre, knowing that at the bottom of the dive the British bomber would have to sacrifice speed in order to gain height and rejoin the other aircraft. At the very point when L-7576's airspeed had dropped and she was almost motionless in the air, the waiting German pilot pounced, squeezing off a long burst of tracer fire, which tore into the rear end of the bomber's fuselage. Fiddick felt the aircraft shudder, as repeated bursts ripped through the plane.

'We did a corkscrew and came back up, and almost immediately as we levelled off we were hit,' Fiddick remarked. 'I still remember the bullets hitting the airplane – just a steady stream.'

The German gunner had found his mark, the bullets shooting away 'all the tail controls, so there was no control of the airplane anymore', Fiddick recalled. Fearing that those towards the rear must have been killed – seemingly confirmed, when no answer came from the rear and upper gunners, Buckley and Proulx – Peabody fought to keep the stricken warplane in the air. But as further bursts tore into them, the surviving crew realised they had no choice – they would have to bail out.

Extricating himself from the cramped forward turret, Fiddick was joined in the nose section by Flight Lieutenant Wishart, who had clambered down from above. They needed to jump before Peabody lost control of the aircraft, or they would lose any chance of getting out at all. Wishart lifted the release handle of the escape hatch, which tumbled away into the night. A freezing wind tore through the gaping aperture at their feet, as Wishart pushed himself through the opening and was gone, whisked away into the howling darkness.

Fiddick moved into position to follow, yet he just couldn't bring himself to jump. Loyalty and friendship trumped his desire to save himself. Turning away from the hatch, he crawled up into the cockpit, to join his friend above. That way, he figured he could at least help Peabody free himself from the notoriously tight pilot's seat when he activated the auto-pilot, which meant they might both stand a change of getting out alive. Fiddick clambered into the seat beside Peabody, trying to help as he fought to keep the dying warplane airborne.

'I held the airplane steady as long as I could,' Fiddick remarked of this desperate moment, as the stricken Lancaster juddered and shook horribly. But eventually the damage proved too much. There was a massive jolt to the aircraft, as he and Peabody lost all control. From his seat, he was 'more or less thrown into the nose compartment and out through the escape hatch', Fiddick recalled.

He had had zero time to strap himself in, and he'd been catapulted out of the cockpit, the arc of his fall taking him through the escape hatch that Wishart had left hanging open. 'The next thing I knew I was falling through the air,' Fiddick recalled.

Recovering his senses, he triggered his 'chute, which snapped into shape above him, capturing the air with a crack like a ship's mainsail. He gazed around. Though the night was brightly lit by the moon, he could see no sign of the other crew members, Peabody included. He figured they must have been 'scattered to the four winds'.

As he drifted towards earth Fiddick reckoned he was coming down in the far north-east of occupied France, in what looked like the Vosges Mountains. France and Germany had been battling over this rugged terrain for centuries, and populations of neighbouring valleys tended to be staunchly loyal to one side or the other. Those of the western slopes generally harboured French loyalties, those of the eastern valleys had German sympathies. If he made it safely to the ground, Fiddick might either be welcomed by friendly Maquis – French resistance fighters – or handed over to the enemy by villagers loyal to the Fatherland.

As luck would have it, he came down into an isolated glade of saplings, which bowed under his weight. 'I landed in a forest about 8 miles SE of Cirey-Sur-Vezouse [sic],' Fiddick's escape report noted, Cirey-sur-Vezouze being a village in the central Vosges region. 'I remember breaking branches off trees as I fell, but I went right to the ground.'

Fiddick's survival instincts kicked in right away as he set to work concealing his presence, for there was a good chance that he had been spotted bailing out. 'I buried my parachute and my vest,' he explained. That vital task done, he simply sat on his buried parachute for the remainder of the night hours, stunned by the rapid series of events that had deposited him alone and unarmed in the depths of remote and hostile territory. As he well knew, the nearest Allied positions were several hundred miles away across occupied France.

'It was the next day when I decided I'd better do something about getting myself out of this mess,' Fiddick recalled, 'so I got up and I started to walk.' It was only as he began to move that he became aware that one of his knees had been injured and that he had lost his boots. He figured they had either been ripped off as he had tumbled out of the aircraft, or torn away with the shock of his parachute opening.

Getting on the move as best he could with no footwear, and hampered by his injury, Fiddick found his bearings using his escape compass. He set a course back along the same direction as the Lancaster had flown in on and began his barefoot march. The journey through the thick forests felt never-ending, especially as he tripped and stumbled painfully. But Fiddick had been a woodsman back in his native Canada, and he knew how to drink from the streams that cascaded through the terrain, to keep himself going. While the human body can do without food for days, it cannot last for long without water.

Finally, he limped into the outskirts of a village. Of course, he had no way of knowing exactly where he was or whether the inhabitants were loyal to the French or the German cause. Should he simply declare his presence and risk capture? Or stay hidden and try to formulate a plan?

In his escape report, Fiddick described how he 'lay up outside the village for two days', keeping to a copse of trees in the middle of a field, from where he had a clear view of the comings and goings. He was keeping a close eye, trying to work out which houses any German troops might be paying attention to and those 'which they didn't bother with'. That way, he hoped to work out the best of the villagers 'with which to make contact'.

At mid-afternoon on his second day in hiding, Fiddick's hand was forced, when 'a young chap about 10 years old brought a couple of cows into the field'. The youth, spotting the mystery watcher in his battered uniform, promptly turned tail and fled. Fiddick knew it was only a matter of time before the child told someone what he had seen, so he approached a nearby farmstead and slipped into the loft of a barn, crawling deep into the hay.

'Now all I had to hope for was that [the farmer] didn't hit me with the pitch fork,' Fiddick remarked. With that thought in the back of his mind he fell into an exhausted sleep.

He awoke the next day to the sound of life all around him. Dragging his fatigued body across the hay bales, he managed to position himself where he could observe the comings and goings. But though he was well hidden, Fiddick was becoming increasingly weak from hunger and thirst. He wondered whether he should simply knock at the nearest house and seek assistance.

Eventually, his hand was forced. The villagers had roused the Maquis as soon as the mystery man in uniform had been spotted. A patrol led by one Raymond Freismuth tracked Fiddick to his hayloft hideout. Freismuth made it clear to the wounded and exhausted Canadian how close he had come to falling into the clutches of the enemy. Clearly visible from the hideout, one of the nearby buildings was actually a Gestapo outpost, for they were doing all they could to counter Maquis activity in the region. Had Fiddick approached that place, the game would have been well and truly up.

Freismuth took the fugitive to the nearby farmhouse, which turned out to be occupied by a man called Leonard Barassi. Italian by birth, Barassi had moved to France and taken French citizenship, and he was a stalwart of the resistance. Barassi took Fiddick in, hid him and fed him – which was fortunate, for the downed Canadian airman was famished. As luck would have it, there was a strong Resistance spirit throughout the village, which Fiddick learned was called Cirey-sur-Vezouze.

Fiddick would stay with Barassi for several days, as the locals checked out his bona fides. They fetched a village priest, Father Rohr, who was clearly there to determine whether Fiddick was the genuine article or not. Father Rohr had spent thirty years living in Fraser Valley, a point on mainland Canada lying just across the sea from Fiddick's home, on Vancouver Island. This strange coincidence proved a streak of good fortune for Fiddick, for the priest was able to probe the airman's story with the kind of questions only a man familiar with the area would be able to answer.

With his identity thus verified, Fiddick was relieved of his RCAF uniform and given some civilian clothes. Thus attired, he stood more chance of being able to pass as a local, while being shepherded between cellars, attics and other places of hiding. But changing out of uniform was a decidedly risky move, Fiddick recalled, for 'it would have been unhealthy for me had I been picked up.' Any Allied serviceman caught in civilian clothes behind the lines would be seen as a spy or saboteur. But likewise, this was the only way to stand any chance of evading capture.

Fiddick marvelled at the courage and spirit of the villagers of Cirey-sur-Vezouze. He knew all too well the risks they took in concealing him, his presence there being a veritable time bomb. An official SAS report from the time described how, if the Germans had any suspicions that French civilians might be helping downed Allied airmen or parachutists, 'they razed the house to the ground and shot the occupants'. Regardless, the villagers risked their lives to keep Fiddick safe, providing medical attention for his injured knee and feeding him up so he might regain his strength.

The locals here were known as 'Les Loups' – The Wolves. Fiddick soon got to appreciate why: they were fierce, loyal and fearless, plus they lived off the mountain and acted as a pack. Step by step, Les Loups arranged to smuggle Fiddick towards the headquarters of the local Maquis, concealed at a secret location deep in the mountains to the south of Cirey-sur-Vezouze. Unlike Les Loups, who had regular 'day-jobs' alongside their secret resistance work, the Vosges Maquis were mostly full-time partisans. They were dedicated to resisting the Germans and fighting the Milice, the militia of French Fascists who were in league with the Nazi occupiers.

'On the afternoon of 4 Aug a member of the Maquis came and took me to a Maquis camp in the forest,' Fiddick would go on to write in his escape report. That man, René Ricatte, was the local Maquis leader, and he turned out to be daring and resourceful. Ricatte arranged for a pair of French gendarmes, resplendent in their police uniforms, to convey Fiddick towards La Scierie de la Turbine, a sawmill set deep in the woods. They did so on their police motorcycles, as if Fiddick were under some kind of official escort.

At the sawmill, Fiddick was handed over to another group of Maquis, masquerading as French woodsmen. From there they continued on foot, making for the Maquis headquarters, set high in the mountains at the Col des Harengs. But en route they stumbled into a German patrol. Fiddick had no idea what he should do, fearing that dressed as he was, if taken captive he would be executed. But masquerading as French countryfolk, Fiddick and his escorts managed to walk right past the enemy sentries. And so, with enormous relief, they 'headed out into the hills'.

Reaching the Maquis headquarters, Fiddick finally found himself at a place of relative safety. But for the spirited and brave role that he had played within the resistance of Cirey-sur-Vezouze, including sheltering a fugitive Allied airman, Leonard Barassi was to pay the ultimate price. Along with two other resistance members, Andrew Legendre and Roger Roualin, Barassi would be rounded up by the Gestapo and shot on 11 September 1944, not far from the village where he had granted a desperate Lou Fiddick refuge.

Further bad fortune lay ahead, or at least for Fiddick's Lancaster crewmates.

The Canadian pilot had hoped that others of L-7576's aircrew might also have survived their warplane being shot down and be brought into the Maquis camp, but then came terrible news. The remains of the Lancaster were discovered in some woodland, and at the crash-site three bodies had been found. The two gunners had been killed in the hail of fire from the Junkers Ju 88, of that Fiddick was certain, but whose was the third corpse?

Fiddick wondered about the fate of the remaining three aircrew, wherever they might be, if they were even still alive. Then came further, shattering news. Reports filtered in to the Maquis camp that two Allied aviators had been captured by the Germans, and shot out of hand 'by the side of the road'. Fiddick could only imagine that was the horrific fate that had befallen some of the Lancaster's ill-fated aircrew.

Fortunately, he did not have long to dwell upon such dark thoughts. On the night of 13 August 1944, the Maquis camp where he was staying almost entirely emptied. Fiddick sensed that something significant was afoot. The Frenchmen returned with news that a stick of British paratroopers had landed in the forest near by. The Maquis leader asked Fiddick if he would like to join the newcomers. Fiddick replied that he would very much, for at least it would give him 'somebody to talk to', as hardly any of the Maquis spoke English.

Fiddick's escape report tells of how, on 15 August, he made the journey 'to another Maquis camp about 8 miles away', where he 'met 15 SAS troops . . . The Frenchmen knew where they were and took me right to the camp.' These were the advance party of 1 Squadron, 2SAS, engaged on reconnaissance for a major SAS mission, codenamed Operation Loyton. They were there to pave the way for a far larger contingent to drop into the area, tasked to cause chaos and havoc behind enemy lines.

'The operation was planned against enemy road and rail communications in the eastern frontier area of France,' the Operation Loyton mission report outlined. 'It was intended that parties should operate against the main lines westwards from Strasbourg, and in addition harass soft transport on the road network complimentary to the railways.' The city of Strasbourg straddled one of the few road routes that led through the Vosges and across the River Rhine, the natural barrier delineating the Franco-German frontier.

The SAS planned to drop into the mountains in such numbers that, aided by the Maquis, they might create enough mayhem and bloodshed to convince the enemy that their lines were disintegrating, and to give the impression that Allied forces had broken through. Their ultimate goal was to drive German forces from the area, for if the Vosges fell, then Allied forces – now massed to the west of the mountains – could punch through this bulwark of Nazi Germany's defences and advance into the Fatherland itself.

Deep in the forested highlands of the Vosges, Fiddick was introduced to a stocky, dark-haired twenty-three-year-old dressed in the khaki battledress of the British Army. 'I met a chap there – a captain – by the name of Henry Druce,' Fiddick recalled of the commander of the SAS advance party. This fortuitous meeting would lead to a lifelong friendship, one that would not only enrich the lives of both men and their families, but also play a crucial role in the coming chapters of the war here in the Vosges.

Captain Henry Carey Druce was born in The Hague, the Netherlands, to a wealthy British father and a Dutch mother. Sent to Sherborne School in leafy Dorset, in the south-west of England, he had gone on to complete officer training at Sandhurst. After graduation, he was commissioned into the Middlesex Regiment, a line infantry unit founded in 1881. Craving adventure, he'd volunteered for the Glider Pilot Regiment – those tasked to fly gliders packed with airborne troops into battle – but was seconded to SOE, where he could make better use of his fluent French, Dutch and Flemish on clandestine operations.

Inserted into Nazi-occupied-Europe to assist downed Allied airmen to make it back to friendly lines, he was captured after his cover was blown by a Dutch double agent. Following a daring escape from enemy captivity, Druce had crossed hundreds of miles of hostile territory to get home to England. But once his true name and likeness was known to the enemy a similar role was out of the question, and he'd found himself at something of a loose end. By chance, he happened to meet 2SAS's commander, Lieutenant Colonel Brian Franks, during a train journey to Scotland. By this time 2SAS were 'very short of operational men', Franks reported. Upon making the acquaintance of someone so eminently qualified for Special Forces operations, Franks invited Druce to join the ranks of the SAS.

It was similar qualities to his own – dash, daring, bluff and front – that Druce recognised in the downed Canadian airman who had been brought before him in the Vosges. Writing of their chance meeting in the Operation Loyton War Diary, Druce noted: 'August 15. A Canadian pilot called Fiddick joined us. He had been shot down and had injured his leg, which made walking difficult.' As Colonel Franks had done for him, Druce promptly invited Fiddick to join their ranks. His instinctive assessment of Fiddick proved accurate. He 'would turn out to be one of our best soldiers', Druce would remark. For his part, Fiddick was overjoyed at his reception. 'I was finally among people I could understand! I was also impressed by the fact that they had dropped into an area so rife with Germans!'

The tenacity and dedication of the SAS team to parachute into an area teeming with the enemy demonstrated the core qualities of men like Druce and his fellows. Yet Captain Druce had not been the original choice to lead this mission. Indeed, the officer slated to command the advance party had contacted Colonel Franks the night before departure, admitting: 'I really don't feel I can do this operation. I have just lost my nerve . . .' Hence Franks had turned to Druce – fresh into the SAS – asking him to take over command.

Druce considered his predecessor 'a most courageous man', for having had 'the guts' to admit that he was not up to the task, and that his nerve had gone. Many of the SAS had been on numerous behind-the-lines missions for three years or more, and it was little wonder their nerves were shot. They had a term for what had happened: they called it 'crapping out'. But far better to have done so before mission departure than in the field, whereupon the officer would have become a burden upon the men supposedly under his command.

Druce had immediately accepted Franks' offer, noting that he 'came rushing like a stuck pig out of god knows where', and made a beeline for the departure airfield. Now, barely seventy-two hours later, and as he was still struggling to remember the names of those under his command, he had a new and wholly unexpected arrival – a Canadian airman, dropped in from out of the blue.

It fell to Druce and his patrol to prepare for the much larger force of SAS operatives slated to drop into these mountains. Or not, as the case might be. Franks had given him carte blanche: if he determined the Vosges to be good guerrilla territory and target-rich, he could call in the main body of raiders. If not, he could stand the mission down, at which point he and his men would make their own way back to friendly lines.

'Our task was to recce the area in the Vosges as to its suitability as an area for operation "Loyton", and also to find and establish a safe base and fresh DZs [drop zones] for re-supply and personnel dropping,' wrote Druce, in his mission report. Time was of the essence, for 'we reckoned that the Americans would over-run us in about two weeks' time . . .' In fact, Druce and his fellow commanders' view – that American troops and armour would shortly punch through the Vosges, driving all before them – would prove mistaken.

For Druce, it was crucial to forge a good working relationship with the local Maquis. They had established a basic camp in remote terrain, 'consisting of wooden huts made from cut down trees . . . on top of a hill in a good defensive position', Druce reported. 'The camp seemed well organised and well run, and the Maquis in the camp consisted of about 80 men who . . . had about 10–15 assorted old and rusty rifles.' While the Maquis were pitifully armed, the SAS had dropped in complete with container-loads of weaponry, and they set about training the Frenchmen how to use the new Sten guns, Bren light machine guns and the grenades that they had brought with them.

From intelligence reports, Druce had understood the Maquis to be 'well organised', but shortly he realised that there were several groups, 'some good some bad'. Colonel Brian Franks' report would go further, describing the Maquis as being 'infiltrated with informers and with no fighting spirit'. Whatever the truth, within days of the SAS team's arrival, word reached German commanders of British parachutists having linked up with local resistance forces. The enemy reaction was swift and decisive.

Not long after Fiddick's arrival, Druce learned that German troops were sweeping the area in a force some 5,000 strong. Fiddick's own escape report noted of this moment: 'After we had been at the camp for three days, the Germans got wind of us, and came to search the forest.' The nearest German patrols were barely a few miles distant, the SAS's position becoming ever more unhealthy, according to Druce.

These enemy forces were no second-class units. Colonel Franks reported that they were made up of 'Special Troops brought from

Strasburg. These troops combed the woods and did not keep to the paths and tracks.' Those 'Special Troops' included Gestapo and Einsatzgruppen – paramilitary 'death squads' that specialised in wiping out the so-called enemies of the Nazi state. They had been brought in specially to hunt for the British and French fighters, for, as Franks noted portentously, 'The Germans had all their experience of the rest of France behind them to deal with Maquis and SAS.'

With the enemy drawing close, Druce had little choice but to abandon the camp. He arranged for Fiddick to be issued with British Army battledress complete with regimental flashes on the shoulders, to replace his peasant attire. That done, on the morning of 17 August 1944 he gave orders to move out. The hundred-strong force of Maquis, plus the dozen SAS – thirteen, with Fiddick in their number – grabbed all they could and melted deeper into the forest. Druce hand-picked a small group to bring up the rear, and Fiddick was chosen to be one of them.

Clutching an American-made .45 calibre pistol, Fiddick waited uneasily, giving the main column a head-start. Finally, his party moved out, tracing the same path that the rest of the fighters had taken, their movements screened by dark woodland. Druce reported that 'after two hours difficult marching across the hills', they came upon a path. After following this for some time, his men stumbled upon a German patrol that had taken a rest break, the troops gathered at the side, eating.

Moving as silently as possible, Druce, Fiddick and the rest of the men 'got off the track and hid, with the idea of moving on once the patrol had finished eating'. But as they crawled into the undergrowth, a cry of 'Achtung' pierced the quiet. One of the Germans had spotted the last man in the column, a Frenchman. The Maquis fighter had opened fire, at which the entire mountainside erupted into a blazing firefight. The SAS men threw themselves flat, just as the foliage all around them was torn apart by bullets. Fiddick got into cover hunched behind a tree, fumbling for his pistol. He knew it was next to useless at this range, but at least it made him feel better, as he unleashed eight rounds into the woods where he assumed the enemy were hidden.

'Neither side could really see each other . . .' Fiddick recounted later, 'so we just fired when we saw movement in the bushes and hoped we hit someone.'

With his pistol now empty, he set about reloading, the action keeping his mind off the ferocity of the gunfight. Just then he heard the fearsome sound of an enemy machine gun opening up from above. Judging by its high fire-rate it had the signature of a Maschinengewehr 42 'Spandau', which made a noise like a buzz-saw chewing its way through wood. As the Spandau swept the terrain, Fiddick saw the foliage around him disintegrate under the sheer power of the weapon.

'I was standing behind a tree with bullets going all around it,' Fiddick recalled. 'It was a little unusual to have so many bullets flying . . . I hadn't expected such a thing, although there were plenty of bullets flying around on the night we got shot down.'

He was joined by an SAS trooper with a shock of bright red hair, who was armed with a Sten submachine gun. At the sound of rustling in the undergrowth the trooper lowered his weapon and emptied the thirty-round magazine in five furious seconds. Agonised cries emanating from the bushes told Fiddick that the man had found his mark. Fiddick was about to speak, when a hail of return fire ripped through the undergrowth, tearing into the SAS trooper's abdomen, his legs caving under him as he hit the forest floor.

Under such a fierce onslaught, Druce gave the order to split up. Prior to moving out from the Maquis camp, he had set an emergency rendezvous for just such an eventuality. 'Fearing that the enemy would soon be on the lower path also,' he reported, 'I decided it best to make for the RV in small parties, since my task was to bring in the reinforcements for the area and therefore I was not keen on risking our necks . . .' Those who survived would need to make for the emergency rendezvous.

On Druce's order, Fiddick rose to his feet and dashed off down the mountainside, there being little choice but to leave the body of the red-haired trooper where he had fallen. The Canadian ran full tilt through the trees, firing his pistol at anything he perceived to be a threat, before throwing himself into a dense patch of vegetation. His escape report noted that by now, the whole party were 'split up and were on the run'.

This represented the lowest point for Druce and one of the darkest moments during the entire operation. As they hurried downhill, he and his men got increasingly separated, no one knowing where the best route of escape might lie. Bit by bit, the survivors managed to slip away from the enemy. But it would be fully five days before what remained of the force was able to gather again. Those left alive – they had lost two others during the fierce firefights – were in a very sorry state. They were without radios, ammo, explosives and most importantly food, as most of their supplies had been lost during the melee.

The Maquis led the survivors to a new camp, where they could recover and reorganise. The usually gregarious and cheery Druce was uncharacteristically sombre. 'Feeling very depressed and very helpless,' he wrote. However, if he was going to avenge those who had lost their lives, the only way to do so was to get more SAS troopers, weaponry and supplies dropped in. Via a radio provided by the Maquis, Druce managed to communicate the situation to Colonel Franks, and he arranged for a vital resupply drop. They were desperate for food, weapons and ammo to replace all that had been lost.

On the night of 1 September, Druce, Fiddick and the other survivors found themselves in a mountain field fringed by forest, awaiting an air-drop that might or might not materialise. Navigating to such a remote spot through such rugged terrain would test the skills of any airman. Then Fiddick, lying prone in the damp grass, caught the distant thrumming of an aircraft. He recognised the engine note at once.

'Captain, there's a couple of Stirlings approaching,' he whispered.

Sure enough, a four-engine Short Stirling bomber hove into view. Druce, impressed that the Canadian could tell what type of aircraft it was by the note of its engines alone, flashed a signal to the pilot to confirm their position. To his delight the heavy warplane began to double back, presumably to drop their much-needed supplies. As the Stirling passed over, Fiddick heard the unmistakable crack of 'chutes opening. Seconds later, he became aware of a figure descending close by. A tall, athletic-looking paratrooper landed squarely in front of him. As he unhitched his harness, the new arrival eyed Fiddick – an unknown trooper dressed in SAS uniform – in surprise.

'Who the hell are you?' he demanded.

This, it turned out, was none other than Lieutenant Colonel Brian Franks, the commanding officer of the 2nd SAS regiment.

Franks had chosen to parachute in with twenty-three of his men, to bolster Druce's force. As succinctly as he could, Fiddick explained how he had come to join Druce and his team. The SAS colonel listened with interest, before formally inviting Fiddick into the ranks of the SAS.

'Don't worry, you'll pick it up as you go along,' he counselled affably.

Now it was official: Canadian airman Lew Fiddick was the newest member of the illustrious SAS. Colonel Franks' reputation as a fearless and intensely loyal Special Forces commander went before him: he had served as Signals Officer with Layforce, in the Mediterranean, and led specialised reconnaissance missions in the Middle East, before commanding a force of Army Commandos in the Italian Campaign, at Taranto and Termoli.

'Brian Franks was super,' Druce remarked. 'He was imaginative, quick to understand the situation and ready to do anything . . . I must admit when he arrived I felt that we'd let him down pretty badly . . . but he appreciated the situation right from the start . . . always cool, always ready to listen to anyone's story.'

The immediate priority was to get away from the drop zone. 'There had been a rumour of Germans moving . . . in force, so I was very anxious to get clear of the field as quickly as possible,' Druce noted in the Operation Loyton war diary. 'I wanted to get Col Franks and new arrivals away immediately, but knew we did not have a camp.'

Harassed though they were, with Franks in charge and building to a force of eighty SAS paratroopers, morale rapidly improved. As more supplies, weaponry and men were dropped in, Franks established a new basecamp on the high ground. From there they began a fierce campaign to harass and ambush the enemy.

German troops were massing in the area in ever greater numbers, charged by Hitler to hold the Vosges at all costs, and prevent the Allies from marching into Germany. Though his forces were massively outnumbered, Franks conceived of daring hit-and-run missions to sabotage and demoralise enemy forces, while seeking intelligence that the Allies could use to secure a breakthrough.

He despatched clandestine information-gathering teams, seeking to make the best use of the SAS's versatility, bravery and cunning. The most effective way to discover what was going on in any area was to garner information from the locals. At one juncture, Franks sought intel about enemy activity from the nearby hamlet of Pierre-Percée. Though there had been no reports of Germans in the area for weeks, the streets were rumoured to be awash with the enemy, so they would need to approach the village using stealth and guile.

The mission rightly fell to Captain Druce. During his time with SOE, Druce had been captured while on an undercover mission, but had managed to outwit his captors and make a daring escape, jumping through the window of his Gestapo interrogator's office and dashing off into the streets. Thanks to his talent for languages and his innate fearlessness, he'd passed himself off as a French peasant thereafter, flitting through the French countryside largely unscathed. As luck would have it, Druce's escape had taken him through the heart of the Vosges, the exact region where Operation Loyton was now in full swing.

'I had been there before "en passant,"' Druce wrote, of his time in the Vosges, adding, 'I knew fairly well what to expect.'

But when he strode into Pierre-Percée dressed in civilian clothes, hoping to mingle with the locals, Druce was met with a chilling sight. The place was swarming with German troops, any number of whom regarded his arrival with open suspicion. Druce knew it was crucial to remain calm and collected. If he were stopped and questioned, he 'only had a gun for papers', and there were too many enemy to shoot his way out of this one. One wrong move, and he would not only endanger his own life, but he might blow the cover of the other SAS hidden in nearby woodland.

Without so much as a falter in his step he walked right up to one of the nearest German soldiers and asked to bum a light for a cigarette. Receiving only a scowl by way of response, for a moment Druce was sure he had been rumbled, before the man produced a book of matches from the pocket of his field-grey uniform and turned away unconcerned. Druce's bold move seemed to have worked, but danger lurked at every turn. What were these enemy troops doing here and in such numbers, Druce wondered? Surely, this increased military presence could not be a coincidence? Sure enough, it turned out that they were searching for the location of the SAS's base.

As soon as he could Druce hurried back to deliver Franks a stark warning, prompting a quick decision to move. This led to a series of dramatic narrow escapes, as the SAS split into smaller groups and changed position repeatedly, attempting to avoid discovery, criss-crossing the high ground with hunter troops dogging their every step.

At one stage, teams of enemy soldiers led by German Shepherd search-dogs tracked the SAS. It was only the enemy's reluctance to venture off well-trodden paths and into wilder parts, doubtless fearing ambush, that gave the SAS the edge. By sticking to remote, inhospitable and seemingly uninhabitable terrain, Franks and his men managed to evade their pursuers, but doing so had taken a heavy toll, both physically and in terms of morale. To make matters worse, the weather turned, and it began to rain incessantly – not uncommon conditions in the Vosges in autumn. At altitude the rain became icy blasts of sleet and snow. Lacking waterproofs and cold weather equipment, spirits plummeted. Franks and his men were soaked to the skin and running short of ammo, food and dry clothes.

Druce was gripped by a deep sense of unease and the feeling that he had let Colonel Franks down. 'We were sent in to do a job, which was to bring in a large number of people to operate, and we had failed dismally . . . Whether it was our fault or not wasn't the point.' Every day was a struggle to survive with, the men thrown onto the back foot. They were lacking supplies, permanently soaked to the skin, with nowhere to dry out or warm themselves. Having no safe refuge, they were forced 'up one valley one day and up another valley the next', Druce lamented.

A note from Druce in the Operation Loyton war diary gives a sense of the desperate straits facing them and their French brothers-in-arms. 'We were forced to move camp owing to the possibility of German attack. Men were coming in from all corners wishing to join the Maquis [the resistance], mostly because the Germans were combing the villages. The volunteers were all without arms and . . . the danger of unarmed, untrained Frenchmen became apparent to everyone.' Though the French villagers were keen to fight, they had little with which to wage war, which meant they in turn became more of a burden.

At daybreak on 31 August Druce again found himself on the move, leading a party of some dozen SAS laden with heavy packs down into a valley, aiming to creep across one of the main highways in an effort to give the enemy the slip. Even as they pushed through the trees, they 'heard shellfire directed onto an old camp'. The enemy were attacking those locations that the SAS parties had just vacated. 'Most of the packs were too heavy and unnecessary material had to be abandoned . . . We crossed the valley that night and slept in the woods. It was becoming hard to sleep at night without sleeping bags.'

But by the end of the second week in September, the hue and cry seemed to have abated somewhat. Through sheer grit and determination, Franks, Druce, Fiddick and most of the Operation Loyton force had managed to evade capture. On 14 September, after nearly two weeks of being almost constantly on the run, Franks was able to report that they had 'found an area in which we were left in comparative peace'. They established a new camp in a high-walled gully, in an area known as Les Bois Sauvages – the wild woods. There, 'conditions appeared to be quieter', and they regarded this inhospitable, steep-sided chasm as a secure place in which to recover, await vital resupply and from which to launch counter-strikes.

On the evening of 18 September, the men of Operation Loyton were out in the dead of night, awaiting an air-drop. They were joined by villagers from the nearby settlement of Moussey, a veritable stronghold of the resistance. 'All the villagers of Moussey were first class,' Franks recorded, with great admiration. 'In Moussey we were welcomed, we were obvious[ly] looked upon as the spear-head of the Liberation Forces.'

That night the Moussey villagers were about to get a taste of the ingenuity and daring that set the SAS apart. They were expecting to intercept the usual crates of food and ammo, but Colonel Franks had requested something distinctly different – something to give his men the edge they hungered for here in the

Vosges; something to enable the SAS's mantra – speed, aggression, surprise – to be made a reality.

The assembled crowd marvelled as a clutch of jeeps, suspended from parachutes, floated down towards them from a Halifax bomber. The US-made Willys Jeep had become the SAS's preferred means of transport behind enemy lines, ever since David Stirling had first used them in the deserts of North Africa. In the SAS war diary from that time, Stirling asserted how the 'astonishing agility' of the Willys Jeep allowed them to reach almost any target over almost any country, enabling his force to be very 'much more flexible' in how, when and where they operated.

Bristling with mounted machine guns, Stirling considered the jeep to be perfect for wreaking destruction and 'getting away again at high speeds'. Now, deep in the French mountains, the SAS were deploying an ingenious method of delivering those versatile vehicles. Each jeep, with its steering wheel removed, was bolted onto a giant steel tray, mounted on springs. Rigging lines were attached at each corner, which were connected to a central parachute above. Four more 'chutes were set at each of the corners.

Like that, the first of the jeeps released over Moussey touched down, bang in the centre of the designated drop zone. But others floated off over nearby woodland. 'One jeep dropped in the trees and was very difficult to extricate,' Franks reported. Luckily for him, 2SAS now boasted a seasoned Canadian woodsman in their ranks. Thanks to his upbringing on the family farm, nestled in the temperate rainforests of British Columbia, Lew Fiddick possessed some considerable skill at woodcraft.

Having participated in a number of SAS operations, Fiddick found 'the dropping of the jeeps' the most fascinating yet. He was ordered to go off and find the second jeep, discovering it far up a hillside, 'with all the parachutes caught up in trees'. Together with a party of around a dozen Moussey villagers, Fiddick observed the vehicle itself, which had 'landed upside down, in a tree, well off the field'. They began work on cutting it down, all 'in the pitch dark of course'. Under Fiddick's expert instruction the Frenchmen systematically lopped the branches, enabling the jeep to drop in a controlled manner, until it ended up safely on the ground.

Exhausted, scratched but flushed with success, Fiddick recalled how they had 'eventually got this jeep out of the tree and onto its wheels', at which point he triumphantly 'got in it and drove it away'. Altogether six jeeps were parachuted into the Moussey drop zone, and they would transform operations, allowing the SAS to do what they did best, striking hard and fast and disappearing swiftly before the enemy knew what had hit them.

Fiddick joined Druce's jeep team. 'We went around looking for German settlements – establishments they had set up to harass the French, so we harassed them with the Jeeps ...' Fiddick remarked, although of course 'you were pretty exposed yourself in a jeep.' It was a little different from flying bombing missions at high altitude. 'You seemed so remote from things in an airplane, whereas here you were directly involved.' Despite the immediacy and ferocity of the action, Fiddick knew it was a case of 'either stay with Henry [Druce]'s group . . . or just stay back at the camp.' Fiddick, with his wish to be useful, 'found it more interesting to be involved'.

The main aim was to target senior enemy commanders – to 'cut the head off the Nazi snake', as the SAS termed it. From their jeeps they aimed to ambush German staff cars, cutting down the high-ranking officers who rode within. That would spread fear and uncertainty among the lower ranks, for not even the top German commanders seemed safe from the British raiders, who seemed everywhere but nowhere, all at the same time. The first such 'jeeping' raid would typify the tactics that were involved, and the bloody carnage that resulted.

At dusk on 22 September, Franks and his force removed the cut branches with which they had camouflaged their vehicles. Six jeeps set off from their hidden base, loaded with twenty-one fighters, pushing south of Moussey, engine fumes hanging thick and heady on the cold, dank air. Franks divided his force into three groups, each with two vehicles. The first to strike would do so on the road that wound its way through the high-sided Celles Valley. There, they set up hidden ambush positions at a crossroads, where any passing traffic would be forced to slow as it approached the junction.

Backing into the thick undergrowth, the SAS hid the two jeeps in such a way that their vehicle-mounted Vickers machine guns could still be brought to bear. Eight muzzles menaced the road . . . and so the wait began. Finally, there was the grunt of a distant engine. As all vehicles had been requisitioned by the Germans – the locals were reduced to travelling by horse and cart – only the enemy could be driving on the roads hereabouts. The ambushers heard the whine of the engine, as the driver changed down through the gears, slowing his vehicle. Fingers tensed upon triggers.

A sleek bonnet emerged around the distant bend, a black cross over white – the sign of the Wehrmacht – emblazoned on its side. As luck would have it, this was a staff car. Eight pairs of gunsights tracked the vehicle, but shortly the grunt of a second engine could be heard. Unbelievably, a second staff car followed the first. The SAS men let the first draw level with their hidden position, waiting to bring the second within their field of fire. But just as they were about to open up, as if by magic a third staff car rounded the bend. The three were travelling in convoy, the last being followed by a heavier vehicle – a three-tonne German Army truck – stuffed full of escorting soldiers.

The ambushers reckoned all three staff cars could be hit, still allowing themselves time to get away. Holding their fire until the very last moment, they opened up at the closest range possible. The twin-muzzles of the Vickers let rip, dozens of .303-inch rounds tearing into gleaming bodywork and shattering glass. Keeping their fingers hard on the triggers, and swinging the weapons on their pivot mounts, the SAS men raked the staff cars from bonnet to boot with murderous fire. Within moments all three vehicles had ground to a halt, rent with long lines of ragged, jagged holes. The lead staff car, slumped low on its flattened tyres, burst into flames, as tracer rounds sliced into its fuel tank.

Only one figure managed to drag himself from one of those stricken vehicles, and he was cut down before he had made it a few yards. By the time the ambushers had ceased fire, hundreds of rounds had been unleashed onto the targets – the truck being the last to take the full brunt of the SAS jeeps' guns. Above the savage crackle and pop of the flames, the throb of further engines was audible now. Further vehicles were approaching. Four more trucks hove into view, and others could be heard behind. The staff cars clearly formed the vanguard of a long enemy convoy.

In typical SAS fashion, the shoot-'em-up had been executed admirably: it was high time to execute the scoot stage of the attack. All surprise was lost, and as the SAS men fired up their engines and raced for a track winding its way into the high ground, bullets tore after them. The staff cars had been leading a twenty-five-vehicle convoy, but fortunately the heavy trucks were no match for SAS jeeps over the kind of terrain they were heading into. Shaking off any pursuers, the ambushers executed a mad dash through the mountains, making it back to their lie-up deep in the woods. They left behind them a pall of oily smoke billowing high above the Celles Valley, where four vehicles were burning fiercely.

Captain Druce proved particularly adept behind the wheel of a vehicle bristling with pairs of mounted Vickers machine guns. Colonel Franks reported of his achievements: 'Over 400 rounds expended at different groups of Germans at close range; minimum killed 15/20.' Speaking later of Druce's leadership and his fearlessness during such hit and run strikes, Fiddick stated simply: 'His job was to create havoc, which he did.'

Indeed, the havoc wrought by these swift, wide-ranging attacks proved so daunting that German commanders began to fear a far larger Allied force was concealed within the dark forests. Not unreasonably, German officers began to argue that if the SAS possessed the capacity to carry out such brazen missions across so large an area so far behind the lines, surely they must constitute a force at least several hundred strong. Meanwhile, the German rank and file began to fear that no one, no matter what their status, was safe. The SAS had accomplished exactly what they had set out to achieve.

'On the whole the Germans seemed very scared of us,' Franks reported. 'Judging by local reports our numbers had been much exaggerated ... the appearance of the jeeps astounded and irritated the Germans, and made them redouble their efforts to destroy our party.' The SAS's summary report noted of the successes scored: 'The parties sent out were able to do considerable damage and kept a large number of enemy troops occupied.'

Unsurprisingly, senior enemy commanders seemed to have had more than enough of these fearsome raiders who struck by surprise from the shadows. Struggling to seek out and destroy the SAS force, they reasoned that such a fighting unit could not be operating without help from the locals. Accordingly, they began to take savage reprisals, rounding up villagers accused of supporting the SAS and despatching them en masse to the concentration camps.

On the 24 September, German commanders unleashed their dark predations on Moussey, the village that lay closest to the SAS base, not so far away in Les Bois Sauvages. At gunpoint, the inhabitants were herded into the square. As luck would have it, at that very moment Druce happened to be heading into the village, returning from a jeep sortie. As his two-vehicle convoy drove into the village square, the German troops gathered there momentarily mistook them for friendly forces. That gave Druce and his men the chance to open fire, unleashing a devastating broadside from the jeep's machine guns.

The two vehicles made it through to the far side unscathed, whereupon they hightailed it to the SAS base, to warn Franks and the others. Back in the village, the surviving German commanders were seething. They proceeded to order all males between the ages of sixteen and sixty to be deported from Moussey and environs. A total of 210 were shipped off to the concentration camps, and only a few dozen would ever return, earning this area the poignant nickname the 'Valley of the Widows'. Yet in spite of such horrors, members of the resistance continued to take the gravest risks imaginable, in order to assist the SAS and to provide them with vital intelligence.

It was thanks to their ceaseless efforts that Colonel Franks came into possession of a sheaf of papers of incredibly high value to the Allies. It consisted of documents outlining the complete order of battle for the 21st Panzer Division, a formidable armoured unit that had achieved a near-legendary status during the German expeditionary campaign in the North African deserts. Pulled back to occupied France, the 21st had reformed on the flanks of the Vosges, charged with achieving similar levels of success against the Allies here as they had when serving with the Afrika Korps.

The papers were too detailed and complex to transmit via radio, and in any case Franks' wireless sets had proven temperamental and highly unreliable. Yet he knew that he must somehow get them into Allied commanders' hands. They constituted a crucial source of intelligence via which to locate and obliterate a key asset of Nazi Germany's defences, detailing just about every position held by the 21st in the Vosges. US General George Patton's forces were situated just to the west, facing the German frontline defences, where they had become bogged down due to fuel and ammo shortages, plus the intensity of the fighting. But if Patton had these documents, he could target the enemy's armour with airstrikes and artillery barrages, so hastening a breakthrough.

Franks knew there was only one viable option: the documents would have to be taken on foot to Patton, the hard-charging American general. The only way to attempt such a fraught journey would be to pose as French civilians, the risks of which were legion. If the courier were caught, he would very likely get classed as an 'unlawful saboteur' or 'spy' and sentenced to death without trial. It was a horrendously risky mission, and as far as

Franks was concerned there was only one choice for such an undertaking – Captain Henry Carey Druce.

When asked, Druce readily accepted. Franks requested a volunteer to accompany him. This would be no easy task, he explained, for it would involve traversing an area that was crawling with enemy troops, with no chance of backup or rescue. Once the party left Les Bois Sauvages they would be entirely on their own. They would need to move many miles undetected to approach the German frontline, and somehow to slip beyond it unseen. Even if they made it that far, they would then be faced with a death-defying dash across no-man's-land, to reach the Allied frontline. And there, they might even encounter 'friendly fire', for the Americans would have no idea they were coming.

Over the weeks that he had spent soldiering with the SAS, Fiddick had grown very close to Captain Druce. Having heard Colonel Franks' appeal, he initially 'hesitated, to see if anyone would put up their hands'. When nobody did, the Canadian airman-turned-SAS-trooper did the only right and proper thing and volunteered, declaring simply: 'I'll go with Henry on this journey.'

'On 29 Sep Captain Druce, 2SAS, and I started off to try to get through to the American lines,' Fiddick's escape report noted. At 0300 hours, the two men set forth, moving stealthily through the dark forest in a westerly direction. It was now fully two months since Fiddick had bailed out of his stricken warplane over France, and it was a bonus that this Canadian farmer's son felt so at home amid such dense and isolated woodlands.

At first, he and Druce made slow progress across the heavily wooded terrain. Even when it became less thickly vegetated and easier to navigate, enemy patrols thronged the area and spotter aircraft criss-crossed the sky. If nothing else, the ever-increasing German presence told them that they must be nearing the frontline. By the following evening, Fiddick and Druce found themselves approaching the village of Saint-Prayel. It lay less than ten miles from their point of departure as the crow flies, but up hill and down dale it had proven a far longer journey.

Saint-Prayel was little more than a scattering of farms and cottages, but the hamlet marked a key point on their journey, for adjacent to it lay the only bridge thereabouts that crossed the River Meurthe – a major tributary of the River Moselle – beyond which lay their objective. The official Operation Loyton report noted how 'the American advance had been halted west of the River Meurthe,' and as Druce and Fiddick knew full well, the German frontline lay somewhere on the far side. The banks of the Meurthe were sure to be bristling with German defences, yet if the two men were to have any chance of delivering their documents, they must risk a dash through the village and over the bridge.

As they observed the hamlet from cover, Saint-Prayel appeared quiet enough, but its strategic position meant it simply had to be well guarded. When darkness fell, Druce motioned Fiddick forwards. Sticking to the darkest terrain, they darted from the cover of buildings to trees and to more buildings. They had almost reached their objective when they heard the pounding of footsteps from behind. The noise of their footfalls must have attracted hostile attention. Fiddick looked to his partner and following Druce's lead he stepped into the deepest shadows, making ready the submachine gun that he carried.

Two black-clad members of the Milice Française – the local militia of French Fascists, raised in part to combat the

Maquis – came rushing down the road, each brandishing a pistol. Clearly, they had heard the sound of someone moving through the village after curfew and had come to investigate. The two figures slowed as they neared Druce and Fiddick's place of concealment, their voices ringing out, demanding that their quarry show themselves.

Without warning Druce and Fiddick stepped out of the darkness, each with their weapon trained on the chests of their pursuers. They uttered no words, but their steely expressions conveyed that they were more than ready to shoot. 'We were armed and they were armed,' remarked Fiddick, 'so we had this kind of cowboy-style stand-off where we just stared at each other. Then they backed slowly off.' Faced with what appeared to be two seasoned fighters wielding formidable-looking firepower, the two Frenchmen seemed to lose confidence in their pistols.

'We clung to our guns and were ready to shoot our way out,' Druce recalled, 'which I'm glad to say we didn't have to do, because we were not very good shots and we couldn't see in the dark. Anyhow, they disappeared and we went on . . .'

As they edged towards the bridge, the blackness of the night provided welcome cover. Fiddick and Druce were certain they could hear a German patrol moving on the far bank. They waited for the moment when the noise seemed to die away, before creeping forward to cross the bridge, but barely had they started to scurry over when a voice called out a challenge from the opposite side. Both men dropped to the ground. Fiddick scanned the far end of the bridge, desperate for any clue as to who had spoken, but he could make out very little. He turned to Druce, the more experienced of the two, seeking an indication as to what they should do next.

But the SAS captain seemed rooted to the spot. When 'that bloody man on the river' threw out his challenge, Druce found himself frozen with indecision, fearing that he and Fiddick 'really had had it'. They had an enemy patrol moving backwards and forwards 'within . . . yards of us', and now a sentry had yelled out a direct warning. It was 'a bad moment', Druce declared. But luck was with them, for no one seemed able to locate the hiding place of the two SAS fugitives. Indeed, it went back to being 'mousey-quiet' all along the banks of the Meurthe, as Druce remarked.

'It was ticklish for a little while,' Fiddick added, with typical Canadian modesty, but finally they were able to set off again and crept across the bridge. Having flitted over the river like hunted fugitives, Druce and Fiddick managed to slip into thick foliage on the far side. They were now in the heart of the German military's frontline positions here on the western wall of the Vosges. Pushing on through the darkness at a painfully slow pace, inching ahead at a stealthy crouch, they half-stumbled and half-fell into an unseen ditch.

'We encountered . . . slit trenches and several Germans,' Druce reported. 'We decided this was the frontline . . .'

'Stumbling into the German trench was . . . unsettling,' Fiddick added, as they feared discovery at every move. 'We retired back into the bush a little distance.' There they decided to lie low and observe the passage of German patrols, to try to ascertain the best route ahead. Eventually, senses on high alert for any sign of the enemy, they picked their silent way forwards once again.

After what seemed like an eternity, the two figures reached the last trench, before what appeared to be no-man's-land. Ahead stretched the churned and blasted territory lying between the opposing sides. The once-fertile earth had been torn up by explosions, crops were scythed by shrapnel, and everywhere the terrain bore the scars of war.

Druce cleared the final parapet, crawling on his stomach like a stalking cat with his body almost entirely flat to the ground. After about ten yards he became still again, checking the lie of the land. Friendly forces had to be somewhere up ahead, but he had no way of knowing how far away, or how watchful they might be for enemy patrols. Behind him, Fiddick kept watch from his position in the final trench. When he saw Druce move off again – their prearranged signal to follow – he pushed himself up over the edge and began to slither after him.

'A thing I guess I'll always remember was crawling across that open field just on the far side of the trenches,' Fiddick recalled. The two men remained as low as possible, sticking to the cover of what remained of the furrows. Moving like that, crawling on their bellies, they finally reckoned they'd covered enough ground to be out of the enemy's line of sight. They were leaving one threat behind, but their problems were far from over.

There was a high likelihood that either one side or the other would have sown this no-man's-land with landmines that, if disturbed by scrabbling hands and knees, would detonate with deadly force. Fiddick and Druce pressed onwards through the peaks and troughs of churned-up earth, fearing at any moment that a hand or knee placed down might meet with an excoriating explosion. But finally, seemingly miraculously, they reached the cover of some trees on the far side.

They crawled in the woodland, Druce reported, remaining there 'until the morning' to ensure they 'really were past the frontline'.

Come sunrise, they reckoned it was time to face the next potentially deadly challenge: to make contact with whatever 'friendly' forces might lie ahead. As matters transpired, they had crawled across no-man's-land to end up at a section of the Allied front held by 'the 1st Spahis Regt. of General Leclerc's Division', Druce recalled. The 1st Spahis were a battle-hardened element of the Free French forces, commanded by veteran French leader General Philippe Leclerc de Hauteclocque, who had been one of the first to make his way to Britain to raise an army under De Gaulle.

The 1st Spahis had fought with distinction in North and East Africa, before forming part of the British Eighth Army to secure victory at El Alamein. Now tasked to help liberate France, they were standing shoulder to shoulder with the American troops of General Patton's forces. A tough, well-experienced and disciplined fighting unit, the men of the 1st Spahis took Fiddick and Druce into their lines, holding their fire until the two mystery arrivals could properly identify themselves. Fiddick could barely believe that they had completed the fabled 'home run', as it was called among fliers – an epic escape from enemy territory, to arrive safely back with Allied forces.

But his elation was tempered with regret. Although he had been a wholly accidental and honorary member of the SAS, he had been thrilled by the weeks that he had spent soldiering with them in the Vosges. Hitting targets from 10,000 feet in a Lancaster had been all well and good, but operating with the British raiders had proven so much more real and visceral. Despite the intense discomfort, and the near-permanent fear of being hunted, 'cutting the head off the Nazi snake' had proved to be heady and intoxicating work. Now, for Fiddick at least, all of that was over.

Fiddick and Druce were taken direct 'to a French Headquarters, and from there to the American ... HQ', where Druce was able to hand over the all-important documents. Unsurprisingly, for his actions in the Vosges he would win 'not only the admiration of all British troops with whom he came into contact, but also of the local French people amongst whom his name became a byword', Druce's later medal citation would state of his actions. For now at least, this was to be his and Fiddick's parting of the ways. Incredibly, while Fiddick was ordered to return to the RCAF, Druce was poised to make an about-turn and head back the way he and Fiddick had just come.

'I decided to return to the Colonel and put him fully in the picture of the situation for our future operations,' Druce remarked, of his move back towards the SAS base. 'Also to take ... [the] badly needed [radio] set and new crystals.' Colonel Franks' last working radio had just gone on the blink, leaving him with no choice but to ask this quite extraordinary SAS captain to sneak back across the lines, bringing with him the spare parts that he so desperately needed. Druce had also learned what he deemed to be vital information regarding General Patton's impending offensive. And so, laden with his precious cargo of radio spares and armed with this new intel, Druce headed back via 'the same route' but this time alone and 'moving rather slowly in view of a 60–70lb pack'.

Unscathed, undetected, Druce returned to the last known location of his unit, only to find the Bois Sauvages camp deserted and a key French resistance leader's 'house burned', plus Moussey village itself swarming with Germans. From a trusted member of the Maquis he learned that the SAS had been attacked and that Franks and the others had split into small groups to attempt to slip back to the Allied lines. The official Operation Loyton mission report states that, 'on the 9th October, as the winter was approaching in this inhospitable area which was now being prepared by the Germans as an alternative frontline position, Col. Franks decided to order his parties to exfiltrate independently.'

However, during the time that Druce had been away, the resistance had 'procured further information about the arrival of three new German Divisions near St Dié'. Knowing that 'the Americans were supposed to be starting an attack' in that area very soon, Druce decided that this intelligence 'was so important that it had to be transmitted to the Americans immediately'. With that priority spurring him on, Druce returned through enemy lines 'on the same route for a third time', an utterly extraordinary achievement by anyone's reckoning.

Having made it back to the Allied forces in the same manner as before, Druce 'met the French, who were alarmed at the information and passed it on to the Americans'. The citation for Druce's Distinguished Service Order, earned during Operation Loyton, sums up his absolutely astonishing achievements: '29 September, Capt. Druce was ordered to contact 3 US Army carrying important documents and much useful information of enemy dispositions. Not only did he succeed in this mission but on receipt of information from 3 US Army which he considered vital to his Commanding Officer, he decided to attempt to pass through the enemy lines once more. This was accomplished successfully. In all, Captain Druce passed through the enemy lines on no less than three occasions.'

The citation goes on to praise Druce effusively, highlighting 'this officer's skill, energy, daring and complete disregard for his own safety'. Druce was also awarded a Croix de Guerre with

Palm for his services to the French people, who would never forget the SAS captain's courage and sacrifice during the long weeks that he had spent in their midst.

For Fiddick, that crawl through no-man's-land would mark his final act of daring as an honorary member of the SAS, and indeed as a Canadian flyer. He was grounded for the remainder of the war, for he was deemed to know far too much about the inner working of the SAS and the French resistance to risk him falling into enemy hands. He would spend the rest of the war training new bomber crews, before returning to his civilian life in Canada.

On his return to the UK from France, on 2 October 1944, Fiddick was debriefed by MI9. His report typifies the modesty and can-do attitude of the man. In describing his joining up with the SAS and exploits, plus his epic escape thereafter, Fiddick wrote: 'Twice we were ambushed by the Germans but managed to get away. From the time I joined up with the SAS troops until 29 September I worked with them doing sabotage etc. On 29 September Captain DRUCE, 2nd SAS, and I started off to try to get through to the American lines, as we had special information for the Americans. We started West, crossed the lines and joined the French Army at DOMPTAIL, after walking for 40 hours. We first went to French Headquarters, and from there to the American and French HQ.'

In time, Fiddick would learn what had befallen the rest of his Lancaster crew. George Wishart – the flight engineer who bailed out ahead of Fiddick – was severely injured upon landing, apprehended by the Germans and lived out the rest of the war as a POW. The rear gunner, Percy Buckley, had been killed by the fire from the German night-fighter, during which the mid-upper gunner, Richard Proulx, was also hit and mortally wounded. The radio operator, Arthur Payton, bailed out of the aircraft at too low an altitude and did not survive. His body was found with the wreckage.

Amazingly, pilot Harold Sherman Peabody managed to crash-land the stricken 'K for King' without triggering her explosive cargo. He and navigator James Harrington Doe made it out of the wrecked aircraft but were captured by the Germans. They were secretly transported to nearby Natzweiler-Struthof concentration camp where they were executed by a Nazi death squad. This terrible fate also befell many of the SAS men captured on Operation Loyton. Under Hitler's notorious Kommando Order, they were to be shown not the slightest mercy. Several were tortured terribly, before being murdered in cold blood and thrown into unmarked graves in the forests of the Vosges.

After the war, Henry Druce emigrated to Canada, where he struck up a lifelong friendship with Lew Fiddick. The pair remained close until Druce's death in 2007 at the age of eighty-five. Fiddick passed away in 2016, surrounded by his loved ones, in his one-hundredth year and after a brief illness.

On 8 October 1944, General Dwight D. Eisenhower, Supreme Commander of the Allied Expeditionary Force in Europe, sent a letter to the SAS's Commander, Brigadier Roderick 'Roddy' McLeod, noting 'the close of phase one of SAS operations in Europe'. In it, he paid a 'very fine tribute' to the men of the SAS, adding, 'I wish to send my congratulations to all ranks of the Special Air Service Brigade on the contribution which they have made to the success of the Allied Expeditionary Force. The ruthlessness with which the enemy have attacked Special Air Service troops has been an indication of the injury which you were able to cause to the German armed forces, both by your own efforts and by the information which you gave of German dispositions and movements. Many Special Air Service troops are still behind enemy lines; others are being reformed for new tasks. To all of them I say: "Well done, and good luck."'

Operation Loyton epitomised the kind of mission that Eisenhower had in mind when writing that letter. But despite such accolades as that delivered by Eisenhower, at the end of the war the SAS was summarily disbanded. Senior figures in the British military and political hierarchy had never really warmed to its freewheeling, meritocratic, piratical nature, which characterised many of its foremost operations. This sense is perhaps best summed up by an exchange that took place between Winston Churchill and the then Conservative Member of Parliament for West Dorset, in the House of Commons, several years into the war. 'Is it true, Mr Prime Minister,' demanded Simon Wingfield-Digby, 'that there is a body of men out in the Aegean Islands, fighting under the Union Flag, that are nothing short of being a band of murderous, renegade cutthroats?'

He was referring to SAS and SBS units operating in and around the eastern Mediterranean. While confirming that it was indeed true, Churchill's response to Wingfield-Digby was typically robust: 'If you do not take your seat and keep quiet, I will send you out to join them.' But by the summer of 1945 Churchill had been voted out of power and by the autumn of that year the naysayers had finally got their way: the SAS was summarily disbanded, as was the SBS. Officially, the SAS and SBS were only reformed in the 1950s, when guerrilla-style conflicts in Malaya (present-day Malaysia), Indonesia and Oman showed the pressing need for such specialist units.

In time, the entry criteria for the SAS and SBS were refined into what became recognised as 'Selection' – a formal, regimented test taking several months, which is designed to push a man to the limits and beyond. Crucially, Selection built upon the lessons first learned by the pioneers of Special Forces soldiering, in the Second World War training camps of Kabrit and elsewhere. In essence, Selection took what Stirling, Lewes, Mayne, Almonds and others had achieved by trial and error in the early years and shaped it into a structured, gruelling and merciless entry test.

One of the key constants of both the SAS's Second World War procedures and today's formalised Selection is that they are designed to test a recruit's mental strength and stamina as much as their physical prowess. Speak to any SAS figure – whether a Second World War or a modern-day veteran – and they will invariably say the same thing: during the punishing Selection process, there inevitably comes a time when the individual 'hits the wall'; when the body tells the mind it just cannot take any more. At that stage, it is only *mental* strength and stamina that keeps the individual going. That mental toughness is the key constant of those who make it into the hallowed ranks of the regiment.

Likewise with our seven great escapers, when all seemed lost, when the odds seemed impossibly stacked against them, when capture and death seemed all but certain, each man found himself possessed of an inner strength to go above and beyond. Each tale is epitomised by such moments: when George Paterson headed back into war-torn Italy, on SOE business, having escaped once already; when Roy Farran refused to give up and die of thirst on the caïque, instead cobbling together the DIY still; when Jack Byrne, apparently facing death in the Sahara, heated the sludge in his water bottle with brandy and forced it down; when Thomas Langton and his men crossed the seemingly impossible barrier of the Qatarra Depression by sheer strength of will; when Jim Almonds crawled into a minefield for the second time in the war, to delineate and circumvent it; when Jimmy Hughes, despite his recent injuries, leapt from the train, to avoid being spirited away to Germany; and when Lew Fiddick, downed airman and honorary SAS, crossed the most heavily fortified frontline in all of Western Europe.

Each escapee endured an impossible-seeming odyssey by drawing on deep reserves of strength and fortitude. Indeed, the selection process was designed to favour such individuals, and to weed out those not blessed with those attributes. But other factors were also key. One of the SAS's mottos – as true then as it is now – is to 'expect the unexpected'. In essence, recruits had to be ready for anything when embarking upon behind-the-lines operations. By actively promoting the use of thievery, bluff, deception and rule-breaking wherever necessary, the training process rejected those not inclined to such unorthodox mind-sets, while favouring those who were of the firm belief that such things were acceptable – indeed necessary – in times of war.

By stressing the value of 'merit above rank' – that respect was not automatically conferred by position but had to be earned – the training process encouraged recruits to think and act on their feet and for themselves. This self-starting, independent-minded spirit fostered a sense of personal responsibility that was vital to our seven great escapees, as they wandered alone through wild terrain, surviving off their wits and what they could beg, borrow or steal.

Combined with valuing merit above rank, camaraderie was also seen as being sacrosanct. Repeatedly, our great escapees made the extraordinary efforts that they did, going well above and beyond, due to a burning desire to return to their fellows and to the fight. In the SAS, the brotherhood of warriors ran deep. Yet at the same time there was a rigorous pragmatism, embodied in the acceptance that sometimes, if the mission demanded it, a fellow operator – wounded or captured – might have to be left behind. Maintaining that balance, between a fierce, unyielding loyalty and hard-headed pragmatism, was crucial.

There was another type of camaraderie – another brotherhood – that was a founding principle of the SAS in the Second World War, one that underpinned the great escapees' exploits, one that is summed up in the phrase 'hearts and minds'. Each of the great escapees had that quintessential factor in common – their ability to build alliances with, and to call on the assistance of, those local to the area of their escape and evasion. In each case – Paterson with his Italian mountainfolk, Farran with his Greek resistance network, Byrne with his Bedouin nomads, Langton with his Senussi tribesmen, Almonds with his rural farming family, Hughes with his Italian partisans, and Fiddick with the villagers of the Vosges – being able to work with and rely on the assistance of strangers was absolutely vital. Arguably, none of the seven would have made it without being open to seeking such help on the ground.

In short, the great escapees depicted in these pages embodied the kind of qualities that made the regiment so special then and now. As just one example of how the free-thinking, unorthodox, audacious mindset that developed during the Second World War has endured, consider the SAS's 1991 operations in the western Iraqi deserts, when those undertaking jeep-mounted patrols realised the best way to slip past enemy convoys was to gird their faces in Arab-style *keffiyeh* – headscarves – wrap themselves in thick sheepskin coats to ward off the chill, and speed past the enemy vehicles waving, as if they were friendly troops. With so many different Iraqi units in the field, any number of which used civilian-style 4x4 vehicles and Arabic dress, the ruse proved to work time and time again.

While the weaponry, vehicles, insertion techniques and escape and evasion kit might have changed greatly, the basic tenets of the SAS remain the same today as they were in 1941–45 – proving absolutely that 'who dares wins'.

Acknowledgements

I could not have written this book without the help of the following people, and please forgive me for any individuals I may have inadvertently forgotten.

Thank you Eve Warton, Second World War WAAF, and Jamie Robertson, her son, for first alerting me to the incredible wartime escape story of George Paterson, who was a family friend of Eve's husband and godfather to her eldest son. Thank you also to you both for introducing me to longtime family friend Teresa Bonfiglio, George Paterson's daughter.

Thank you Teresa Bonfiglio, the daughter of George Paterson, for corresponding with me from the USA over your father's wartime story and for sharing with me what documents, photos, recollections and other materials you were able to, for which I am immensely grateful.

Thank you David R. Farran, son of Roy Farran MC, for corresponding with me over your father's war years and for sharing with me the documents, photos and family memorabilia such as you were able to.

Thank you Christopher Langton, the nephew of Thomas Langton MC, for kindly allowing me permission to quote from your uncle's diary and private papers, and for sharing with me family documents and photos, for which I am immensely grateful.

Thank you Brett Fiddick, grandson of Lew Fiddick, and Rod Fiddick, son of Lew Fiddick, for corresponding with me over Lew Fiddick's war years and for sharing with me the documents, photos and family memorabilia such as you were able to.

Enormous thanks to the family of Lt Quentin Hughes, and particularly his cousin, Mrs Morrie Conant, his wife, Mrs. Jo Hughes, and his daughters Ceri Howard, Sian Davenport and Alice Hughes, who cherish Lt. Hughes' memory and tales of his wartime exploits greatly. Also to Lt. Hughes' great friend Conrad Thake, in Malta, for all your help and support.

Heartfelt thanks also to Lorna Almonds-Windmill, whose books about her father's long and distinguished wartime career with the SAS are so superb – namely *Gentleman Jim*, and *Escaping The Ordinary*. Meeting up and chatting with you has been an enormous pleasure and very enlightening, of course.

Thank you Jonathan Peck, for corresponding with me and sharing documents and photos regarding your cousin, Harold Sherman Peabody, the pilot of the Lancaster Bomber which was shot down over the Vosges, and his aircrew. Thank you Sean Rae Summerfield, for sharing with me and permitting me to quote from your superlative research document *Swallowed into Dusk: Missing Airmen during the Second World War*.

Thank you once again to LRDG, SAS and SBS veteran Jack Mann, who at ninety-five years of age soldiered through an early draft of the manuscript of this book, to scrutinise it for any mistakes I may have made. To have a Second World War veteran of the unit portrayed do so was invaluable and very greatly appreciated, and especially as the last great escape portrayed, that of Lew Fiddick and Henry Druce, in the Vosges, remains so very dear to your heart.

Thank you Peter Forbes, of the Newtownards War Department Film Club, for reading and checking the manuscript in an early draft and for your perceptive comments.

The staff at various archives and museums also deserve special mention, including those at the UK National Archives and the Imperial War Museum.

My gratitude is also extended to my literary agent, Gordon Wise, of Curtis Brown, for helping bring this project to fruition, and to all at my fantastic publisher, Quercus, for same, including, but not limited to: Charlotte Fry, Hannah Robinson, Bethan Ferguson, Ben Brock, Fiona Murphy and Jon Butler. My editor, Richard Milner, deserves very special mention, as always, as does Luke Speed, my film agent at Curtis Brown.

Thanks also to Tean Roberts, Julie Davies and Phil Williams for your research into the stories as portrayed in these pages. I am also indebted to those authors who have previously written about some of the topics dealt with in this book and whose work has helped inform my writing; I have included a full bibliography.

Finally, of course, thanks are due also to Eva and the ever-patient David, Damien Jr and Sianna, for not resenting Dad spending too much of his time locked away ... again ... writing ... again.

Sources

Note: this book contains public sector information licensed under the Open Government Licence v3.0.

CHAPTER ONE

1. Personal communication, Eve Warton, 17/10/2018 – letter of 3/2/2000, opening 'Dear Eve and Robin, Thank you very much for your card. In this country . . .'
2. Personal communication, Jamie Robertson, 18/10/2018 – 'SOE Italian Missions'.
3. Personal communication, Eve Warton, 14/10/2018 – 'George Paterson Canadian 3 x MC SOE Ops Italy'.
4. Personal communication (various), Teresa Bonfiglio, November 2019–February 2020, concerning her father, George Paterson's war record.
5. Personal communication, George Paterson with Eve Warton (undated), held in Eve Warton's private papers.
6. Personal communication, Eve Warton, 25/10/2018 – 'George Paterson SAS and SOE'.
7. Personal communication, Eve Warton, 15/10/2018 – 'George was Godfather to my eldest son'.
8. Personal communication, Eve Warton, 17/10/2018 – 'He was a POW with David Stirling in Italy.'

9. Personal communication, Jamie Robertson, 19/11/2018 – 'More research on George Paterson's SOE exploits.'

CHAPTER TWO

1. National Archives Catalogue Number: WO 373/4/341 – Recommendation for Award.
2. National Archives Catalogue Number: WO 373/148/427 – Recommendation for Award.
3. National Archives Catalogue Number: WO 373/27/289 – Citation for Military Cross.
4. National Archives Catalogue Number: WO 373/61/692 – Citation for Bar to Military Cross.
5. National Archives Catalogue Number: WO 106/3240 – Crete: Battle of Crete.
6. National Archives Catalogue Number: WO 106/2136 – Operation Compass: Situation and Operational Reports.
7. National Archives Catalogue Number: WO 106/3121 – Forces of Greece: Order of Battle.
8. National Archives Catalogue Number: PREM 3/212/8 – Order of Battle in Greece.
9. 'Kokkinia Prisoner-of-War Hospital' from 'Medical Services in New Zealand and the Pacific' – http://nzetc.victoria.ac.nz/tm/scholarly/tei-WH2PMed-pt2-c1-2.html.

CHAPTER THREE

1. National Archives Catalogue Number: WO 208/3314/1355 – Jack Byrne Escape Report.
2. National Archives Catalogue Number: WO 373/62/565 – Jack Byrne Recommendation for Award.
3. National Archives Catalogue Number: WO 106/2136 – Operation 'COMPASS': situation and operational reports.
4. Imperial War Museum Catalogue Number: 29806 – 'The Archive Hour: SAS The Originals': Gordon Stevens presents previously un-broadcast interviews with SAS founder David Stirling and other surviving members of the original SAS, recorded in 1987, BBC Radio 4.
5. Imperial War Museum Catalogue Number: 30103 – Lecture entitled 'Desert Survival Experiences' given by British civilian J. W. Sillito at SAS Regimental Association, date unknown.
6. Imperial War Museum Catalogue Number: 18032 – Oral History: 'John Edward "Jim" et al Almonds' (Windfall Films), Recorded in 2001.
7. *Daily Telegraph* obituary, Jack Byrne: https://www.telegraph.co.uk/news/obituaries/1542897/Jack-Byrne.html.
8. Army Apprentice Memorial: http://www.armyapprenticememorial.org.uk/.
9. *Shropshire Star* article, 'Shropshire SAS Hero's Medals': https://www.shropshirestar.com/news/2010/09/22/shropshire-sas-heros-medals-sell-for-72000/.

CHAPTER FOUR

1. National Archives Catalogue Number: WO 201/751 – Operations Agreement, Bigamy + Nicety.
2. National Archives Catalogue Number: WO 201/748 – Report on Combined Operations Bigamy, Nicety, Agreement.
3. National Archives Catalogue Number: ADM 223/565 – Operation Agreement
4. National Archives Catalogue Number: WO 373/46/62 – Langton MC Recommendation.
5. National Archives Catalogue Number: WO 373/46/6424 – Hillman MM Recommendation.
6. Imperial War Museum Catalogue Number: Documents.241 – The Private Papers of Colonel T. B. Langton.
7. Imperial War Museum Catalogue Number: 30103 – Lecture entitled 'Desert Survival Experiences' given by British civilian J. W. Sillito at SAS Regimental Association, date unknown.

CHAPTER FIVE

1. National Archives Catalogue Number: WO 373/46 – Citation for Military Medal.
2. National Archives Catalogue Number: WO 201/751 – Operations Agreement, Bigamy + Nicety.
3. National Archives Catalogue Number: WO 201/735 – Reports on Operations at Benghazi September 1942.
4. National Archives Catalogue Number: WO 244/7 – Operation Avalanche: Lessons Learned.
5. National Archives Catalogue Number: WO 204/1424 – Operations Goblet and Slapstick: outline plans and orders of battle.

6. National Archives Catalogue Number: WO 201/2778 – Avalanche, Buttress, Goblet, Slapstick: orders of battle.
7. National Archives Catalogue Number: WO 170/7573 – Altamura Camp.
8. National Archives Catalogue Number: WO 224/118 – 51 Italian POW Camp Altamura.
9. National Archives Catalogue Number: WO 361/1898 – Prisoners of war, Italy: Camp 65, Gravina Altamura; International Red Cross reports.
10. National Archives Catalogue Number: WO 224/127 – 65 Italian POW Camp Gravina Altamura.
11. National Archives Catalogue Number: WO 224/130 – Campo 70.
12. Imperial War Museum Catalogue Number: 18032 – Oral History: 'John Edward "Jim" et al Almonds' (Windfall Films), Recorded in 2001.
13. Imperial War Museum Catalogue Number: 29806 – 'The Archive Hour: SAS The Originals': Gordon Stevens presents previously un-broadcast interviews with SAS founder David Stirling and other surviving members of the original SAS, recorded in 1987, BBC Radio 4.
14. Imperial War Museum Catalogue Number: 30103 – Lecture entitled 'Desert Survival Experiences' given by British civilian J. W. Sillito at SAS Regimental Association, date unknown.
15. *Daily Telegraph* obituary, Major 'Gentleman Jim' Almonds, 13/09/2005: https://www.telegraph.co.uk/news/obituaries/1498251/Major-Gentleman-Jim-Almonds.html.
16. *Independent* obituary, Major Jim Almonds, 07/09/2005: https://www.independent.co.uk/news/obituaries/major-jim-almonds-310747.html.

CHAPTER SIX

1. National Archives Catalogue Number: WO 204/1810 – Operation Shingle.
2. National Archives Catalogue Number: WO 204/6856 – Operation Pomegranate.
3. National Archives Catalogue Number: WO 373/25 – Military Cross Citation for Major Edward Antony Fitzherbert Widdrington.
4. National Archives Catalogue Number: WO 373/96/457 – Military Cross Citation for Lieutenant Quentin Hughes.
5. National Archives Catalogue Number: WO 208/3484 – 'Escape from Italy of Brigadiers Armstrong, Stirling, Vaughn, Todhunter, Coombe'.
6. National Archives Catalogue Number: WO 208/3320/94 – Escape Report from Brigadier Douglas Arnold Stirling.
7. National Archives Catalogue Number: WO 208/3373 – Escape Operations.
8. Imperial War Museum Catalogue Number: 29806 – 'The Archive Hour: SAS The Originals': Gordon Stevens presents previously un-broadcast interviews with SAS founder David Stirling and other surviving members of the original SAS, recorded in 1987, BBC Radio 4.
9. Imperial War Museum, '13/18 Hussars in 1940 Campaign: Part 1' by Douglas Arnold Stirling, as part of the unclassified papers of D. A. Stirling held at the IWM.
10. *Daily Telegraph* Obituary, Quentin Hughes, 18 May 2004: https://www.telegraph.co.uk/news/obituaries/1462120/Quentin-Hughes.html.

11. Battle of Britain Historical Society: 'Aircraft of the Luftwaffe: Junkers Ju 88 Specifics': https://www.battleofbritain1940. net/0016.html.
12. Remembrance NI: 'SAS men from Northern Ireland executed by the Gestapo': https://remembranceniorg.files.wordpress. com/2018/04/remembrance-ni-sas.pdf.
13. Paratrooper.Be, 'Escape Compasses': https://www.para-trooper.be/articles/escape-compasses/.

CHAPTER SEVEN

1. National Archives Catalogue Number: WO 218/202 – Operation Loyton Report.
2. National Archives Catalogue Number: WO 208/3324/189 – Fiddick, R. L. Escape/Evasion Reports.
3. National Archives Catalogue Number: AIR 14/34112 – 'Bomber Command Night Operations 28th/29th July 1944'.
4. National Archives Catalogue Number: WO 218/222 – '2nd Special Air Service Missing Parachutists'.
5. National Archives Catalogue Number: WO 208/3324 – 'M19 Evaded Capture in France'.
6. Imperial War Museum Catalogue Number: 18033 – Oral History: 'Lew et al Fiddick', TVS (Gordon Stevens), Recorded in 1987.
7. Imperial War Museum Catalogue Number: 18032 – Oral History: 'Henry Carey Druce', TVS (Gordon Stevens), Recorded in 1987.
8. 'The War Years' by Lew Fiddick, unpublished memoir, personal communication.

9. 'Fiddick, Lew: My Bomber Command Experience' – interviewed by Isabelle Carey, 26 March 2015, http://contentdm.library.uvic.ca/cdm/ref/collection/collection13/id/2880.

10. 'Remembering Sherman Peabody', Bishop's University blog, 26 July 2017, Dr Michael Childs, Sean Summerfield and Megan Whitworth: https://blog.ubishops.ca/remembering-sherman-peabody/.

11. 'What Happened to Sherman Peabody', 2018 Bishop's University film. Directed by Sarah Fournier and Produced by Michael Childs: https://www.youtube.com/watch?v=gs-rxrSUrSoc&feature=youtu.be.

12. 'A Second World War Mystery Solved: 75 Years Later, A Transatlantic Team Retraces Two Lost Canadians', Eric Reguly, *The Globe and Mail*, 06/07/2019: https://www.theglobeandmail.com/world/article-a-second-world-war-mystery-solved-75-years-later-a-transatlantic/.

13. 'Swallowed into Dusk: Missing Airmen during the Second World War', Sean Summerfield, 2018, Sean Summerfield, personal communication.

14. *Daily Telegraph* obituary, Major Henry Druce, 07/02/2007: https://www.telegraph.co.uk/news/obituaries/1541780/Major-Henry-Druce.html.

15. *Times Colonist* obituary, Lew Fiddick, 26/11/2016: https://www.legacy.com/obituaries/timescolonist/obituary.aspx?n=lewis-fiddick&pid=182767811.

16. Private papers of Fred 'Dusty' Rhodes, personal communication from Phil Rhodes, including various Operation Loyton war diary entries.

Bibliography

Lorna Almonds-Windmill, *Gentleman Jim: The Wartime Story of a Founder of the SAS and Special Forces*, Pen and Sword Military Press, 2011.

J. V. Byrne, *The General Salutes A Soldier: With the SAS and Commandos in World War Two*, Robert Hale, 1986.

Roy Farran, *Winged Dagger: Adventures on Special Service*, Arms and Armour Press, 1986.

Roger Ford, *Fire From the Forest: The SAS Brigade in France, 1944*, Cassell Military Paperbacks, 2003.

Phil Froom, *Evasion and Escape Devices Produced by MI9, MIS-X, and SOE in World War II*, Schiffer Military History, 2015.

Jimmy Quentin Hughes, *Who Cares Who Wins: The Autobiography of a World War Two Soldier*, Charico Press, 1998.

Malcolm James, *Born of the Desert: With the SAS in North Africa*, Greenhill Books, 2001.

David Jefferson, *Tobruk, A Raid Too Far*, Hale, 2013.

Damien Lewis, *The Nazi Hunters: The Ultra Secret Unit and the Hunt for Hitler's War Criminals*, Quercus, 2016.

Damien Lewis, *SAS Ghost Patrol*, Quercus, 2017.

Damien Lewis, *SAS Italian Job*, Quercus, 2018.

Damien Lewis, *SAS Shadow Raiders*, Quercus, 2019.

Ben Macintyre, *SAS Rogue Heroes*, Viking, 2016.

Charles Messenger, *The Middle East Commandos*, William Kimber, 1988.

Gordon Stevens, *The Originals: The Secret History of the Birth of the SAS in Their Own Words*, Ebury Press, 2005.

Alan Hoe, *David Stirling: The Authorised Biography of the Creator of the SAS*, Little, Brown, 1992.

George Windsor, *The Mouth Of The Wolf*, Hodder and Stoughton, 1957.

Index

Pritchard, Major Trevor Allan 'Tag'
4, 5, 6–7, 8, 9
promissory notes 82, 163
Proulx, Flight Sergeant Richard 261,
264, 301

Damien Lewis is a very active supporter of charity
Blind Veterans UK:

Blind Veterans UK helps ex-servicemen and women of every generation rebuild their lives after sight loss. It has provided rehabilitation, training, practical advice and emotional support to tens of thousands of veterans since being formed in 1915.

The charity now supports more veterans than ever before, ranging from those who served in the Second World War and on National Service and have lost their sight through age-related conditions to those injured in Iraq, Afghanistan and other military conflicts. Blind Veterans UK provides services and support across the UK via a network of community teams and has centres that provide training, respite and residential care as well as recreational facilities.

It was established by Sir Arthur Pearson, founder of the Daily Express, *in response to blinded soldiers returning from the Front during the First World War. Having lost his own sight through glaucoma, Pearson was determined that they should have the training and rehabilitation to allow them to live independent and productive lives.*

The same work continues today, and while originally formed to help those who lost their sight on active service, it is now open to veterans no matter what the cause of their sight loss, or the length of their service.

*To find out more about the work it does,
visit blindveterans.org.uk*

CHURCHILL'S HELLRAISERS

Perfect for fans of Erik Larsen's *The Splendid and Vile* and Alex Kershaw's *The Forgotten 500*, here is the thrilling account of one of the most daring raids of WWII—the untold story of the heroic hellraisers who stormed a Nazi fortress and helped turn the tide of the war. Bracingly tense, brilliantly researched, and truly unforgettable, *Churchill's Hellraisers* is a must-have for every World War II library.

It is the winter of 1944. Allied forces have succeeded in liberating most of Axis-occupied Italy—with one crucial exception: the Nazi headquarters north of the Gothic Line. Heavily guarded and surrounded by rugged terrain, the mountain fortress is nearly impenetrable. But British Prime Minister Winston Churchill is determined to drive a dagger into the "soft underbelly of Europe." The Allies' plan: drop two paratroopers into the mountains—and take the fortress by storm . . .

The two brave men knew the risks involved, so they recruited an equally fearless team: Italian resistance fighters, escaped POWs, downed US airmen, even a bagpipe-playing Scotsman known as "The Mad Piper." Some had little military training, but all were willing to fight to the death to defeat the Nazi enemy. Ultimately, the mission that began in broad daylight, in the enemy's line of fire, would end one of the darkest chapters in history—through the courage and conviction of the unsung heroes who dared the impossible . . .

Available from Kensington Publishing Corp. wherever books are sold

CHURCHILL'S BAND OF BROTHERS

Award-winning war reporter and internationally bestselling military historian Damien Lewis explores one of WWII's most remarkable Special Forces missions during the Normandy landings on D-Day—and the extraordinary hunt that followed to take down a cadre of fugitive SS and Gestapo war criminals.

On the night of June 13th, 1944, a twelve-man SAS unit parachuted into occupied France. Their objective: hit German forces deep behind the lines, cutting the rail-tracks linking Central France to the northern coastline. In a country crawling with enemy troops, their mission was to prevent Hitler from rushing his Panzer divisions to the D-Day beaches and driving the Allied troops back into the sea. It was a Herculean task, but no risk was deemed too great to stop the Nazi assault. In daring to win it all, the SAS patrol was ultimately betrayed, captured, and tortured by the Gestapo before facing execution in a dark French woodland on Hitler's personal orders. Miraculously, two of the condemned men managed to escape, triggering one of the most secretive Nazi-hunting operations ever, as the SAS vowed to track down every one of the war criminals who had murdered their brothers in arms...all with Churchill's covert backing.

With Nazi Germany's lightning seizure of much of Western Europe, British Prime Minister Winston Churchill had called for the formation of specially trained troops of the "hunter class." Their purpose was to incite a reign of terror across enemy-occupied Europe. Churchill's warriors were to shatter all known rules of warfare, taking the fight to the enemy with no holds barred. In doing so, the Special Air Service would be tested as never before during the pivotal D-Day landings, and the quest for vengeance that followed.

Breathtaking and exhaustively researched, Churchill's Band of Brothers is based upon a raft of new and unseen material provided by the families of those who were there. It reveals the untold story of one of the most daring missions of WWII, that not only had ramifications for the war itself but led to the most extraordinary and gripping of aftermaths.

Available from Kensington Publishing Corp. wherever books are sold

CHURCHILL'S BROTHERS IN ARMS

#1 internationally bestselling author, war reporter, and award-winning WWII historian Damien Lewis chronicles the birth of the legendary SAS, Winston Churchill's singular band of brothers, and how their extraordinary do-or-die exploits truly turned the tide of war.

In 1941, as World War Two raged, scores of men stepped forward to answer Winston Churchill's call for volunteers for Special Service, a high-risk opportunity to undertake the most hazardous, top-secret duties of war. Comprised of some of the finest fighting units in the entire British Army, these warriors longed to leave behind their mind-numbing garrison duties for battle. They hungered to pit themselves against a seemingly omnipotent enemy and brave a bloody and bruising baptism by fire. A rightfully proud regiment with an unrivalled esprit de corps, they were disavowed as unruly by top brass, unyieldingly vaunted by Churchill, and courageously loyal to the clandestine "butcher and bolt" raids that made their sacrifices—and their triumphs—legendary. But even as the combat-worn ranks of the SAS risked all to deliver the first resounding defeats on Nazi Germany, there were well-founded fears that their fortunes would change.

In *Brothers in Arms,* Damien Lewis pays tribute to the mavericks and visionaries who founded elite-forces soldiering—the SAS. Exhaustively researched from an invaluable trove of never-before-seen documents, wartime letters, diaries, mission reports, rare photos, undeveloped film, plus interviews with WWII veterans and their surviving families, Damien follows one close-knit band of men from the founding of the SAS through to the Italian landings, which truly turned the tide of the war. It is a breathtaking narrative of do-or-die action and unbelievable daring chronicling the exploits of some of the most fearless, revered, and under-the-radar soldiers of the 20th century.

Available from Kensington Publishing Corp. wherever books are sold

FORGED IN HELL

In the summer of 1943, the largest invasion fleet ever assembled sailed for fortress Europe, aiming to bulldoze its way onto Nazi shores. At its vanguard went a few hundred elite forces soldiers, the Royal Navy warship carrying them bearing the iconic winged dagger emblem on its prow, plus the motto 'Who Dares Wins'. Led by the legendary SAS commander Blair 'Paddy' Mayne, these war-bitten, piratical raiders were tasked to do the impossible – to bludgeon their way through the most heavily defended enemy shoreline, so enabling the ensuing forces to follow on.

If they succeeded, it would mark the turning point in the war. If they failed, the consequences were unthinkable. Against all odds, outnumbered some fifty-to-one, and facing a ferocious series of cliffside defenses, they would have to dare all as never before. So begins the incredible true story of the SAS's mission to liberate Europe. Replete with surprise, shock, action, heroic endeavor and glory, not to mention subterfuge, treachery and dismay, this is a classic combination of combat writing and breath-taking narrative non-fiction.

Forthcoming from Kensington Publishing Corp. in fall 2024